Guide to
Funerals and
Bereavement

The Daily Telegraph
L I F E P L A N N E R

Guide to
Funerals and
Bereavement

Sam
Weller

**KOGAN
PAGE**

Although this book has been carefully prepared, regulations, particularly those regarding DSS benefits, certification and notification are subject to change. The information in this book is for general guidance only and should not be treated as a complete and authoritative statement of the law. No responsibility for loss occasioned to any person acting, or refraining from action, as a result of any material in this book can be accepted by the author or publisher.

First published 1999

Kogan Page Limited
120 Pentonville Road
London N1 9JN

British Library Cataloguing in Publication Data

A CIP record for this book is available from the British Library.

ISBN 0 7494 3057 5

Typeset by Jean Cussons Typesetting, Diss, Norfolk
Printed and bound in Great Britain by Thanet Press Ltd, Margate

Contents

Contents

Contents

"When you go home tell them of us and say for your tomorrow we gave our today."

The Royal British Legion is the leading charity providing assistance to ex-Service men, women and their dependants. Founded in 1921 by Earl Haig the Legion has striven to meet the ever increasing needs of the ex-Service community and to keep alive the spirit of Remembrance.

Every day The Royal British Legion receives requests for assistance, and it is only with the loyal and generous support of those who are willing to give so freely of their time and money that we are able to provide the help and security that is so frequently needed.

Last year we were contacted by Mr & Mrs George Wallworth. Mr Wallworth served in the Second World War from the age of 19. During the time in which he fought for his country he was wounded several times but valiantly remained with his division. When the war ended George left the army and settled down with his new wife and young daughter. Their lives continued smoothly enough until, in 1998, they had to make contact with the Legion for assistance. At the age of 82 George was experiencing bad health, stomach ulcers left him feeling constantly weak and sore, coupled to that he had become profoundly deaf. George had lost 4 stone in just twelve months.

Sadly his wife had cancer and was only expected to live a few more months. Despite their situation, George did not want charity but desperately needed a washing machine and some new clothes. The washing machine was vital as incontinence became a result of both their illnesses. The new clothes were needed as those he had previously worn now hung off his diminished frame.

Their situation was brought to the attention of their local Royal British Legion County Field Officer and the much needed washing machine and clothes were provided. We received a letter from George, shortly after the death of his wife, *"I wish to offer my thanks for you, The Royal British Legion, for your kind gifts of a washing machine and £100.00 to enable me to select suitable clothing which enabled me to clothe myself in the appropriate manner ... I once again offer my grateful thanks to all concerned who made these gifts to me."*

Sadly, George is just one case out of the 300,000 requests which the Legion receive each year. As a result, there is increasing pressure to raise sufficient funds in order to effectively meet this need. The annual Poppy Appeal raises a tremendous amount of money each year, thanks to the generosity of those who buy the little paper poppies which signify so much. However, this appeal raises only half of the total funds we need to provide welfare care each year and every year we need more.

If you currently buy a poppy and would like your support to continue beyond your life time one way in which you could help The Royal British Legion to secure the futures of the ex-Service men and women who approach us for assistance is to include a gift in your Will. This could either be in the form of a legacy or by adding a clause stating that any gifts received in lieu of flowers are to be directed to the Legion.

It is vital that your Will is an accurate representation of how you wish your estate to be handled after your death. Obviously it is also the means to provide for your family and loved ones and it could be the time to support the charities which were close to your heart during your life. A legacy to the Legion is not only a fitting tribute to the memory of those who died to preserve our freedom but also provides the means to enable the Legion to remain a symbol of hope for those ex-Service men, women and their dependants who rely on the support of The Royal British Legion today and indeed, those who will tomorrow.

The Legion will only be able to support the service men and women into the next century if you are there by its side. With British forces currently serving in no less than 28 countries across the world it seems certain that The Royal British Legion will continue to play a vital role in the lives of the ex-Service community for many years to come. One way in which you could help to ensure that the Legion is still in a position to help would be to ask those closest to you to direct any gifts made in your memory towards its valuable work.

Should you wish to make or amend your Will, we strongly recommend that you visit a Solicitor for sound and professional advice. In addition to this you may wish to read the Legion's guide to Making and Changing your Will, if you would like to receive a copy, or have any related queries, please contact Perdita Chamberlain on 0171 973 7297 at 48 Pall Mall, London, SW1Y 5JY.

Remember us for our tomorrows, as well as our yesterdays.

For further information, please contact:

**The Royal British Legion
48 Pall Mall,
London,
SW1Y 5JY**

**Registered Charity No.
219279**

The Royal British Legion, one of Britain's best known and most highly respected organisations, is generally acknowledged to be the leading Service charity safeguarding the welfare, interests and memory of those who have served in the Armed Forces.

The word "memory" is significant. As *de facto* custodian of Remembrance in the UK, the Legion is charged - under the terms of its Royal Charter - with organising "Festivals of Remembrance, services and parades to perpetuate the memory of sacrifices made during service with Our Armed Forces in war and peace".

Its custodianship of Remembrance is at the heart of the Legion's activities. For most of this century, it has been an annual tradition that each autumn, as the nights draw in and the leaves fall from the trees, the nation's thoughts turn to Remembrance and to events inspired and co-ordinated by the Legion.

Remembrance is symbolised in many ways. Poppy petals falling gently down onto the heads of the silent Service men and women at the end of one the most popular and emotive televised annual events of the year, the Festival of Remembrance at the Royal Albert hall. The Parade and Service at the Cenotaph in Whitehall on Remembrance Sunday. Poppy Appeal collectors out on the streets in all weathers at the end of October and beginning of November. Most of the population spontaneously pausing from their daily round at 11 a.m. on 11th November and observing a two minute silence to remember those who fought and died or were injured in the causes of peace and freedom.

All these Remembrance acts and events "evoke" The Royal British Legion to the extent that the Legion and Remembrance are virtually synonymous.

Some people felt that with the VE and VJ day celebrations in 1995, fifty years after the end of the 1939-1945 war, the nation would move on to a new chapter, its duty to remember the dead and injured of two world wars fully discharged. But they underestimated the power and importance of Remembrance and the innate desire of the nation to pay regular respect to its Service men and women, past and present.

The revival of support for observance of the Two Minute Silence at the eleventh hour of the eleventh day of the eleventh month demonstrates that, despite the passing of the years and the gradual, inevitable fall in the number of survivors, the nation does still feel strongly about Remembrance and does wish to show its strength of feeling.

Fifty-seven per cent of the population responded to the Legion's 1995 campaign to reinstate the Two Minute Silence on what many always felt was "the proper day". Support for the idea has grown steadily over the last three years; 67 per cent observed the 11th November Silence in 1996, 69 per cent in 1997 and 72 per cent last year.

The level of support among young people is even more substantial. Around 75 per cent of schools and colleges observed the Two Minute Silence on 11th November 1998 or marked Remembrance in some other meaningful way.

Encouraged by this success, the Legion believes that Remembrance will now be marked in the UK in this way permanently and it hopes that in 1999 and 2000, the "millennium years", first the Commonwealth countries, then the rest of the world will join in. There is no doubting many countries' acceptance of the value and meaning of Remembrance and marking it with a period of silence has become a poignant and powerful expression of all that the word "Remembrance" embraces.

The observance of a silence, heads bowed in reflection and prayer - these and other solemn acts transcend boundaries and borders. In themselves, they may amount to small individual acts. Carried out at the same time, they can go from "individual" to "collective" - rare moments when whole nations can stand together, remember and reflect on the price and value of freedom.

For The Royal British Legion, Remembrance is an almost daily occurrence. Formal Legion meetings are preceded by an "Act of Homage" using the words from "The Fallen" by Laurence Binyon: **They shall grow not old, as we that are left grow old, Age shall not weary them, nor the years condemn, At the going down of the sun, and in the morning, We will remember them."**

Two Minute Silence 1998

And in the Legion's own words, to promote the observance of the Two Minute Silence on 11th November,

"If we are to maintain our peace and freedom, we must always remember ."

The greatest Act of
Remembrance

...is to remember The Royal British Legion in your Will.

There can be no greater Act of Remembrance than leaving a legacy to The Royal British Legion. A legacy is not only a fitting tribute to the memory of those who died to preserve our freedom, it's a symbol of hope for the thousands of people who rely on The Royal British Legion today.

Please consider leaving a gift to The Royal British Legion in your Will. For further information please call Perdita Chamberlain now on 0171 973 7297.

Remember us for our tomorrows, as well as our yesterdays.

THE ROYAL BRITISH
LEGION

Registered charity number: 219279

© Bjørn Svenson A-Z Botanical Collections Ltd

Introduction

More Than Just a Funeral

There are more matters concerning death and bereavement than just the funeral arrangements. This book takes a holistic view of death and its aftermath. It spans not only planning for the funeral and what to do when someone dies, but also the longer-term matters of memorialization, ownership and inheritance of grave plots and what to expect in the way of rights and responsibilities in cemeteries and churchyards.

Clear information is provided about arranging a funeral, the pros and cons of cremation versus burial, what you should know about memorialization and the costs involved.

The average cost of a funeral is £1,200–£1,400. A grave and headstone can add more than £1,000. Plus flowers, entertainment for mourners, time off work… the expense mounts up. And it is a purchase no one wants to make. Most of us keep up to date on the prices of other major purchases such as cars, holidays, TVs and PCs. They are advertised and displayed in shop windows. But few of us want reminding about funerals and this information is not readily available.

A Complex Undertaking

The undertaker is the only contact that members of the public will generally have with the 'death care industry'. Lined up behind this gatekeeper are crematoria and cemeteries, which may be owned and operated by private or local authority concerns, churchyards, which are managed by the clergy in accordance with ecclesiastical law, and monumental masons, with an ancient craft that is increasingly adapting to modern technology. In between times, one has to cope with the bureaucracy of hospitals, doctors, coroners, registrars and, for some, the Department of Social Security.

The UK undertaking service, whose members prefer to be called funeral directors, comprises the Co-op (25 per cent), the US-owned Service Corporation International (SCI) (13 per cent) and independent small groups and individual traders (62 per cent).

Some funeral directors' groups also own crematoria and cemeteries. There is concern about monopolistic practices, prices being forced up and standards and levels of choice cut down. The funeral directing trade is not licensed or regulated and this is being investigated by both the Office of Fair Trading (OFT) and the Department of Trade and Industry (DTI).

This book spans the entire industry and lays out the likely benefits and disadvantages of dealing with large, small and combined undertakings.

Early Payment, Insurance and Benefits

The death grant was removed years ago and replaced with social security payments for funerals, which were gradually reduced. Regulations about who may be eligible for benefits have been tightened up.

Pre-purchase funeral plans and insurance schemes have become big business. The prepaid plans are not regulated, although the government has proposals to do this. The plans are heavily marketed by the Co-op, SCI and independents' groups. However, planning your funeral can be completed without prepayment. Savings and insurance schemes may be better.

This book examines the pros and cons of pre-planning funerals and pre-need purchase schemes, insurance and savings and gives a guide to what financial assistance may be available from the Benefits Agency.

Plan Well in Advance

Forward planning can provide more than peace of mind. It can ease the burden on the bereaved and bring them consolation. It can avoid mistakes being made under pressure of the urgent demands of arranging a funeral, which can be grievous and costly.

Rules and regulations about graves and gravestones are varied and confusing with very little harmonization. Burial in your garden may be possible but carving 'Dad' on a headstone in a churchyard prohibited. The costs of grave plots and cremation are rising faster than inflation. Pitfalls and ways to avoid them are pointed out for you.

Ritual and Changing Attitudes

Attitudes to death are changing, with fewer ceremonies being held in church and more secular services being conducted. Environmentally friendly 'green' funerals and woodland burials are increasing in popularity. Ashes are launched into space. Charters setting out the rights of dead citizens and the bereaved have been produced.

More people want to take control of 'their' funeral. While a traditional ceremony is still preferred by the majority, they are often being personalized in small but significant ways. Other people would like to do something radically different, or even cope without a funeral director.

These social developments are reviewed and advice offered about how funerals may be improved.

The Role of Memorialization

In the UK, there are 600,000 funerals every year and 70 per cent end in cremation. Virtually every one of the 180,000 burials will have an inscribed stone memorial. In 1997, the ashes of the cremated were taken away from the crematorium in 44 per cent

3

of cases in order to conduct some personal act of commemoration. Many of those left at the crematorium will have a plaque or a rose bush within the grounds. If interred without a marker, the crematorium garden itself becomes a place of remembrance.

Remembrance need not take the form of a conventional monument. Planting a tree, donations to charity or a Web site may be satisfactory for some.

Memorials historically and psychologically can play an important part in the holistic approach to death and bereavement. What they can mean to you, what is available and the costs and responsibilities are all considered.

I hope this book will help to guide you through the mystique of death care services, and enable you to cope more effectively during this sad and difficult time.

What to Do When Someone Dies – A Summary

The vast majority of deaths in the UK (approximately 90 per cent) occur within hospital or care home environments. However, a significant minority of deaths do occur elsewhere and these can, of course, be either expected or unexpected. Although there are similarities, the exact procedures for certifying and registering a death, which must be followed before a funeral can proceed, do differ according to the circumstances at the time of death and whether or not a cremation is required. The most common categories of procedure are summarized below and are also discussed in detail in Chapter 3 and illustrated in Figure 3.1 on page 47.

Procedures Following a Death in a Hospital or Care Home

▌ Bereaved relatives and the duty/family doctor are informed.

▌ An appointment is made for the bereaved to complete the formalities with the hospital/care home authorities and to collect any personal belongings.

▌ The attending doctor issues a medical certificate giving the cause of death.

▮ The bereaved, or a recognized representative (the informant), registers the death with the registrar of births, deaths and marriages.

▮ The registrar issues a certificate for burial or cremation (the green form), allowing the bereaved to proceed with burial arrangements either with or without a funeral director (see Chapter 15).

▮ If cremation is required, another four forms have to be completed. These are obtained from a funeral director, crematorium or doctor. They include certificates confirming cause of death (forms B and C) each signed by a different doctor. With these, cremation arrangements may now be finalized.

▮ Sometimes the coroner is involved after a death in a hospital: if it was following an accident or injury, an industrial disease, during a surgical operation, under anaesthetic, from cause unknown or sudden and unexplained. A coroner's investigation or a hospital deciding on their own post mortem may delay the issue of the medical certificate of the cause of death.

Procedures Following an Expected Death Elsewhere

▮ Person or persons present inform the doctor and bereaved relatives.

▮ The attending doctor may issue the medical certificate of the cause of death in which case the qualified informant may proceed with the registration of death and then the funeral arrangements, as above.

▮ If there is any doubt about the cause of death, the coroner is informed.

▌ If death by natural causes is confirmed, the coroner releases the necessary documentation (form 100) to allow registration and subsequent funeral to proceed, as above.

▌ The coroner may elect to hold an inquest (and possibly a post mortem) in order to establish the cause and circumstances of the death.

▌ If so, you may be given an order for burial (white form 101) or a certificate for cremation (yellow form E). Either document will enable the funeral to take place before the inquest is over and should be given to the funeral director (or the staff at the crematorium or cemetery) as soon as possible.

▌ When satisfied, the coroner will send a certificate to the registrar (form 99 rev) stating the cause of death. This allows the death to be registered without the attendance of an informant.

When an unexpected death occurs, the procedures are as above with the possible additional involvement of the police (definitely if foul play is suspected). Death may occur in exceptional circumstances, or while abroad, and the procedures that apply here are covered in Chapter 13. Some specific rules apply in Scotland with regard to certification and registration and these are detailed in Chapter 14.

Brian Moody/Scope

SOME MEMORIES SHOULD
NEVER BE ALLOWED TO FADE

The debt we owe all our ex-soldiers and soldiers is beyond measure.

What they have done for us must never be forgotten or dimmed by the passing of time.

Nor should we forget that sometimes these soldiers and their families find themselves in real need and are often too proud to ask for help.

When you make your Will, or are advising people on legacies or giving a gift in memory, please remember the Army Benevolent Fund.

TO: THE ARMY BENEVOLENT FUND, DEPT. DTF, 41 QUEEN'S GATE, LONDON SW7 5HR.

☐ I would like to make a donation ☐ I would like information on covenants and legacies

Signature _____

Name _____

Address _____

_____ Postcode _____

I enclose a cheque/PO or debit my credit card Visa/Mastercard/CAF card number

Reg. Charity No. 211645

Expiry date _____ **Or phone our donation line on**

Amount _____ **01634 226 210**

Data Protection Act: We may occasionally wish to contact you about our work. If you would prefer that we do not, please tick the box ☐

9

Sherrie, the smiling seven year old in this picture, is one of 23,000 young people with cancer supported by Sargent Cancer Care for Children since 1968.

Sargent is the only UK-wide charity that supports young people with cancer and their families from the moment of diagnosis.

The charity responds quickly to the many problems that the children and their families may experience. Fifty Sargent Social Workers, attached to cancer units across the country, provide psychological and social support and practical care to these families. Child Cancer Specialists consider our work to be essential in the fight against cancer.

Sargent directly offers families practical financial help to alleviate hardship that may result during the fraught treatment periods. We also provide respite breaks at our special holiday homes.

We depend entirely on public donations. If you would like to remember us in your Will or require a copy of our free legacy information pack 'Looking at the future - Why YOU need an up-to-date Will', or require any further information please contact:

Claire Buchanan
Legacy Information Officer
Sargent Cancer Care for Children
Griffin House
161 Hammersmith Road London W6 8SG
Tel: 0208 752 2880

Cancer Care for Children
Sargent

Registered Charity No. 256435

Funerals in Perspective

Funerals are, in the natural way of things, just as important as weddings, christenings and birthdays: all milestones along the path of life. Unlike weddings, with 4 out of 10 ending in divorce, funerals are for ever. But, as is often the case, we rush through the arrangements, skimp on the ceremony and wonder afterwards if we had done the right thing.

There is a lot to be said for having a good funeral. An event to look back on and remember with a fondness akin to the memories of your loved one. That does not mean it has to be expensive. The average funeral at a cost of £1,650 may be less than is spent on a wedding, but it is often begrudged and thought a 'RIP-off'.

It's not what you spend so much as the way that you spend it. Think about the funeral and plan it with the same consideration that you would give to a wedding, 21st birthday party or golden wedding anniversary. Be involved with the detail. Take care with the guest list, seating plan, music and socializing – just as you would with other important occasions. Many people find this approach therapeutic, with the benefits being two-fold in that it not only has the immediate effect of taking their mind away from dwelling on the sadness of their recent bereavement, but it also helps later on, when they can reassure themselves that they played a significant part in the final farewell.

Like other major life events, such as christenings, Easter and Christmas celebrations and harvest festivals, funerals used to involve the whole community. Friends and neighbours rallied round with practical help and moral support and there would be a community resource of funds as well as goodwill to draw upon.

Today, trade and commerce have replaced that community spirit and nowhere so significantly as in the funeral service. Death and its demarcation as a rite of passage are hidden from view. More than 80 per cent of people die in hospital; another 10 per cent in nursing homes or sheltered accommodation. The few who die at home don't lie there to be visited one last time, but are whisked away to a funeral home. Society hides death and shields itself from it.

This corporate cling to immortality and rejection of death is quite a modern phenomenon. The Victorians are renowned for their lavish funerals and legacy of monumental cemeteries. Our modern 'traditional' funeral continues to be based on the Victorian model. Churches have historically been the focus for burial grounds. Many were built on sites of pre-Christian burials where, according to archaeologists, the bodies of our ancestors were much revered.

What are the reasons for this change in public attitude? Some believe it is a reaction to the slaughter of young men in the two great wars. British war dead stayed in those foreign fields. There was no soldier's body brought back to be buried with due ceremony. Grieving was suppressed.

As modern cemeteries followed the pattern of war graves' architecture, so the British attitude to death changed to reflect that they are made of stuff stern enough to turn the tide of war. Wartime rationing made it right and proper for things to be kept plain and simple. The Victorian celebrations of death gave way to a more austere ceremony. As some poor families had been known to add to their deprivation by trying to keep up with the Joneses in paying for elaborate funerals, this was, in some ways, no bad thing.

Cremation, however, is the single most dramatic influence on the British way of death. Only a handful of people, about 9 per cent in England and Wales, were being cremated at the end of the last war. By 1967, for the first time, more were being cremated than buried and the figure had reached more than 70 per cent by 1990. In recent years, the nationwide average of those being cremated has remained fairly static. There has even been an increase in burials in some parts of the country.

Until the mid-19th century, when the first cemeteries were

constructed, all burials had been in churchyards. The ceremony and ritual of burial in a churchyard, enshrined in Christian liturgy, translated freely to interment in cemeteries. The body being lowered into a hole in the ground, committed to mother earth, the ancient words spoken and soil dropped into the grave is a ritual familiar to us all. It is embedded in our folklore. It comforts the bereaved with the Christian promise of resurrection and the pagan affirmation of nature's gift of rebirth from the soil. But cremation is new to our society and bereft of conventions.

We have a duty to dispose of our dead, but there is no law to say how it must be done. Once upon a time there was no problem: except at sea, everyone was buried – and nearly everyone in a churchyard.

The church was a communal meeting place and the church-yard a collection of individual plots combining to create a central communal memorial. A repository not only of the community's dead, but also of memories and memorials of them, of how they had contributed to the life of the community, a historical monu-ment to the life and times of the place.

The parish priest was in charge. Family, friends and neigh-bours looked after the practicalities of the funeral and tended the churchyard. There was no question of what had to be done, or who would do it. There was a well-understood routine that took care of the necessities and formalities. The grave was nearby and could be tended and visited as frequently as need be.

The Changing Role of Memorials

At first only the very wealthy had stone memorials. In the 18th century they became more plentiful and today hardly any burial is without at least a headstone. The grave, and for many the memorial, can play an important role in the life cycles of the family, the community and even a nation. Gladstone is said to have declared, 'Show me the way a nation disposes of its dead and I will measure... the level at which their society exists'.

The most basic function of a memorial is to be a grave marker, simply some means of identifying the location, name and probably dates of birth and death of the body interred there. But, for most people, a memorial and gravesite is much more.

During the period soon after a death, the bereaved, and especially close partners, spouses and parents, will often relate quite closely to the grave and memorial. Tending the grave, placing flowers, cleaning the headstone, even talking alone at the graveside can be ways of coming to terms with the loss. They can be gestures of continuing care for the dead person (deceased) that enable the grieving parties to demonstrate their love while gradually adjusting to the changed circumstances of their life. Most graves have a similar cycle of frequency of visits: regularly and often at first, then increasingly spaced out until visits are just made on special anniversaries, such as the date of death, birthdays, Mothering Sunday, Easter and Christmas.

Dr Frances Clegg, a clinical psychologist, believes it is possible that, for some individuals, this kind of interaction with a burial place or memorial obviates the need for any kind of bereavement counselling or grief therapy.

Later, the grave may become a place for occasional pilgrimage, for a journey of remembrance and contemplation. A haven of peace, tranquillity and meditation.

Another role for a memorial is as a special link for a family, a tangible reference to one's roots and inheritance. Often, children who have agreed to their parents' urgings not to waste money on a memorial have regretted this when their own children have enquired about their grandparents' family history.

As well as being part of a family's genealogy, a memorial can be part of the communal monument by adding to the structure of the landscape in a churchyard or cemetery. It can be a personal contribution to enhance the place where a community has gathered together the remains of their people to create somewhere that is special to everyone.

In the longer term, a memorial can make a contribution to the ecology, sometimes as a support for ivy or a host for lichens. Even, reminding you that nothing is for ever, in a secondary, recycled role as part of a wall or footpath.

Commemoration after Cremation

Virtually every burial nowadays results in an inscribed stone memorial of some sort. This cannot be said of cremation. During the race for cremation in the post-war years, the cremationists positively discouraged memorials. Local authorities operate most cemeteries and crematoria and they are motivated to avoid the burden of maintenance of stone memorials. Monuments were simply not permitted at virtually all crematoria. An Audit Commission survey in 1989, when cremation accounted for just over 60 per cent of funerals, revealed that 22 per cent of crematoria offered no more than a book of remembrance or cards for commemoration. Others offered different temporary memorials such as a rose bush, shrub, flowering bulbs or maybe a tree or bench. A few offered small wall- or kerb-mounted plaques. The attitude of those in charge at crematoria was 'scatter and forget'.

In the last decade, responding to public pressure, numerous cemeteries and churchyards have set up cremation memorial sections where cremated remains can be buried and a flat plaque or small upright monument can be erected.

Though still called a funeral, the service and method of committal at crematoria are far removed from the rites performed in conducting a burial. For a lot of people, leaving the coffin at the crematorium does not provide similar solace to that derived from seeing it lowered into a grave. The history and tradition surrounding a churchyard is missing from the modern crematorium buildings, no matter how tastefully designed and decorated. And the unremitting flow of traffic providing for cremation services at 20-minute intervals throughout the day can impart a production-line impression.

The way we take care of our dead is no longer a clear-cut, simple matter. First, there is the big question of whether to cremate or bury. The church today is not the only place to go. The vicar hardly ever takes charge and the community is not committed, nor even possesses the skills, to rally round and help. We have come to rely on the professionals, but there are still many decisions to be made.

People often say, 'I'll be dead. I won't worry, so don't you bother.' But funerals are more for the living than the dead.

Psychologists have found that the ritual, and the memorial, can have a profound effect in helping people through the period of grief. And the degree of therapeutic help they experience can be related to the amount of involvement they have put into creating the funeral occasion or the design of the memorial.

Funerals need not be so much the end of a journey as the start on a road that is full of fond memories for family and friends. A good funeral can mean a bereavement that is mourned in sadness but remembered with gladness.

2 Choices to be Made

How the Funeral Will be Managed

Who Will Take Charge?

Someone has to take charge of arranging the funeral. The most obvious choice is the immediately bereaved person, a spouse or partner keen to carry out a last ministration. In this case it is a good idea for someone else to help out as well, as the bereaved person may not be focusing too clearly on the details. A close relative or friend would be an ideal companion.

If the nearest and dearest is too distraught or indisposed, the relative or friend can take the lead. Make a pair of it, or three if you can. Organizing a funeral is a complicated business and quite expensive. You are probably less knowledgeable about it than the other major purchases you have made and most likely you took someone with you when buying that car or suite of furniture. Even if companions don't have much, or any, experience of buying funerals, they can provide moral support and remind you to think twice before reaching a decision.

The person in charge of the funeral need not be one of those who are looking after the deceased's affairs, those named as executors in the will, though it often is. Logically, the person who is going to pay will take control, and providing there is sufficient money in the estate, the costs of the funeral will be paid out of that. It is important to understand that the person who signs the bills and forms will be taking over responsibility for grave and memorial rights, or placement of the ashes, as well as for paying up.

Pre-planned, Prepaid Funerals and Guardians

More people are planning for their own funeral and sometimes even paying for it in advance. Prepaid funeral plans are selling at the rate of 40,000–50,000 a year. If the deceased did make such arrangements, he or she may also have appointed someone to be in charge of the funeral. If you haven't been told about a pre-arrangement ask around and look through the papers just in case. The existence of a prepaid funeral plan doesn't mean you won't need someone in charge. Such a plan will make dealing with the funeral director more straightforward but there will still be plenty of other decisions to make and things to do (see Chapter 17).

However, if a person to be in charge has already been appointed, this 'funeral guardian' will have been fully informed about what the deceased would like to happen and how to go about it. With a guardian's help, things will be able to proceed much more smoothly (see Chapter 16).

Executors and Next of Kin

A person definitely not in charge is the one who is dead. The executors or, if there are none, the next of kin have the right to decide on burial or cremation and funeral details, whatever arrangements had been made previously. The deceased cannot enforce any contracts taken out when alive, nor can anyone else enforce them on behalf of a person who is dead. This could become quite complicated if, for example, a funeral director refused to carry out a contracted prepaid funeral plan that had been purchased by the deceased.

Officials at the crematorium or cemetery, and the funeral director, will assume that whoever is making the arrangements is aware of the deceased's wishes, the next of kin's and whether there is a will and executors.

A dead body cannot be owned by anyone, nor does it have any rights. The next of kin is expected to take responsibility for dealing with the body in a decent and lawful manner. The next of kin, says the dictionary, is the person's closest relative. First in priority is the husband or wife, then children, parents, brothers and sisters and other relatives. But if the death occurs in hospital, staff will contact whoever the deceased named as next of kin. This need not be a relative, though it often is.

The Informant for Registration

In certain circumstances, the person in charge of the body may be the informant who registers the death. A death has to be registered, usually by someone going in person to the office of the registrar in the district where the person died. Only certain people will qualify as the informant for the purpose of making this registration. The place of death has a bearing on who may qualify.

When a death has occurred in a house or public building, there are seven ways by which an informant may be qualified. These are set out in order of precedence. The first three are a relative present at the time of death, a relative present during the last illness or a relative who lives in the district where the death occurred.

Then comes someone who is not a relative but was present at the time of death; the occupier of the building where the death occurred, if aware of the details of the death (perhaps a matron or warden); any inmate of the building, if aware of the details; and, finally, the person accepting responsibility for arranging the funeral.

If a person has been found dead elsewhere, there are five qualifications for informants. These are: any capable relative; any person present at time of death; the person who found the body; the person in charge of the body, which will be the police if the body cannot be identified; and, finally, the person accepting responsibility for arranging the funeral. When a coroner's inquest is held (see Chapter 13), the coroner becomes the informant.

Common-law wives or husbands don't count as next of kin or relatives. This can be particularly distressing for long-term partners and gay and lesbian couples. There have been cases when close relatives have refused admission to a funeral to the partner of the deceased. Without a marriage certificate they have no leverage.

Decisions by the Benefits Agency

If the deceased hasn't left enough money to pay for the funeral, the Benefits Agency has a scheme for deciding who is in charge, or at least responsible for footing the bill. The partner, parents or an adult child or other relatives of the deceased may be required to pay, even if the person responsible for the funeral has a right to claim for benefit. The Benefits Agency will make the final decision after their own enquiries into the circumstances of the deceased, the claimant and the other members of the family. If the claim fails, the whole of the funeral account will become the responsibility of the 'person in charge' (see Chapter 5).

In the last resort, if no friends or relatives can be found, the local council has a duty to bury or cremate the deceased.

Fixing who has the responsibility for a dead person has long been a grey area. In some old parish records there is mention of payment for the transport across a parish boundary of the body of a vagrant found dead in a ditch, so the cost of burial would descend on the neighbouring parish where the body was later found.

Style, Price and Value for Money

The first decision the person in charge has to make concerning the funeral (having ascertained there is no prepaid funeral plan in existence) is whether or not to employ a funeral director. No law says you have to and we look at do-it-yourself funerals in Chapter 15. Most people do retain the services of a funeral director and so gain access to facilities, experience and a team of people to help out.

Next, you have to decide what kind of funeral you want to achieve. As with any other purchasing decision you need to lay down some ground rules. Are you looking for something very basic; ordinary, middle of the road; upmarket or out of this world? The majority of funeral directors market three levels of service with names like bronze, silver and gold. Nowadays, more cater for special requests such as unusual vehicles, horse-drawn hearses, jazz bands, ecologically friendly 'green' burials and so on.

Friends, relatives and colleagues are going to take part in the funeral, and neighbours may be watching, so their expectations and aspirations need to be considered as well of those of the deceased. Is this journey going to be tourist, business or club class? The class of travel will establish the ticket price – essentially the quality of coffin provided. Numbers and journey times govern the other costs.

Burial or Cremation?

The decision whether to cremate or bury the deceased is ultimately taken by the person responsible for arranging the funeral. Preferences previously expressed by the person now dead will normally have a major influence, but there are other considerations such as cost, convenience and even the feelings of surviving relatives.

The law says that the executor or administrator of the estate can decide on the method of disposal. There will be no repercussions from the deceased if, for example, cremation rather than the requested burial is carried out. But if the cost of burial is too high to be met out of the estate, or if some of the relatives have very strong objections, then pleasing the deceased can lead to expensive and unpleasant experiences for the living bereaved. And much of such unpleasantness is likely to be directed at the person in charge of the funeral.

Burial is almost always more expensive than cremation and buying a grave in some areas is either impossible or very costly. There are fewer than 240 crematoria in the country and there may not be one conveniently near to where you want the funeral to take place. It is advisable to make enquiries among the family and look carefully into the costs and practicalities before deciding.

In exceptional circumstances, the decision as to cremation or burial may be decreed by the coroner.

More about this matter in Chapters 6, 7 and 8.

Religious, Social and Family Matters

Few funerals are carried out without some religious content. This can range from a church ceremony including the Eucharist to a brief committal in a crematorium or at the graveside. There is no compulsion to include religion in a ceremony to mark a death but the majority in the UK calls for a Christian content, even if those involved rarely attended church.

The mainstream churches in England and Wales have a co-ordinated policy for funeral services at cemeteries and crematoria, pulled together by a group formed in 1980 and called descriptively the Churches' Group on Funeral Services at Cemeteries and Crematoria. They liaise with clergy, funeral directors and crematorium and cemetery staff and have produced handbooks and joint funeral service books that are most commonly used.

Services in particular churches, of course, have liturgy dating from historical times and funerary traditions can vary quite dramatically. The end of a burial service can be marked by the sprinkling of a little dry earth on to the coffin and the mourners walking away from the plastic grass-lined graveside. The mourners at a Caribbean funeral may take shovel in hand and themselves backfill the grave while hymns are sung and a jazz band plays 'When the Saints Come Marching In'.

The ancient Christian prayers and rites have been amended to allow for the committal of the coffin to the incinerator instead of the earth. And there is now a published service for the burial of ashes.

Catholics and some Jews are becoming more flexible about cremation rather than burial. Muslims require burial and orientation towards Mecca. Some authorities provide dedicated areas for Muslim burials. Hindus are always cremated and seek special arrangements to view the coffin going into the cremator and for a family member to light the flames. Most minority religions in the UK have well-defined rites and traditions for funerals with clear guidelines established and religious leaders, family and community knowledgeable and committed to delivering the funeral rites according to those traditions. Some do not use the services of funeral directors at all; others have select funeral directors that specialize in meeting their requirements.

If the deceased or family attended a nearby church or was an active member of a religious community then that minister or religious leader is one of the first people to contact when planning the funeral. They should help with the arrangements, service and care and counselling.

Crematoria, cemeteries and funeral directors will have contact with ministers or officiants who are qualified and experienced in conducting services; if one is not known to you or the family personally, they can make the introduction.

Having decided on burial or cremation, a time has to be agreed between the person elected to conduct the ceremony and the place where it is to be held (for example, the crematorium, cemetery chapel, graveside, church or religious centre).

Inviting and Notifying Mourners and Guests

There are people to be invited and notified about the time and place of the funeral. This probably means spending some time on the telephone, e-mailing and writing letters to immediate family, more distant relatives and people from work, hobbies and pastimes. A press notice is a traditional and effective medium (the local press or dailies such as *The Times* or the *Telegraph*) and can make a comforting keepsake in years to come.

People travelling from afar will probably require accommodation. You could help them with advice from the local tourist office, which can supply a list of different types of accommodation in the area.

A map showing the major places of importance to the funeral will be helpful. This should show where mourners are expected to assemble, the church or other place where the service is to be held, the crematorium, cemetery or churchyard and where the after-gathering or wake and refreshments will be held.

Advice on car parking, bus and train services and stations is also a good thing to have available.

Flowers or Charitable Donations

Mourners will want to know if flowers and floral tributes are expected, or whether donations are to be collected for named charities. Flowers have a long and significant connection with funerals but can be very expensive. You may think the money spent could be put to a better purpose. Whatever is decided, this information should be included in the notice published in the newspapers if you are placing one or, of course, with the invitation to mourners. The funeral director can be instructed to collate and record donations and organize flowers to be in the right places at the right times.

If you do want flowers, you'll have to decide what will be done with them after the funeral. If you don't like the idea of them wilting at the crematorium or on the grave, the local hospital or old people's home may be pleased to accept cut flowers (see Chapter 10).

The Reception, Wake and Catering

Holding the reception at home is typically more work than organizing a venue at a hotel or club. Sometimes, residential homes or funeral directors will have facilities. There'll be a charge but it may be worth it to save you the task of buying in food and drink, making tea and coffee, serving and clearing up afterwards. That said, having friends and relatives in your home can be more personal and especially comforting – and some will most likely want to join in to lighten the load of chores.

The Church of England funeral service allows for returning home after the funeral and offers a prayer at the door for peace and comfort and to drive away all darkness.

A Memorial Service

Timing is sometimes a problem when people anxious to pay last respects are unable to attend the ceremony at short notice, perhaps having to travel from overseas. A memorial service can be the answer. At a convenient time, a period after the cremation or burial, a service of remembrance and thanksgiving can be held.

Cremation has made this a convention in some countries. The cremation is carried out quickly with a minimum of ceremony. The ashes are placed in an urn and this, rather than a coffin, becomes the focus for a ceremony similar to a memorial service at a later date. The culmination can be a service of committal and interment of the urn or whatever other choice of placement of the ashes is preferred.

Special Rituals and Traditions

Find out if there are any family traditions to be followed. Sometimes special rituals have evolved within the closeness of a family and it can be quite hurtful to those familiar with them if they are missed out. It may be a small thing, such as a particular type of flower on the coffin, the flower being taken away to be pressed and saved, but the omission can be distressing for some.

A daughter was greatly upset to discover, on the catafalque, that the coffin in which her father was lying was made of chipboard. He was a cabinetmaker and lover of natural timber with a hatred of artificial materials. The coffin had appeared to have a natural wood grain finish in the picture in the catalogue from which it had been chosen.

There are probably some elders in the family who have strong views about how things should be done. They will quite likely have attended a number of funerals and so think they know what to expect. Even if you are planning something different, or especially if you are, it is a good idea to discuss the arrangements with the gurus. If you cannot persuade them to agree with you, they will at least have prior warning of what to expect.

Other traditions can be peculiar to certain regions of the country or to certain nationalities. Particular goods, flowers, herbs or spices or even coconuts, may go into the coffin, although coconuts are discouraged for cremation as they can explode with the heat. Coffins are carried on the shoulders of bearers in some counties but low to the ground at arm's length in others. Gifts of food and money (to help you through to the other side) are the norm in some societies with pennies being placed on the eyes or in the hand. You may even be asked to follow the words of the New Orleans St James's Infirmary anthem: 'Put a 20-dollar gold piece on my watch chain so the boys will know I died standin' fat'.

Last Respects and Viewing

Viewing of the body is another tradition that varies according to religion, nationality and region of the country. It may be that you, or family members, would like to see the deceased just one more time before the coffin lid is fixed in place.

This is best done on a day before the funeral. You should make an appointment with the funeral director who will make arrangements for the coffin to be placed in a chapel of rest, or viewing room, where friends and relatives may pay last respects.

You may decide to have the coffin closed for this leave taking. Sometimes the funeral director will recommend this. It is possible to have caskets with a split lid so that only the upper part of the body is on view.

There will probably be an extra charge for preparing the deceased for a viewing, to cover staff time and use of the chapel of rest (see the section on embalming below).

Removal of Christian Symbolism

If not religious, the deceased may have been very anti-religious and it would be offensive to those in the know if Christian artefacts decorated the crematorium or cemetery chapel.

Although many of these chapels were built to replicate British church buildings and Christian symbols are the norm, the management is invariably sensitive to religious preferences nowadays and these can be removed or covered up if a request is made in good time.

Photographs

Photographs were frequently taken to commemorate funerals in Victorian times. Studies show family groups in Sunday clothes including children and babes in arms standing formally around the coffin. Cameras at funerals then became a rarity until, quite recently, they started to make something of a comeback.

Parents of deceased children, in particular infants and still-born, are encouraged to have photographs as a tangible reminder of the child they brought into the world, if only for so short a time.

When viewing the encoffined body is a tradition, photographs of this event, and of the person lying in state in the coffin, may be taken to send to relatives unable to attend the funeral as well as for a memento.

Video cameras are also sometimes in evidence at modern funerals. A horse-drawn hearse and cortége of gleaming limousines can make an impressive moving picture of a memorial event.

Even if the funeral ceremony itself is thought inappropriate for photography, the gathering afterwards can be a grand opportunity to record the meetings of long-lost family and friends. Such pictures can revive happy memories of the sad occasion in times to come.

And, of course, photographs can be mailed to those unable to attend the funeral or, as is increasingly possible, dispatched via the Internet.

Whether or Not to Embalm

Embalming as it is normally carried out in the UK bears no resemblance to the mummifying processes of ancient Egypt or the preservation of the bodies of Russian dictators. Sometimes described as 'hygienic treatment', it involves replacing blood in the veins and arteries of the body with embalming fluid. This delays the decomposing process by a matter of days and imparts a healthier colour and appearance to the deceased.

At the same time, 'cosmetic treatment' is often carried out. This involves washing, shaving, hairdressing and applying make-up so that the deceased looks decent and attractive if there is to be a viewing.

Embalming has advantages for the funeral directors. It will

ensure the body remains in good condition while it is in their care. They can also charge an extra fee and make more profit by doing it.

There are clear advantages to the bereaved if the deceased is to be viewed. Some funeral directors, understandably, will not arrange for viewing a body unless embalming and cosmetic treatment is performed.

When there is not to be a viewing, the need for embalming is questionable. In modern times one can expect a body to be kept under controlled temperature conditions, which would make embalming unnecessary for the purpose of short-term preservation. Even if there is to be a viewing, providing it is within a few days of the death, cosmetic treatment may be all that is compassionately required.

There is a growing lobby against embalming for ecological reasons. Embalming fluid is very toxic and some people don't like the idea of several pints of it leaching into the ground or, with cremation, having the poisonous chemicals released into the atmosphere. There are other worries about what happens to the blood that is drained away (see Chapter 15). Again, some people simply don't like the idea of the body being needlessly interfered with.

Many funeral directors will automatically carry out embalming without you asking for it and include the cost in the overall price they charge. If embalming is not required you should make this condition clear when commissioning the services of the funeral director.

Planning for Memorialization

Well-intended, but misinformed, advice is often given about when to think about memorials. Something like this is frequently said: 'Wait until after the funeral is over, when the pressure is off, and you can think calmly about what kind of memorial would be best – and not too expensive.'

The Charter for the Bereaved, published by the Institute of Burial and Cremation Administration in 1996, says this on the subject of memorialization: 'Decisions over a memorial should be taken during the period of reflective adjustment following the funeral. There is no rush. Some funeral directors sell memorials at the time of the funeral, and advice may be biased towards recommending a certain grave type, which may have future commercial advantage in the supplying of a memorial.'

I have found funeral directors quite resistant to requests for them to give advice about memorialization at the time of arranging the funeral. They say they have enough matters to consider and resolve in planning the funeral without introducing side issues like memorials at this time. Church incumbents also say that they consider it inappropriate to tell people about churchyard regulations on memorials at the same time as arranging a funeral and burial. They are all wrong.

If a memorial is likely to be wanted, even at some future date, it is very important to consider it before the funeral takes place. The memorial will be installed in the grounds of a crematorium, cemetery or churchyard where strict rules and regulations are enforced. They can dictate the style, material, shape and position and even the wording on a memorial. These rules are not the same throughout the country or even from place to place in the same town. And the rules can change over a period of time.

Invariably the memorial is wanted in the same place that the person is buried or where the ashes have been placed. Looking around and deciding on something similar to what is already there may not be wise. The style of memorial allowed in the past may no longer be permitted.

Once committed to a certain cemetery or churchyard, because that is where the interment has taken place, you will be bound by the current regulations about memorials – and these could prohibit the memorial you really want. The only solution may be to exhume the body or ashes and take them to a place with more accommodating rules about memorials.

This has happened on several occasions. One of the best known of such tragedies is the much-publicized case in a churchyard in Freckleton in Lancashire in 1994. The incumbent insisted that the formal 'Father' and 'Grandfather' must replace the names 'Dad' and 'Grandad' in a headstone inscription. After an appeal to a consistory court failed, the family applied for an exhumation licence and removed the body to a local cemetery where the offending words were not offensive.

It must be better to find out all you can about what sort of memorial might be desired, and what is permitted in the cemetery, churchyard or crematorium you will be using, before you make that virtually irreversible commitment to inter the remains in any particular place (see Chapter 10).

The Essentials of Managing a Funeral

If you are in the position of organizing a funeral, these are the seven essentials, described in detail above, which you should address:

1. Be aware of your responsibilities. When organizing a funeral you take on a long-term and financial commitment. Know how the costs incurred will be met.

2. Before commencing preparations, check whether any sort of funeral plan, requests or arrangements have already been made.

3. Establish who is the person properly qualified as the 'informant' and register the death.

4. Make a cost/value decision about: the style of funeral service; the use of embalming; if it is to end in cremation or burial; whether or not to retain a funeral director.

5. Contact and instruct the funeral directors or other essential service providers.

6. Liaise with those concerned and as appropriate about family and religious matters.

7. Consider the possible implications of memorialization.

THERE ARE MORE THAN 10 MILLION REASONS TO LEAVE US A LEGACY

HERE'S JUST ONE

Every year, the Red Cross Movement cares for more than 10 million men, women and children in crisis all over the world. We provide food, medical aid and longer term assistance to whoever needs it, wherever it is needed. But we rely on the money we receive from legacies to continue this vital work.

Whether you have already made a Will or have yet to make one, please think seriously about leaving a legacy to the British Red Cross. Send for our free, straightforward guide to making or updating your Will by returning the coupon below. And help millions more children like the one above.

For all our tomorrows

Will you help the Red Cross with a legacy?

☐ Please send me your legacy guide, *For all our tomorrows*.

Name (Mr/Mrs/Miss/Ms*)

Address

(*delete as applicable)

Postcode

Please return this coupon to: Legacy Manager, Room BM99, British Red Cross, FREEPOST, London SW1X 7BR. Or telephone 0171 201 5047.

British Red Cross
Caring for people in crisis

2109   Reg. charity no. 220949

3 Things that Have to be Done at the Time of Death

Notification and Certification

Follow the Red Tape Road

Death unfurls a bundle of red tape that has to be followed through before the funeral can commence. The various procedures are illustrated in Figure 3.1 at the end of this chapter.

Nothing can begin until the green form (or if a coroner was involved a yellow form E or white form 101) has been handed to the funeral director or the management at the crematorium or cemetery.

The registrar of births, deaths and marriages issues this crucial green form, the certificate for burial or cremation. To get it, an appropriate person has to make a journey to the registrar's office equipped with the answers to specific questions, which the registrar will ask, and a certificate of cause of death, which may be issued by the doctor or hospital if everything is clear and straightforward.

If there is any doubt surrounding the death, you won't be given a certificate of cause of death by the doctor or hospital. The coroner has to investigate. If after the coroner's post mortem death is found to be by natural causes, the coroner may issue the pink form (form 100). With this you can register the death and be given the green form. A pink form is usually sent direct to the registrar but the coroner may give it you to deliver. If you want the body to be cremated and the coroner agrees to this, you will be given the yellow certificate of cremation by the coroner.

Should the coroner decide that an inquest must be held, you may be given an order for burial (white form 101) or a certificate for cremation (yellow form E). This will enable the funeral to take place before the inquest is over, unless, of course, the body is required for further examination. When satisfied, the coroner will send a certificate to the registrar (form 99 rev) stating the cause of death. This allows the death to be registered without the attendance of an informant.

But by now you may not need to collect a green form from the registrar – you could have previously obtained a white or yellow one from the coroner. The registrar may also give you some other useful documents and, for a fee, copies of the death certificate (see below). After 50 years of being printed with a grey tint background, the death certificate changed in 1999 to a blue tint background featuring a central design of the rose and daffodil emblems of England and Wales. The birth certificate, previously with a red tint, has changed to a matching design and colour blue. The majority of certificates, including short birth certificates, are to be the standard A4 paper size.

Death in a Hospital or Rest Home

Most deaths, about 80 per cent, occur in hospital. Probably half the remainder are in either a nursing home, sheltered residential accommodation or a hospice. When someone dies in one of these places, under professional care as it were, then a member of staff (usually the matron or warden) will contact the person who had been named by the deceased as their next of kin. This may be a relative but not necessarily.

If the death was in the evening or during the night, an appointment will be made for the following day to deal with the formalities. The deceased's possessions will have to be collected by the next of kin or an authorized representative, usually from the hospital's property office. A signature on a receipt for the property will be required.

The hospital will have a mortuary, and the rest home most likely a contracted undertaker with mortuary or chapel of rest, where the body will be kept. And there it must stay until the procedure for collecting the documentation for release of the body is completed.

Certification of cause of death

The first essential is a certificate of cause of death. In hospitals and many homes, a doctor will automatically be notified and, if the cause is quite clear, he or she will fill out and sign a medical certificate of cause of death.

If the body is to be cremated, the hospital should be told as soon as possible. Arranging for cremation may cause a delay, sometimes up to 48 hours, or more over a weekend, while a second doctor who did not attend the patient examines the body and the additional forms for cremation are completed. The hospital staff can make the arrangements and sometimes save the cost of one of the two certificates.

There is no charge for a death certificate but there is a charge for issuing the forms for cremation (£41 for each certificate in 1999). This doctor's fee, known in the trade as 'ash cash', is usually paid by the funeral director and included in the disbursements added to the funeral account.

If there is any doubt and the hospital requires a post mortem to be carried out to confirm the cause of death, the next of kin will be asked to authorize the operation. Sometimes it is necessary for organs to be retained and doctors should give full information when asking you to sign the authorization document. The incident of babies being buried without their hearts after surgery in a Bristol hospital, and the distress caused to parents when this was later discovered, is a well-publicized case in point.

Sometimes the coroner is involved after a death in a hospital: if it was following an accident or injury, an industrial disease, during a surgical operation, under anaesthetic, cause unknown or sudden and unexplained. A coroner's investigation or a hospital deciding on their own post mortem may delay the issue of the medical certificate of the cause of death.

Removal and contract funerals

Once all the necessary forms have been issued, the relatives will be able to arrange for the body to be collected from the hospital's mortuary. Your funeral director, if you have decided to use one, can take care of this (alternative arrangements are discussed in Chapter 15).

The person in charge of the funeral, the next of kin or the executor will normally have to sign a form authorizing the transport of the body to the mortuary or chapel of rest at the funeral director's premises. Funeral directors may be expected to have their own controlled temperature facilities for the short-term storage of bodies. Some, however, have no refrigeration equipment and rely on collecting the body at the last possible time from the hospital mortuary.

Some hospitals sub-contract the provision of mortuary facilities, on the hospital premises or elsewhere, to private firms of funeral directors. You do not have to use them as your funeral directors but can choose to have another firm collect the body and provide the services – or carry them out yourself.

Of course, many people simply allow the contracted firm to win the business and carry on with the arrangements. Because of this 'windfall' of extra trade there is competition among funeral directors for contract funerals at nursing homes and hospitals. Large firms have been known to tender at peppercorn prices and provide a collection service during periods when their staff would otherwise be under-employed. Likewise, many local authorities have contracts with funeral directors to collect bodies after accidents or for post mortems for the coroner's office on a similar basis.

The charge on the NHS and the local community is correspondingly reduced, but so is the variety of choice and quality of service as small independent firms are unable to compete on the same terms.

Hospital staff are not supposed to recommend any particular funeral director but can sometimes supply a list of names and addresses of those in the locality. Chaplains and bereavement counsellors, as well as the managers of the homes and hospitals, will be available to help with practical arrangements and coping with grief.

Expected Death Elsewhere

If a doctor has recently attended a person who dies at home, you should contact that doctor. Do this immediately if there is any doubt about whether the person is actually dead. But if the death had been expected and is certain, there is no need to disturb the doctor in the middle of the night. A visit may not be necessary but it is advisable, though not essential, to have the doctor's permission before the body is removed. Some doctors see the body of every patient who has died as soon as this can be arranged. Others prefer to carry out the examination at the funeral director's mortuary.

If the doctor can certify the cause of death you will be given a medical certificate (in a sealed envelope addressed to the registrar) and a formal notice that states that the doctor has signed the medical certificate and explains how to register the death. Tell the doctor as soon as possible if you know cremation is intended as additional papers will have to be prepared and a second doctor, who had not attended the patient, brought in to make another examination.

Public health regulations come into force if the person has died of AIDS or HIV or other notifiable diseases (cholera, plague, relapsing fever, smallpox or typhus). To avoid the health of others being put at risk, a Justice of the Peace (JP) can order the body to be taken to a mortuary or immediately buried or cremated. There may be special concerns about handling the body after a death following illness from HIV or AIDS. Organizations that can help in these circumstances include London Lighthouse, FACTS Health Centre and the Terrence Higgins Trust.

Unexpected Death

If the death is sudden or unexpected, or you have discovered a body, first of all contact the family doctor if you know who that is. If you do not know how to contact a doctor then dial 999 for the emergency ambulance service.

You should then advise the deceased's nearest relative and, if appropriate, minister of religion. The police will help find the people to contact if necessary.

The police should always be informed, at once, if death appears to have been caused by an accident or violence or other unnatural or suspicious circumstances. The police will notify the coroner if they consider it necessary.

If the police are called, do not touch or move anything in the room until they give permission. They will almost certainly want to take statements from anyone involved but no one is obliged to give one. Anyone who has made a statement, or who the coroner believes may be able to give information about the death, may be called as a witness if there is an inquest.

The coroner must be informed if circumstances surrounding the death are unusual or if no doctor has attended for some time. There are other specific reasons for notifying the coroner and these are listed in Chapter 13.

The coroner will decide whether an inquest, and perhaps a post mortem, is to be held. Most cases are found to be due to natural causes and no inquest is called. However, these investigations take time and if the coroner is involved you must not arrange the funeral until proper authorization is received from the coroner's officer.

If there is to be no inquest, the coroner will notify the registrar of births, deaths and marriages that the death can be registered. The next of kin or qualified informant will have to visit the registrar in person to do this. If an inquest is to be held, the coroner may give you a certificate for cremation (form E, yellow) or an order for burial (form 101, white). Either document will allow the funeral to take place before the inquest is completed. It should be given to your funeral director or delivered to the crematorium or cemetery as soon as possible.

Registration of a Death

Who Has to Do It and When?

Deaths should be registered within five days in England, Wales or Northern Ireland. Someone who knows about the deceased (the informant) has to attend in person at the offices of the registrar of births, deaths and marriages, preferably in the sub-district where the death occurred or where the body was found. If there are problems then the task may be delayed for a further nine days by submitting written confirmation that a doctor has signed a medical certificate of cause of death. There are different regulations in Scotland (see Chapter 14).

The doctor who has been attending the deceased will normally give you the signed medical certificate. This will state the cause of death, the last date the doctor saw the patient alive and whether or not a doctor has seen the body after death occurred.

The informant has to formally, and in person, deliver particular details about the deceased to the registrar. There is a checklist with the certificate, which the doctor will fill in to ensure the informant is fully briefed. This part of the form is headed 'notice to informant'.

Where You Must Go to Register

Armed with this information, and if possible the documents listed below, you will have to visit the office of the appropriate registrar. The entire country is divided into areas from within which people are elected for local councils and national government. Each sub-district within this network keeps a record of the births, marriages and deaths that occur within its boundaries. The registrar is appointed with responsibility for keeping this register. This is a government requirement and is quite separate from parish registers.

It is best to find out where the relevant registrar's office is located (the receiving registrar) and go there. However, if this presents difficulties, it is possible in England and Wales (but not in Northern Ireland or Scotland) to take the information to a more conveniently placed registrar who would be known as the attesting registrar. Everything is sent on by the attesting registrar to the receiving registrar by post, along with a cheque for the number of death certificates required, and the necessary documents posted back to the informant or any other specified address. This toing and froing in the post will obviously cause delays.

Most probably the doctor will write the address of the relevant registrar on the envelope you are given. Alternatively, you can find the address in the local phone book under 'Registration of Births, Deaths and Marriages' or from the doctor, local council, post office or police station.

The registrar is usually a solicitor and may be operating from the offices of the practice or, sometimes, from an office in the town hall, library or other local government building. They are probably open for registrations at set hours on set days so it is as well to check. An increasing number of offices are operating an appointments system, which can cut down your waiting time. You could probably just turn up during office hours and wait until the registrar is free to see you, but interviews can be lengthy. The people concerned are recently bereaved and care and compassion are of the essence. You have quite a lot of organizing to do in a short space of time, so anything that will reduce waiting time is to be welcomed.

You should also check whether you are properly qualified as the informant for the registrar or whether someone other than you will be needed to give information (see Chapter 2). The responsibility cannot be passed on to someone not qualified under the law to act as informant. Should this happen, the registrar will refuse to register the death and insist that a qualified informant makes an appearance.

What You Should Take With You

As the informant registering the death, you will need to take with you the medical certificate of the cause of death and, if available:

▪ the deceased's medical card;

▪ any pension orderbook, certificate or document relating to any pension allowance that was being received from public funds by the deceased;

▪ birth and marriage certificates of the deceased.

You should be prepared to tell the registrar:

▪ the date and place of death;

■ the deceased's last (usual) address;

■ the deceased's first names and surname (and the maiden name where appropriate);

■ the deceased's date and place of birth (town and county if born in the UK, country if born abroad);

■ the deceased's occupation and the name and occupation of the spouse and of previous spouses (if appropriate);

■ whether the deceased was getting a pension or allowance from public funds;

■ the date of birth of the deceased's surviving widow or widower if appropriate.

A friend or relative can go into the meeting with you but it is the qualified informant who has to answer the questions that the registrar asks. Your answers are written down in a draft form, which you will be asked to approve, before being copied into the actual volume of the register.

How the Meeting Will be Conducted

First, the registrar will check that the death occurred in the relevant sub-district; a death cannot normally be registered if it took place, or if the body was discovered, somewhere outside the registrar's sub-district.

Next question will be to establish how you qualify as the informant – as a relative, being present at the time of death, taking responsibility or some other reason.

The registrar may ask if you have all or any of the documents listed above. It is not essential to have these but they can be helpful.

Other questions will cover the date of death and where it occurred, the sex, first names and surname of the deceased. All the names by which the person was ever known should be given, and they should relate to those on birth and marriage certificates and other official documents. If names are different, there could be difficulties over identity in connection with probate, pensions, bank accounts, insurance policies and other important documents. The registrar will go on to collect answers to all the questions in the above list.

Then, the medical cause of death will be copied from the doctor's certificate or the coroner's note, including the doctor's or coroner's name and qualifications.

Some of the information the registrar requires is for the population statistics and not entered in the register of deaths. The deceased's medical card is required to update the NHS register.

You will be asked to approve the information in the draft, which will then be copied by the registrar into the register proper. You will be asked to sign that the entry is correct, in your usual signature using special ink. Finally, the registrar will sign it off. Look carefully for any errors before that final signature; it is difficult to make alterations after it.

The death certificate is a certified copy of the entry in the death register. Once the entry has been signed off, the registrar is able to supply you with copies, but you will be charged a fee for each copy.

Organizations such as banks and building societies, insurance companies and pension providers need a copy of the death certificate before they will release funds. They are pretty good at returning the certificate quickly, so you probably won't need more than three copies.

The fee for copies in the register currently being entered is, in 1999, £3.50 each. After the particular volume of the register is full and bound, probably after about a month, the price goes up to £6.50. If at some future date, when particulars of the registration may have been lost, obtaining a copy requires a search, the fee will be £18. It is a good idea to make a note of the details – the district, date and number of entry in the register – in case you need them later.

There may be some keyboard activity surrounding the filling out of the draft form. Computers are used in many registrars' offices and the particulars will probably be fed into the system and copies printed out. The entry is still made in the register in the usual way and you will have to sign it. Computerized copies can be certified but photocopies will not be accepted.

Without charge, the registrar will also give you a certificate for burial or cremation, known as the green form. That is unless the coroner is involved and you have received a certificate for cremation (form E) or an order for burial (form 101). The funeral cannot proceed without one of these forms, which should be taken to the funeral director, if you are retaining one, or direct to the crematorium or cemetery.

The registrar will also give you a certificate of registration of death (form BD 8 rev) which is for social security purposes. Read the information on the back of the certificate and, if any of it applies, fill in the appropriate sections and send or give it to your social security office.

You can also obtain from the registrar leaflets about widow's benefits and income tax for widows.

Registration of a Stillbirth

A stillborn baby is one born dead after the 24th week of pregnancy. Earlier loss of the foetus is technically a miscarriage and does not legally constitute a stillbirth (see Chapter 13).

The event of a stillbirth should be registered within 42 days at the office of the registrar of births, deaths and marriages preferably in the relevant sub-district. The registrar will make the entry in the stillbirth register.

You can ask to have a first name for the baby entered. The baby's name will be written on the certificates if it is recorded in the register. Certified copies of the entry of stillbirth can be obtained but this does require permission from the Registrar General.

Those qualified to register a stillbirth are the same as for live births: the mother, the father if married to the mother, the occupier of the premises where the stillbirth occurred, a person who was present or who found the body.

A doctor or midwife who was in attendance, or examined the body, will sign and issue a medical certificate of stillbirth. If no doctor or midwife was involved, a responsible person has to sign a declaration (form 35) saying that to the best of his or her knowledge and belief the child was stillborn.

The coroner must be notified if there is any doubt. There could then be an inquest or post mortem and the coroner would issue a certificate of the cause of death.

The doctor or midwife will give you a 'notice to informant' setting out details of who should register the death and what particulars are required. Assuming the coroner is not involved, you will have to take the medical certificate or declaration of stillbirth along to the registrar and be prepared to answer the questions set out in the 'notice to informant'.

You will have to tell the registrar the name, surname and maiden name of the mother, her place of birth and address at the time of the stillbirth. If she was never married, her occupation is required. If married to the deceased child's mother, the name, surname and occupation of the father and his place of birth are required. Unmarried parents are also able to include the father's details but the process is more complicated.

Information for population statistics is required if the father and mother were married to each other. This is the date of marriage, number of the mother's previous children and whether alive or stillborn or by any former husband.

A Neonatal Death

If a baby dies very shortly after birth, a neonatal death, the death should be registered within five days. If necessary, the birth can be registered at the same time. You should, as the informant, go with the relevant information to the office of the registrar of births, deaths and marriages, preferably in the relevant sub-district. The registrar will enter both the birth and the death in the appropriate register.

The procedure will be similar to that described above.

The Essentials for Certification and Registration

1. Obtain a certificate of cause of death from the doctor (unless a coroner is involved).

2. Go as or with the qualified informant to the appropriate registrar's office, taking with you the certificate (if provided) and required information.

3. Obtain from the registrar or coroner the necessary documentation to allow the funeral to proceed and to release any possible funds.

4. Take documents to the funeral directors or other service providers.

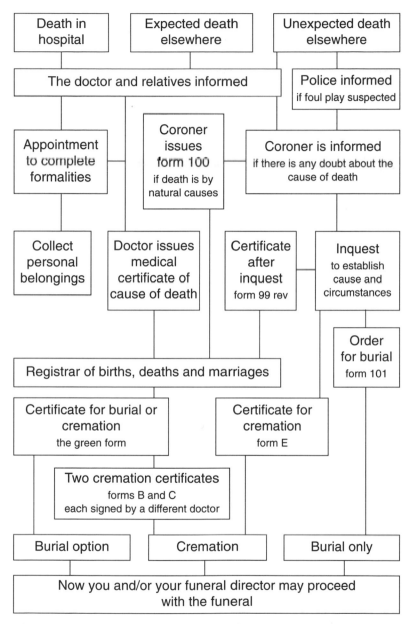

Figure 3.1 *Procedures when someone dies*

4 *The Undertaking*

Choosing Your Funeral Director
The Trade Prefers a Low Profile

Shopping around for a funeral director is not easy. The trade has a low profile and likes to keep it that way. With most purchases you are going to make you have a pretty good idea of what is available, at what prices and what kind of service to expect – and what your consumer rights and protections, warranties and guarantees should provide.

This information is all around you, in advertisements, shop windows and shopping centres. You are welcome to browse in car and furniture showrooms, warehouses and discount stores where helpful people will guide you through the complexities of modern machines, explain why some are twice the price and exactly what the shop will or won't do in the way of delivery and installation. And you are free and easy to walk out and choose the same model next door at a lower price.

Stores are brightly lit to attract your custom, designed to be warm and welcoming with a shop front that makes a statement about the establishment and the quality and style of products and services you can expect. You can tell at a glance the type of organization you would be dealing with: country crafts, state-of-the-art, multi-national, family owned, commission sales or service orientated, discount house or designer label.

But look at funeral directors. Sombre dingy colours, rarely even a smart black. The shop window is obscured by blinds or opens on to a narrow peepshow of dried flowers and drapes. You can't push open the door and walk in for a look around. You have to push a bell-button and wait for someone to descend from upstairs or come from a back room. Inside is a reception room with a couple of chairs and a table or desk.

Of course, it is not a shop. There are no displays of ranges of funerary products neatly set out and clearly labelled with prices. No showcards giving the hire price of a hearse and driver at £X per mile. You are face to face with a businessperson in selling mode. And, unless you have a body for removal, you will be no more knowledgeable about funeral costs when you leave than when you went in.

A Major Business Transaction

The funeral trades associations' codes of practice state that funeral directors must provide price lists that potential customers can take away with them. Consumers' Association researchers visited 78 funeral directors to see if they did. Fewer than half, 31, gave out a price list when first asked. When asked again after a discussion, 23 still failed to provide one. Lists, when they were obtained, were rough estimates of total costs on scraps of paper or the back of business cards. Many gave no details of disbursements, that is, fees paid on behalf of the customer.

The findings were published in _Which?_ in February 1995. At a trade conference in July of that year, the industry's response to the criticism was described as 'breathtaking complacency' by Colin Brown, deputy director of research at the Consumers' Association. Funeral directors said that the sample was too small to be representative and that the 'mystery shoppers' had been recognized as researchers and refused information for that reason. 'Industry leaders just don't understand where the consumer is coming from,' said Colin Brown.

Arranging a funeral is a business transaction and should be treated as such. It is a 'distress purchase', one that must be made rather than one made for pleasant reasons. It is made by distressed people dealing with professionals who are neither prepared nor equipped to enable them to make a fully informed choice.

Funeral services are totally mysterious to the consumer and conducted in an atmosphere that militates against consumer choice. Funeral directors prefer to do too much, to spoon-feed their clients, and at such a vulnerable time the consumer is often over-receptive to suggestions or unaware that this is happening.

Selection of Time, Place and Transport

Mystery Militates Against Choice

People have been known to walk past the door of a funeral director several times before gathering the determination to go inside. Once over the threshold, the environment is unlikely to put you at ease. It may be austere wood-panelled walls or pastel colours, deep pile carpet, soft lighting and plump furniture. There may be a bowl of sweets on the table or a friendly dog. You feel as if you are intruding into someone else's home and, not wanting to seem rude, are inclined to agree with anything you are told.

In contrast, the salesperson, for that is what the funeral director is at this time, is comfortable in familiar surroundings and fully in command of the situation and the subject about which you know very little.

Some funeral directors make a point of visiting you in your own home to make the arrangements. This also gives a salesperson a territorial advantage of a different kind. Your ability to pay, and within what price band, can be easily assessed by a professional looking round your home. You are inclined to be welcoming and polite to someone in your own home and not in a business, negotiating or shopping frame of mind. If the welcome is overstayed you may feel pressured into signing up to persuade the person to leave.

And, of course, with a home visit you won't be able to see the actual premises or products, just pictures in a catalogue or photographs.

You may not in fact decide for yourself on the date and time for the funeral you are arranging, but be steered to a slot that suits the funeral director's timetable. By allowing the funeral director to make all the direct contacts with crematorium, vicar and cemetery you give away much of your ability to negotiate over important points. For example, early morning times at the crematorium may be available at a cheaper rate. They are not popular with the public or with the funeral director, who would rather be doing other things at the start of the business day. The funeral director may be motivated not to tell you that early times are available. The more popular times, like Fridays, may be pre-booked by the funeral director and reserved for high-paying customers.

Most funerals are completed within five days or a week of the death. But do not be pressured into making a date too soon for important things to be arranged and for mourners to congregate. It is better to take another day or two to organize an event that will be meaningful.

Visit the Places Beforehand

The choice of crematorium, cemetery, church or hall for the ceremony and wake or after-gathering can be very important for the convenience of you and your guests. The style and aesthetics of the place can have a major bearing on the success of the event and, given memorialization, for a long time afterwards.

The funeral director has a different agenda. Quickness and convenience are business priorities. The more round trips that can be completed in a day, the higher the profit.

There may be commissions connected with certain establishments. Some funeral directors are part of companies that also own crematoria and cemeteries and may therefore have a vested interest in directing you there.

Try to visit the crematorium, cemetery or churchyard and find out what the place is like and what is going to happen and where. The staff are there to help, guide you through the rules and regulations, explain costs and, if circumstances allow it, make changes to suit your needs.

As well as aesthetics, you should consider journey times. A long journey when at a low ebb, closeted in a car with relatives you haven't seen in ages, and perhaps don't want to, can be unnecessarily stressful.

Journey's Start, Middle and End

You should be prepared to tell the funeral director where you want the ceremony or ceremonies to be held and the most suitable day and time.

The rendezvous for the start of the funeral needs to be established. It may start from the home of the deceased or of a relative, from a church or meeting hall, the funeral director's premises or directly at the crematorium, churchyard or cemetery. You may want a procession behind the hearse from home to church for a service, then from church to the crematorium for a committal service and then cars to take guests to the reception, either back home or at a hotel or other venue.

The funeral director will know the district and the times it should take at certain times of day to travel from one point to another. It is essential to get this timing right, especially for cremation as the crematorium is likely to have the chapel booked for services one after the other all day. If you are late it will interfere with the bookings that follow.

Things the Funeral Director Should Provide

Check Out the 'In-house' Facilities

Most funeral directors will have what they call a 'chapel of rest'. This name is given to different kinds of places. It may be rather like a chapel: a meeting room with rows of chairs and a catafalque or bier on which the coffin can be displayed and where the funeral service is conducted before transport to the cemetery or crematorium. It may also be where the body can be viewed before the funeral.

Not many funeral directors have such a large room and the chapel is more likely to be more of a 'side chapel': a small room just big enough to hold a coffin on a bier and a chair or two. This will be available for viewing the body and may be where the body rests prior to transport to the cemetery or crematorium. 'Chapel of rest' is sometimes used as a euphemism for a mortuary.

A reasonable-sized funeral directors will have a mortuary, a preparation or embalming theatre and several viewing rooms. Those with a large room for holding services may rearrange the room for gatherings and receptions before and after the committal. Funeral directors, once generally known as undertakers, have evolved from other trades such as jobbing builders and carpenters. Many have been operating from the same house where generations of the same family have lived and facilities remain old fashioned. Bodies may sometimes be kept in an outbuilding at the end of the garden, which doubles as a garage. Viewing is in the front parlour of the house as it would have been in the bereaved person's family home. Indeed, undertakers' establishments have long been known as 'funeral homes' or 'funeral parlours'.

This kind of 'homely' family business may be just the sort of funeral service that will suit you. But if you are concerned about what may be behind the scenes, don't be afraid to ask to be shown. And read some significance into a refusal.

Hearse and Limousines

The type of vehicles, hearses and limousines can vary considerably from one funeral firm to another. Some have just one hearse and following car, others have none of their own but hire in from carriagemasters whatever transport is needed. The vehicles may range from a lovingly tended family heirloom, such as a vintage Rolls-Royce or a middle-aged Daimler, to customized stretched limos from the latest Volvo model.

Ask about the vehicles and see them if you can. You need to know they are well kept and serviced. The last thing needed is a breakdown during the funeral.

If you need a number of vehicles and want them all to match in model and colour then you may have to settle for a large firm's standard fleet or find a flexible firm that is prepared to hire in the models you want. Some companies insist you have to use the company's fleet vehicles only, in which case you should find out what they are and decide if you like them. Most are black, but some funeral firms have their own house colour for vehicles.

Check on this if you have strong feelings about what the proper colour should be.

Horse-drawn hearses and mourners' carriages are making something of a comeback. There are operators covering the country and any funeral director should be able to track down a rig.

Uniforms of chauffeurs and bearers should be considered. Pinstripes, frock coats and top hats continue to be conventional, but coloured blazers and trousers or Italian-cut dark suits are also on offer from some firms. There are an increasing number of women entering the trade, so skirts and jackets can also be in vogue.

Monumental Masons

Some funeral directors have a monumental masonry department within their organization. Some have a working relationship with a local mason and will supply memorials made for them on a sub-contracted basis or will direct you to a mason who gives them a commission. Others do not provide any sort of memorial masonry service.

If you are contemplating having a memorial, it is worth checking to see if the funeral director is interested in this aspect and, if so, to what extent (see Chapter 10).

Flowers or Charity Donations

You must tell the funeral director whether or not you will be having flowers. If there are to be flowers, arrangements have to be made for them to be delivered either to the funeral directors or to the home from where the funeral will start. Some funeral directors have their own florists or will take your order and have the flowers made up and delivered. Others will direct you to a florist or leave you to find your own supplier.

If you are having flowers, the funeral director will want to know if they are to go inside the hearse, on top of the coffin, on the roof of the hearse or following cars or travel to the ceremony in the boot. If people are donating flowers, should they be delivered to the funeral director's to travel with the coffin, to the home of the deceased or direct to the cemetery or crematorium? You must also decide what to do with the flowers after the cremation or burial. Give instructions to the funeral director if you want cards collected from the flowers or a note made of the names on the cards.

If you want donations to be made to a charity instead of having flowers, the funeral director can assist by collecting the donations and keeping a record of the donors for you.

Press Obituary Notice and Printing

The funeral director will probably have an arrangement with the local paper to place a notice about the death, time and place of the funeral service and where flowers, if requested, should be sent. The cost of such an insertion in the press will be passed on to you.

You may want an 'Order of Service'. This is a printed sheet to be handed to mourners at the service. It sets out the programme and can include the words of any hymns or songs to be sung, poems and perhaps a photograph and tribute to the life of the deceased. Most funeral directors will be able to arrange for this to be designed and printed. Nowadays, quite a few have computerized desktop publishing packages in order to produce these and other items such as invitations.

Selecting the Coffin

Essential and Most Misunderstood

The coffin is the focus of the funeral. It lies high on the deck of the hearse, entirely on view through the glass windows, and is central to the commemorative and committal service on bier or catafalque. It may be looked on as a statement of a person's lifestyle or a last gift from and to someone much loved.

As a product, it is a much-misunderstood part of the funeral director's itinerary. Commerce is simplified if funerals can be sold as 'package deals'. You are expected to start with the minimum of a hearse, one following car and a full complement of conductor, chauffeur and bearers. More following cars can obviously be added.

The variable cost item is the coffin. To illustrate the difference between the tourist, club and first-class packages, alternative coffins are presented.

More likely than not, they are all identical under the gloss: chipboard beneath a wood veneer-patterned paper. Superficial changes are imparted with medium-density fibreboard (MDF) embellishments and different gold coloured plastic handles.

You may not be able to see an actual coffin. The choice may only be made from colour photographs with studio lighting that makes them look like cabinetmakers' works of art, gleaming with layers of beeswax and shining brass fittings.

While the range of coffins may be basically the same with cosmetic changes, the price differences can be substantial. The packages will have different names but essentially range from the simple funeral with simple coffin ('really only for paupers, sir'), through the standard mid-range product ('this is our best-seller, madam'), to the de luxe ('for someone you loved very much').

Funeral directors' coffin prices bear little relationship to their actual value, more to the level of packaged service, and they may not be priced separately at all. When they are priced separately they are typically £300 to £950. It is possible to buy direct and pay around £100 for a simple chipboard coffin. The funeral director, buying at trade prices, will, of course, pay much less.

United States Influences Increased Choice

Such a limited choice is convenient for the funeral director and has been the normal practice in the UK for many decades. The recently arrived US owners of SCI, however, know that more money can be made by offering a greater variety of coffins. They offer a choice of 12.

In the United States, all coffins are called caskets. In the UK, caskets are rectangular, without any taper from shoulder to head and foot, and containers for cremated remains are sometimes referred to as caskets (these are also rectangular).

More varied and costly coffins and caskets can be bought from other funeral directors that are not part of SCI or the Loewen Group. It is quite possible to spend up to £3,000, or more on a coffin or casket. They can be obtained in solid wood rather than chipboard or MDF and this may be preferred for burial. In the UK, one can also obtain the US-style metal casket with rounded corners and even hermetic seals. These are generally too large for UK-sized graves and may mean the cost of two graves. They cannot be used for a cremation.

There are strict regulations about materials for coffins to be cremated and the handles and fittings are made from brass- or nickel-electroplated plastic. Metal and brass fittings on a coffin, even for burial, are a rarity these days and suitable designs can be difficult to obtain.

Every coffin has to have a nameplate carrying the name of the deceased and this often also includes the (optional) dates of birth and death. Religious or Masonic symbols made from the approved plastic may be fixed on request. You should discuss the use of symbols, even if not required, as a cross may appear if not definitely ruled out.

Some funeral directors buy the coffins already lined and fitted from the factory. Others fit the lining and handles themselves and may allow you to select the type of handles you prefer. The lining, and what is called the gown, may be a one-piece article that envelops the body, leaving just the head showing. You should be able to choose the colour – if only from blue, rose or white. There are dresses and suits designed like a hospital theatre gown, which makes dressing easier, and you may be offered a selection of these. You may like to dress the deceased in his or her own clothes but there are some restrictions, especially if cremation is to be performed.

A Cardboard Alternative

Cardboard coffins have quite recently appeared. They sound cheap but can cost as much or more than basic chipboard coffins. Much is made of them being biodegradable but chipboard also biodegrades, as does all wood over time.

Some cardboard coffins are very good products. I have seen US- and French-made models intended for cremation that are better looking and just as substantial as chipboard.

Cardboard coffins need to be looked at carefully, however. If some types get wet during the funeral, flex while being lowered into a grave or burst when soil is thrown in, the results can be distressing.

Placement of Ashes

If you are going to recover the ashes from the crematorium you should think about a container for them. The convention in the UK has been established by the funeral trade and operates along the same lines as for coffins. Most of the ashes caskets stocked by funeral directors, and therefore offered to the public, are scaled-down versions of the chipboard body casket. In fact, many are made from off-cuts remaining after coffin manufacture. The range on offer is very restricted.

More imaginative and artistic urns are available on the Continent and from the United States in many styles and colours and made from materials such as ceramics, copper, bronze and turned wood. More enterprising funeral directors and crematoria will stock some or have a catalogue from which you can make a selection.

Crematorium staff will probably place the ashes in a plain plastic or cardboard container. You can take delivery in that container or ask the funeral director to transfer the ashes into the casket or urn of your choice.

You should tell the funeral director what you want to happen with the ashes. If you want to bury them in a cemetery, churchyard or the crematorium grounds, the funeral director can arrange for this and you may have an interment service. The ashes will normally be collected by the funeral director a few days after the cremation. If you want them the same day, special arrangements will have to be made well in advance.

Form of Funeral Service
The Most Simple Arrangement

Probably the simplest deal you can do with funeral directors is for them to collect the body (called the removal) from the hospital or wherever the death occurred, prepare and encoffin the body and drive it in a hearse to the crematorium. The mourners make their own way to the crematorium and assemble in the chapel. The coffin is borne in and placed on the catafalque for the duration of a farewell ceremony or service of committal after which the coffin is removed into the crematory by crematorium staff. Even if there is to be no ceremony, the industry's code of practice insists that the coffin enters the crematorium by this route.

A minimum standard for a funeral service, set in 1995 by the Benefits Agency (but deleted from the Social Fund Funeral Payments Regulations in 1997), allowed for the removal, preparation and encoffining, flowers up to a value of £25, bearers, transport in a hearse to a crematorium or place of burial and one following car. You will notice that a following car and floral tribute had been added to the even simpler deal described above. The Social Fund, prior to April 1997, contributed up to a total of £500 to the funeral director's fees for providing this simple funeral, plus disbursements and some other charges.

Along with other significant changes to the Social Fund Funeral Payment Regulations, which came into effect in April 1997, the maximum allowance was set at £600 (see Chapter 5). Obviously, it had been calculated that the funeral director ought not to be out of pocket in providing a basic service at £500–£600, so this can provide a benchmark against which to measure the absolute minimum of what you can expect to pay.

You should find out the funeral director's stance on embalming (see Chapter 2). Some will do this automatically as part of their overall fee, others will charge extra.

Conductor and Bearers

You may have to pay for a complete complement of driver and four bearers with a hearse from some firms. Others will let you find bearers from among family and friends and reduce the hire price accordingly. Perhaps the driver will double as a bearer and show you a saving that way.

The funeral conductor is another individual who may be dispensed with. This is the character who stalks in front of the procession and takes the lead in organizing the funeral director's team and contact with the chief mourners. If you don't want the show of a spare person walking in front or overseeing the team then the conductor can be dispensed with and a bearer or chauffeur take charge.

If you have in mind some element of DIY then you will need to find a flexible funeral director who is prepared to accommodate your wishes at the risk of some disruption to their normal routines.

A Written Estimate Should be Presented

Whatever plans you agree with the funeral director, these should be written up in detail and presented to you with an estimate of the price you will be charged. It is quite likely that the plans will be changed as you discuss them with relatives or for reasons outside your control, so the final event, and costs, will also change. But that first estimate will give a basis from which to work and some idea of the probable cost so that you can cut out some items if necessary or add on extras in the knowledge of what they will cost.

The estimate may be only for the funeral director's own charges and not include the disbursements, which can add £300–£400 to the cost of a cremation and twice that amount to a burial.

Codes of practice say you should be given this written estimate. You are unlikely to get one 'on spec', rather only after you have contracted with the funeral director to carry out the funeral service for you.

Not all funeral directors are members of a trade association or signed up to a code of practice and some may not be prepared to give you a written estimate. There are regional differences of practice and habit. Some take the attitude that it is inappropriate or demeaning to go into detail of prices for such a solemn occasion.

While it will give an indication of what the funeral is likely to cost, the estimate is not a bill. The final account will almost certainly be different when it is submitted after the funeral. The Consumers' Association and the Office of Fair Trading have been pressing for transparency of accounting from funeral directors, that is, requiring them to provide a breakdown of items in the account they send you. Most invoices now split out disbursements from the funeral director's fees but few go into more detail about expenditure.

How the Costs are Made Up

Fees and Disbursements

The funeral director's items on the bill are made up of:

▋ The fee to cover overheads, wages, the cost of products purchased to complete the service and an operating profit.

▋ Products sold to you at a profit such as the coffin, gown, container for ashes, flowers, grave marker and order of service sheets.

▋ Disbursements, which are payments for services purchased on your behalf and passed on to you at cost. Some are unavoidable such as the charge made by the crematorium, the cost of a burial plot, grave digging and doctors' fees for cremation certificates. Disbursements may also include optional extras such as a minister's fees, charges for music, bell ringing, choir, advertising in the press, gratuities and memorial permits.

Usually included in the basic costs are:

▋ removal of the body (in daytime) and storage;

▋ supply of a simple coffin and gown;

▌ hearse and driver;

▌ pall bearers;

▌ travel to place for cremation or burial.

Extra charges may be incurred for:

▌ night-time removal of body;

▌ better quality coffin or a casket;

▌ better quality gown;

▌ viewing in chapel of rest;

▌ embalming;

▌ following cars;

▌ additional travel to church or elsewhere;

▌ flowers;

▌ placement of ashes;

▌ memorialization.

Value Added Tax

You should not be charged any VAT for the services of the funeral director, provision of hearse and cars, crematoria, cemetery or clergy fees. If you buy a coffin or ash container separately, which is not part of a complete funeral package, you can expect to pay VAT. You will also be charged VAT for flowers, newspaper advertisements and printed material such as an order of service, condolence or invitation cards. You will be charged VAT on the cost of a memorial and inscription but not on the permit or grant of right to erect a memorial.

Variations in Costs

The prices charged for funerals show huge differences, both in comparative averages across the country and between funeral directors in the same towns. Some example prices are illustrated in Figure 4.1 at the end of this chapter.

The charges for burial or cremation, which are outside the control of the funeral director, also vary considerably and are liable to change from year to year. These are paid by the funeral director and the cost passed on to you as disbursements. A cremation fee may be £150 in one town and £300 in another. Crematoria have recently had to absorb huge capital expenditure to upgrade equipment to meet new standards for environmental pollution control. Increased costs are inevitably passed on to the consumer in higher fees.

Cemeteries are also seeking to recover costs of care and maintenance by increasing charges for burial rights and grave digging. Grave plots can range from, say, £100 in a rural cemetery to £10,000 for a prime site in an inner-city necropolis. The average cost is between £260–£500 (see Chapters 6 and 7).

The Manchester Unity Friendly Society has conducted 13 nationwide surveys on funeral costs over some 16 years. In 1998 the researchers found the national average cost for a burial was £1,657, rising to £2,391 in London and £1,912 in Scotland. Cheapest burial in the country was to be found in the East Midlands at £1,269. Cremations were cheaper at an average of £1,101.

They found the definition of a 'basic' funeral to be flexible. In some cases, for example, a hearse, coffin or bearers was not included in the quote!

The Society of Allied Independent Funeral Directors (SAIF), which champions family firms against the multiple Co-ops and SCI, commissioned its own survey to compare prices between local firms in different types of ownership. In 50 towns across the UK, one funeral director from each group was asked by telephone to quote for a basic funeral. The results, published in December 1998, showed the average price excluding disbursements quoted by SCI was £1,031. The figure from the Co-ops was £920. From the independents it was £791.

In a letter published in a trade journal, the chief executive of SCI (UK), Peter Hindley, said the SAIF research was 'not a comparison of real prices'. He went on to say that while price may be important it is unlikely to be the deciding factor when it comes to client satisfaction.

'A funeral is a highly emotive purchase that people seldom have to make too often, but the basic rules apply: you get what you pay for and top quality products and services often represent better value for money than cut-price offers, particularly when it comes to peace of mind,' said Peter Hindley.

A Multiple Choice

Family Firm or Combine

The choice is yours. But you may have difficulty sorting the multiples from the independents. The Co-ops and the emerging groups, two of which SCI acquired in a couple of coups to establish their bastion in the UK in 1994, created their groups by acquisition of established family firms. But habitually they have never changed the name over the door.

Funeral directors have always relied for their business on reputation built up over years, often over generations, in the local community. Staff may change but the name stayed the same. The deeply ingrained and valuable goodwill would be lost if the name was replaced by 'XY Region Co-operative Society' or 'Service Corporation International (UK) Funeral Services'.

In 1993, the Funeral Standards Council (FSC), created by the Co-operative Funeral Services Association, had National Opinion Polls (NOP) carry out a survey to find out how customers were choosing their funeral director.

Personal recommendation was the main source of influence: 30 per cent said they would ask a relative or friend (who would mention the name of the firm they knew about from past experience) and 18 per cent said they would go to the nearest funeral company they knew about from local knowledge. Of those who had arranged a funeral in the last five years, 26 per cent had returned to the same funeral director. Only 2 per cent searched a directory. Obviously, a lot of potential business would be lost if the name changed.

One way to spot an 'independent' is to look for the SAIF chain-linked emblem within their advertisements in Yellow Pages, on a window sticker or on their stationery. The Co-ops quite often have a Co-op Society emblem alongside the family name on their funeral home signage, while some openly trade as 'Co-operative Funeral Services'.

Under British law, anyone trading under a name other than their own is required to display a notice to this effect on the premises. The SCI (UK) Group says it can be identified by a framed certificate, usually on the wall inside the reception area, and an external sign. So, if you want to know, be sure to look around.

Funeral Supermarkets

The arrival of 'funeral supermarkets' in the UK has had some influence towards a more open approach to funeral retailing. Adapted from a hugely successful development in France, where it has taken 30 per cent of the market in 10 years, funerals are marketed and managed like ordinary products and services.

Memorials, flowers, vases, urns, coffins and other funerary paraphernalia are displayed, with prices clearly marked, in a familiar shopping environment. People are encouraged to browse and buy goods and not only at a time of bereavement. When arrangements are being made for a funeral, all the items can be examined and compared for quality, value and preference.

A pilot project, the Regale Funeral Store, pioneered from 1996–98 in London's East End, proved popular but failed to attract investment for continued development. Adaptations of the concept have appeared in various parts of the country and increasing numbers of funeral parlours are opening up their shop windows and their attitudes to the public.

The Essentials for Choosing an Undertaker

1. Get the facts to enable you to make choices based on information and knowledge.

2. Plan the event and journeys; visit the places.

3. Check facilities and services provided.

4. Select a suitable coffin.

5. Insist on a clear and complete written estimate in advance.

Example No. 1 – Cremation

'Elegy' coffin (wood composite with oak foil finish) + fittings
Hearse
Two bearers
Removal
Arrangement fee

Total (not including disbursements) £620

Example No. 2 – Burial or cremation

'Elegy' coffin (wood composite with oak foil finish) + fittings
Conductor
Hearse
Limousine
Four bearers
Removal
Arrangement fee

Total (not including disbursements) £910

Example No. 3 – Burial or cremation

'Opus' coffin (wood composite with gloss elm veneer)
+ fittings + gown
Conductor
Hearse + two limousines
Four bearers
Removal
Care, presentation & viewing
Arrangement fee
Total (not including disbursements) £1,125

Example No. 4 – Cremation

'Forte' coffin (solid sapele, gloss finish, panelled sides & double raised lid)
+ fittings + tuxedo
Conductor + hearse + two limousines
Four bearers + removal
Care, presentation & viewing
Classic-style steel ashes urn
Arrangement fee

Total (not including disbursements) £1,625

Example No. 5 – Cremation

'Harmony' casket (wood composite with gloss oak veneer) + fittings + dress
Conductor
Hearse + two limousines
Four bearers
Removal
Care, presentation & viewing
Classic-style 'Cupal' ashes urn
Arrangement fee
Total (not including disbursements) £1,845

Example No. 6 – Burial

'Harmony' casket (wood composite with gloss oak veneer) + fittings + gown
Conductor
Hearse + limousine
Four bearers
Removal
Care, presentation & viewing
Arrangement fee

Total (not including disbursements) £1,560

Example No. 7 – Burial

'White Rose' American-style steel casket
+ fittings + tuxedo
Conductor
Hearse + limousine
Four bearers
Removal
Care, presentation & viewing
Arrangement fee

Total (not including disbursements) £3,115

Cremation disbursements – Example

Local cremation fee	£195
Two doctors' fees	£ 76
Vicar's fee	£ 69
Organist's fee	£ 20
Total	£360

(Please note: all disbursements vary according to a variety of factors. Always check the fees specific to your case)

Burial disbursements – Example

Cemetery in East London, exclusive right of burial for 100 years in plot for two local residents in lawn

section including labour	£627
Vicar's fee	£ 69
Total	£696

(Please note: burial fees do vary according to location and specification of the grave. Always check the fees specific to your case)

Figure 4.1 *Typical funeral costs*

Financial Affairs

Who Pays and When?

Terms of Payment are Getting Tighter

Years ago, undertakers would be fairly flexible about payment from families in the community where they lived and worked and probably knew well. It was understood that the bereaved had many things to cope with, wills to settle, property to sell and so on. If the family was having problems the funeral director may well have accepted stage payments. It was not unusual for them to take payment in advance from elderly people and save it for them until needed, rather like the village pub's Christmas fund. Their details would be filed under NYD (Not Yet Dead) and they would be visited or telephoned at intervals to check on their welfare.

Today, credit control regulations don't allow that sort of deposit taking and payment on tick unless the provider is licensed. Some of the larger groups have set up credit facilities and independents may have access to a credit scheme arranged by their trade association. Visa and Access cards are acceptable in many firms. And, of course, there is a cost attached to using credit facilities.

Terms of payment are generally much tighter now. Most firms will send out their invoice immediately after the funeral and expect payment within their standard terms of, say, 14 or 28 days. Increasing numbers are offering a discount for prompt payment. Some insist on at least the disbursements being paid in advance of the funeral while others want payment in full before the service.

The Responsible Person

Whomsoever steps forward and agrees to take over the funeral arrangements becomes responsible for paying the bill. This person need not necessarily be the next of kin nor the executor, but any person who has assumed the responsibility. It is going to cost at least £1,000–£1,500 so if you are the responsible person, first find out where the money will come from, if there is enough and when it will be to hand.

The person who deals with everything owned by the person who has died is known as the personal representative, the executor (if appointed in the will) or the administrator (if there is no will or no executor named). Find that person and discover if there are any requests concerning the funeral arrangements in a will or among the papers and if there is a plan in position to pay for the funeral in advance of probate (see Chapter 17).

The executor or personal representative has the final say in the funeral including whether to employ cremation or burial. You will need to liaise with that person with regard to arrangements as well as to costs.

Powers of Administration

Probate is the process of proving the authenticity and validity of a will and also the name of the certificate, which gives executors power to administer the estate. The estate is the name for the deceased's money, property and possessions.

The costs of the funeral can be included in calculations of the deceased's debts, taxes and other expenses. These are paid out before any distribution of the rest of the estate is made. But the money won't be released until a certificate of probate or letters of administration are issued. An exception may be if the whole of the estate is worth less than £5,000, when probate is not normally required.

The process of proving the will or, if there is no will, obtaining a grant of administration can take up to three months or more while advertisements are placed seeking creditors. Only then will the money be accessible. Not all funeral directors are prepared to wait for this length of time.

Instant Access Funeral Funds

There are various ways in which prudent people can organize their affairs to make sure money will be available to pay for their funeral when it is needed. A funeral savings plan or insurance scheme can be set up so that payment is made into a trust specifically to pay for the funeral. This way it does not become part of the estate and in risk of being held up during probate. Such a trust fund also means the money is used for the funeral as intended and not diverted to some other purpose by the administrators.

A number of Friendly Societies have savings or deposit schemes that provide funeral bonds that can be paid direct to a named funeral director on the death of the member.

Some pension schemes pay out a lump sum to help with funeral costs and, sometimes, benefits for widows and other survivors. Check to see if there was such an employer's occupational pension scheme in place or – particularly if the person was self-employed – a private scheme.

If a pension was being paid from a previous job, find out if it was being paid by the employer's scheme or an insurance company and notify the appropriate representative. Dependant survivors may be able to get funds from the pension scheme. You can find help for tracing an employer's pension scheme from The Pensions Scheme Registry, PO Box 1NN, Newcastle upon Tyne NE99 1NN (tel: 0191 225 6394).

There may be a scheme in place for funeral costs to be paid from a club or benevolent fund with a trades union, provident club or professional institution that pays benefit when a member dies. The Royal British Legion, for example, can sometimes help out with funeral arrangements for an ex-service person member. Membership of the Cremation Society may qualify for a reduction in the cremation fee or a contribution towards the cost.

If there is a prepaid funeral plan in place then a substantial part, though probably not all of the costs, should have been settled. There are almost certainly going to be additional costs for extras and probably for all or part of the disbursements, so don't assume everything will be taken care of by a prepaid funeral plan (see Chapter 17).

Early Release of Funds From the Estate

If there is money in the estate, in certain circumstances you may be able to secure a payment in advance of probate. The bank account will be frozen, unless it is a joint account, but the bank manager may be able to help with a loan. Building societies may pay out up to £5,000. National Savings may release money to pay for the funeral providing there are no other funds available, the value of the National Savings is under £5,000 and a grant of representation is not being obtained.

All these offices will want to see a copy of the death certificate (an original copy, not a photocopy) and probably the funeral director's bill before they will consider releasing any money.

Insufficient Funds in the Estate

If there is not enough money to pay for the funeral in the deceased's estate, the nearest relative is expected to carry the cost. First in line is a surviving partner, then parents, adult children and their partners and all immediate relatives.

Various changes to the qualifications for payments towards the cost of funerals from the Social Fund have been introduced in recent years. The regulations were open to wide interpretation. However, new regulations, published in April 1997, cut back on items that could be claimed for, such as £25 for flowers, and tightened up on the eligibility of those people who could assume responsibility and collect any benefit.

Help From the Social Fund

Rigid Criteria to Qualify for Benefit

The Benefits Agency may release payments towards the cost of a funeral from the Social Fund in cases of extreme hardship. But to qualify, you, and possibly the deceased's relatives and friends, will need to be experiencing considerable financial difficulty. The criteria are rigid.

The adjudication officer at the local offices of the Benefits Agency will assess the merits of your claim. The decision rests there. Qualifying conditions they will look for are as follows.

It must be considered reasonable for you to have put yourself forward as the person responsible for the funeral costs. The most usual reason is that you are the surviving partner. A partner for this purpose is a spouse or someone you lived with as if you were married (but not in a same-sex relationship). If the deceased had no partner, you will be expected to be a close relative or a close friend.

To qualify for a payment, you or your partner must currently be receiving one of the following benefits: income support, income-based jobseeker's allowance, family credit, housing benefit, council tax benefit, disability working allowance.

If you are not a surviving partner, the Benefits Agency will look to a parent or adult children or their partners to see if they can afford to pay. No Social Fund payment will be forthcoming unless all these close relatives are receiving one of the qualifying benefits.

A further test is to make sure that those relatives deemed responsible have no savings that could be put towards the funeral cost, that is, savings in excess of £500 or, if over 60 years old, in excess of £1,000.

Any savings over these amounts will be deducted from an award made by the Benefits Agency as will any available assets, any lump sums due on death for funeral costs and any monies contributed from clubs, grants, charities or collections among friends. If you do get a funeral payment and later on funds are found in the deceased's estate, it will have to be paid back out of those funds.

Another condition is that the deceased must have been a resident in the United Kingdom and the funeral must normally take place in the UK. Under some circumstances it may be possible to get a payment for a funeral outside the UK if you are a migrant worker or have a right to reside in the UK.

Payment for a War Pensioner

You may be able to get help towards the cost of a simple funeral if the person who died was a war pensioner and died from the disablement condition for which a pension was being paid or while being treated for the condition in hospital.

Payment may also be allowed if the war pensioner was receiving constant attendance allowance or a war disablement pension assessed at 80 per cent or more, with an unemployability supplement, at the time of death. A claim for a war pensioner must be made within three months of the funeral by writing to The War Pensions Agency, Norcross, Blackpool FY5 3WP.

How and When to Claim

If you are not sure whether you will qualify for a payment your funeral director should be able to guide you and will probably have some leaflets and a flow chart to help. However, some funeral directors are reluctant to take on this sort of work. Their business may be so structured that very simple funerals are not economic or they may not be prepared to risk incurring bad debts.

If you don't want to go to a funeral director to help decide if it is worth applying for a funeral fund payment, your local social security office will provide advice and the claim form SF200. An information pack and claim form can also be obtained from the registrar of births, marriages and deaths. This form, together with the funeral director's invoice, has to be posted to one of the six Benefits Agency offices listed in the phone book.

A claim can be made from the date of death or up to three months from the date of the funeral. Payments are usually made by girocheque made out in the name of the funeral directors.

You must be aware that only the Benefits Agency officials will decide whether or not you are eligible for a payment from the Social Fund. If your claim fails, you will personally be responsible for payment of the whole cost of the funeral including both disbursements and fees.

What the Funeral Payment Should Cover

Payment from the Social Fund treats necessary costs and the

funeral director's fees as separate items. Necessary costs would normally appear under the disbursements heading of the funeral director's bill. They cover payments made on your behalf (see Chapter 4).

Necessary costs for a burial

If there is to be a burial, the funeral payments scheme will allow for the cost of purchasing an exclusive right of burial in a basic grave.

The lowest cost option has to be followed, which means, for instance, that if there is a choice of graves in neighbouring cemeteries then the grave being offered at the lowest price will be the only one allowed.

The cost of grave digging or the reopening of an existing grave will also be paid from the fund.

Necessary costs for a cremation

In the case of cremation, the necessary costs allowed are:

▌ the cremation fee, including medical references;

▌ the doctors' certificates;

▌ the cost of removing a pacemaker or similar implant.

Extra costs allowed

The following necessary costs for either a burial or cremation are also allowed:

▌ cost of documentation required for the release of funds that result in a deduction from the award;

▌ transport costs (in excess of 50 miles) for the removal of the body;

▌ transport costs (in excess of 50 miles) for hearse and up to one following car;

▌ the reasonable cost of one return journey within the UK for the responsible person to either arrange or attend the funeral.

Funeral directors' expenses

In addition to the necessary disbursements and extra costs allowances, up to a maximum of £600 may be allowed to cover the costs of the coffin, transport and other products and services supplied to provide a simple, respectful, low-cost funeral, normally within the UK. Any fees for clergy, a church service or other items that some people may consider necessary also have to be covered within that basic £600. The only allowable costs extra to the £600 are those necessary charges listed above.

There is no specification of a basic funeral imposed by the Benefits Agency upon you or the funeral director. It is up to you to negotiate with the funeral director the level of service to be provided within the limit.

Going Over the Limit

You may want to improve on the basic funeral by purchasing additional services over and above the capped value of £600. There are only two ways to do this that would be acceptable to the Benefits Agency. One is to pay from your allowable savings (maximum £500 or, if you are over 60 years old, £1,000); the other is to pay by instalments or some other credit agreement with the funeral director over a period after the funeral.

Payment From a Prepaid Plan

If expenses have been covered by a prepaid funeral plan then you may not be entitled to a payment, or perhaps only to a part payment to meet cremation or burial disbursements not necessarily covered by the prepaid plan.

Municipal Funeral Services

Not all funeral directors are prepared to provide their services under such rigid and restricted conditions. However, increasing numbers of local authorities are contracting with a funeral firm in their locality to provide a municipal funeral service for residents in their area.

The authority puts the contract out to tender and selects the best-value service offered to supply a suitable basic funeral. The chosen funeral director can organize his or her business to manage this type of funeral and can also expect increased business from referrals from the municipal cemetery and crematorium. Municipal funeral services are by no means universal but it may be well worth making the enquiry.

Most cemeteries and crematoria will provide you with a direct service, that is, without you having to retain a funeral director. However, very few people are prepared to cope with managing all the arrangements for themselves (see Chapter 15).

No Responsible Person Identified

If no responsible person can be found to pay for the funeral, the local authority or the hospital where the death occurred has to arrange and pay for the funeral. When the death is in a hospital and relatives cannot be traced or are unable or refuse to pay for a funeral, the health authority may take over arrangements. Many hospitals have a funeral fund. They may make a claim on the deceased's estate to reimburse them for the costs.

If the hospital has reason to believe the deceased's relatives have the means to pay for the funeral but are unwilling, they will probably ask the local authority to arrange the funeral. Local authorities have power to recover the costs of a funeral from the deceased's estate or from anyone responsible for maintaining that person while alive.

Most local authorities have an arrangement with a local funeral director to carry out basic funerals under these circumstances. While probably not politically correct, such arrangements are still known as paupers' funerals and there are strict procedures for them to be carried out. If it seems that such a funeral is going to be appropriate, you should not contact a funeral director or begin any funeral arrangements. If you do you will be deemed the responsible person and the costs will hit your pocket. Local authorities have no power to reimburse costs to a third party.

The Essentials of Funeral Finances

1. Ensure funds to pay for funeral costs will be available when needed.

2. The nearest relatives are expected to carry the cost if there are insufficient funds in the estate.

3. Expenditure from the estate may be for the cost of a funeral commensurate with the deceased's lifestyle, not excessive.

4. The criteria necessary to qualify for a contribution towards the cost of a funeral from the Benefits Agency are very strict.

Variety Club's Wills and Legacies programme has raised more than £1 million since it was started in 1997, and now in the Charity's 50th Anniversary year, is one of its most successful fundraising appeals.

Money bequeathed to the Variety Club Children's Charity goes towards supporting its work with sick, disabled and disadvantaged children across the UK. Because Variety Club is a membership organisation of volunteers, with only a small permanent staff, it can ensure that about 90 pence in every pound goes directly to the children who need it most. Every appeal is carefully researched, and grants are made quickly and efficiently.

A bequest to Variety Children's Charity will be spent on improving the quality of life for children who have special needs. It may be used to buy a Sunshine Coach or an electric wheelchair, giving freedom and mobility to disabled youngsters.

Special equipment such as computers could be donated to individual children or schools for pupils with special needs, giving them the opportunity to communicate for the first time.

Variety Children's Charity has given more than £10 million to children's hospitals, including the building and maintenance of the Variety Club Children's Hospital in south London. This hospital has become an international centre for the treatment of liver disease, neurosurgery, sickle cell and cystic fibrosis. Donations are given for everything from toys for the patients, to life-saving equipment, and to build new wards.

Smaller grants are constantly being made to individual children: for example, a few hundred pounds to buy suitable toys for a severely disabled toddler. The Charity is often there when desperate families have nowhere left to turn.

With millions granted every year to hospitals and hospices, schools and respite homes, youth clubs and playschemes, Variety Children's Charity is active throughout the country.

The children Variety Club helps are special, and deserve the chance to fulfil their potential. A bequest to the Charity will make a real difference to children's lives, and offers the chance to give them hope for their future.

For more information, telephone: 0171 428 8100 Or write to: The Variety Club, 93 Bayham Street, London NW1 0AG Email: info@varietyclub.org.uk

USE YOUR WILL POWER TO HELP US

Barry

Gloria

Paul

The Variety Club has just one objective; to raise funds for children who are disabled or deprived, affording opportunities and enjoyment that would otherwise be beyond their reach.

Using the power of your Will, a legacy (no matter how small) will enable the Variety Club to continue providing Sunshine Coaches and Electric Wheelchairs and more - which make a real difference to a disadvantaged child's life.

Please complete and post the form below (with no obligation) to receive further details on how the power of your Will and a legacy to the Variety Club can help.

If the form is missing please write to the following address and we will send you a leaflet:
The Variety Club of Great Britian, FREEPOST 20WD 1707, London W1E 9DH

✂

To : The Variety Club of Great Britain, FREEPOST 20WD 1707, London W1E 9DH.

☐ Please send me a leaflet (without obligation) on how the power of my Will can help disadvantaged children.

☐ I enclose a donation now by cheque/postal order made payable to The Variety Club for £ _____

Name _____ Address _____

_____

_____ Postcode _____

♥ariety Club
The Greatest Children's Charity in the World

RM1   Registered Charity No. 209259

For further information **please insert 8220** on Reader Enquiry Card.

Cancer touches everyone

You may not have cancer yourself but the chances are you know someone who does

Cancerlink
TIME FOR EVERYONE

Cancer now accounts for more deaths in the UK than any other cause, around a quarter of a milion new people are diagnosed every year and the incidence is rising. A cancer diagnosis leaves a person feeling angry, afraid or isolated. To relieve these feelings they need to know what is happening to them and what will happen, they need information in a way thatthey can understand - backed up by emotional support and the opportunity to discuss concerns.

Cancerlink's unique combination of services offfers health professionals, those living with cancer and their families, friends and carers the full range of cancer-related information.

- Cancerlink operates Freephone Cancer Information Helplines aimed at people with general concerns about cancer, children and young people and Asian people.
- We produce a range of publications including booklets, factsheets, video tapes and audio tapes on emotional and practical issues raised by the diagnosis of cancer.
- We act as a resource for over 700 cancer self help and support groups across the UK, help people who are setting up new groups and offer training, development and consultancy.

If you would like to know more about leaving a legacy to Cancerlink, please call 0171 520 2604 for further information or write to Cancerlink, 11-21 Northdown Street, London N1 9BN
Email: cancerlink@cancerlink.org.uk

Cancer Touches Everyone

Cancer can affect people's lives in ways they may not expect. It isn't just about physical illness. It's about your job, doing your shopping, your relationships with friends and family. Often medical professionals will not have the time to discuss all these aspects of your life. Cancerlink has time. Cancerlink's holistic approach not only satisfied people's need for medical information but also meets their psychological and social needs, empowering people to maintain control and improve the quality of life.

Through Cancerlink's Freephone Helplines we offer a calm listening ear alongside sound, practical information. Cancerlink's helplines are staffed by trained cancer nurses, social workers and counsellors. We produce factsheets, booklets and audiotapes which can be sent out to people needing support and information. Cancerlink also acts as a resource to over 700 local self help and support groups across the UK, helps people who are setting up new groups and offers training, development and consultancy.

Anyone can contact Cancerlink, wherever they are in the UK, with questions about any aspect of cancer or for emotional support. We are here for people with cancer, their families, friends and carers.

Cancerlink's Freephone Cancer Information Helplines are:
Freephone Cancer Information Helpline:0800 132 905
Freephone MAC Helpline for young people affected by cancer: 0800 591 028
Freephone Asian Cancer Information Helpline in Bengali, Hindi,

Cancerlink
TIME FOR EVERYONE

Cancerlink
11-21 Northdown Street
London N1 9BN
Tel: 0171 833 2818
Fax: 0171 833 4963
Registered Charity No: 326430

6 Cremation

The Choice of the Majority

A Cultural Revolution

More than 70 per cent of funerals in the UK ended in cremation in 1998. That amounts to nearly 440,000 cremations. They were carried out at 237 crematoria. Six new crematoria were opened during the year (though Arnos Vale at Bristol was closed) and more are under construction and being planned.

In the UK 100 years ago cremation was virtually unknown, in fact it was illegal before 1884. The first UK crematorium was set up in Woking in 1879 but was only allowed to cremate a horse. The first human body was cremated there in 1885. Growth of the movement was very slow. By 1940, there were only 54 crematoria in operation and only 9 per cent of funerals ended in cremation. But in the 20 years between 1947 and 1967 the number had increased to the point where more people were being cremated than buried. The proportion of cremations continued to climb steadily until the early nineties, when it seems to have levelled out.

What has brought about this dramatic swing in deeply held cultural behaviour? Technology? Well, yes. But cremation has been widespread in the world for a very long time: in Genesis, Abraham is ordered by God to prepare a funeral pyre for the sacrifice of his son, Isaac, and the Greek and Roman civilizations generally adopted cremation. It was the spread of Christianity with its belief in resurrection that resulted in burial becoming the norm throughout the Christian world since the fifth century AD.

Then came the Victorian revolutionary enthusiasm for municipal hygiene. Cemeteries were built on the edge of towns.

But cremation was observed by those in the know as being, they considered, an even better solution to the problem of polluted churchyards.

Sir Henry Thompson, surgeon to Queen Victoria, saw a 'cremating apparatus' exhibited at the Vienna Exposition in 1873. He was immediately an ardent supporter and promoter of the concept and gathered a group of friends, all living within partying distance of his home in London's Wimpole Street, to form the Cremation Society of England. They were an elite group from the realms of literature, art, science and medicine, striving to spread information and change the public attitude to cremation. Their purpose, in fact, was propaganda.

Progress was slow and 60 years after its formation, in 1934, the Society recorded an annual total of 8,337 cremations. 'Soon the industrial classes were to be brought within the orbit of the movement,' reports their brochure, *The History of Modern Cremation in Great Britain from 1874.* They had identified that 'the immediate problem was to convince the masses of the people that cremation was suitable for their purposes and that it was not purely a perquisite of the intellectual and moneyed section of society'.

Private to Public Sector Ownership

The first four crematoria to be opened, in Woking (1885), Manchester (1892), Glasgow (1895) and Liverpool (1896), were all private enterprises. The first municipal crematorium opened in Hull in 1901. The Cremation Society commented: 'Now for the first time, a local authority had acknowledged how important it was, both socially and economically, to provide cremation services for the community.' The trend had begun for virtually all subsequent crematoria to be municipal.

In recent years a few municipal crematoria have passed into private hands and a number of new private projects have been built. Still, out of 237 crematoria operational in 1998 there were only 43 in private ownership.

The pressure and propaganda to cremate was increased during the war when, in fear of the havoc that could result from aerial bombing, emergency regulations were passed that allowed the authorities to carry out thousands of cremations. The figures rose from 16,312 in 1938 to 50,000 in 1946. It was clear that, where facilities were provided, increasing numbers of the public would be prepared to accept cremation.

Local authorities were facing something like a rerun of the overcrowding of churchyards which had led to cemeteries being created in the mid-1800s. Cemeteries were filling up and many other social demands were being made on land resources. The cost of maintaining the landscapes of stone memorials was an increasing burden on the rates. Cremation was seen as being able to make a substantial contribution towards a solution. There was an expectation that advancing cremation technology would eventually enable every trace of a body to be vaporized so there would not be even an ash disposal problem. This has not been realized.

Post-war National Policy

The Minister of Health, Mr Aneurin Bevan, was persuaded to relax restrictions on building activities to enable new crematoria to be built. This was the start of a post-war policy of encouraging local authorities nationwide to provide crematoria 'where they would meet the needs both of densely populated areas and of the scattered rural areas'.

In the next 20 years, 150 new crematoria were built. And where they were built, people were prepared to use them. Indeed, they received some encouragement and incentives to do so.

The main argument for cremation advanced by the founder of the cremation movement, Sir Henry Thompson, was a sanitary one. He also believed that cremation would prevent premature burial, keep the human remains safe from vandalism in urns within columbaria, reduce the expense of funerals and spare mourners the necessity of standing exposed to the weather during interment.

Funeral directors were quick to appreciate the reduction in their costs as the time involved in conducting a cremation is much less than for an earth burial. They also were able to enjoy, as much and more often than mourners, the clean, dry and warm environment of the crematoria. They were and are enthusiastic promoters of cremation whenever appropriate.

Local authorities were able to set the cost of cremation favourably against that for burial. They introduced regulations that proscribed stone memorial landscapes. The Cremation Society continued campaigning to 'Keep Land for the Living' and by 1967 more people in Britain were cremated than buried. The tide had turned.

The Crematorium Service

The Place

The vast majority of crematoria were built during the fifties and sixties and bear the marks of the architectural style of the period. They are generally bland, fearsomely functional and, with the inevitable chimney, give the impression of a unit on an industrial estate. Pre-war examples may be Victorian gothic, emulating church/chapel architecture and some with art deco style. Very few aspire to any significant spiritual quality.

They may be within or beside a cemetery, though often on an edge-of-town site, and set in a town park landscape of lawns, flower beds and shrubs. They are usually well signposted with directional signs on approach roads.

The buildings comprise: an administration block of offices, reception and staff rooms; one or two auditoria, usually called 'the chapel', where the committal service is held; the crematory, where the equipment and machinery to cremate the body is housed; a chapel of remembrance, where an inscribed book of names is displayed and probably where floral tributes can be placed; sometimes a chapel of rest, where an encoffined body may be kept before the service; a wreath court or terrace, where floral tributes are displayed after the funeral. Some crematoria have a large reception room where families can gather before and after the ceremony. There may be places for commemorative plaques or rose gardens (see Chapter 10).

The sites are designed to manage a constant flow of traffic, in and out and parking, so there is probably a gyratory one-way route.

The System

Few crematoria do less than 1,000 cremations a year, although five handled more than 4,000 each in 1998 when the average was 1,845. Most are open for business five days a week from 9 am to 4 pm and closed for public holidays. Working days are busy and the time allowed for each cremation service is closely controlled and managed. The most typical time allowed for a service is 20 minutes. Some allow 30 or even 40 minutes. It may be possible to secure two periods if you want to conduct a special, more prolonged ceremony. If you want more time then be sure to make clear arrangements with the management well in advance.

Friday late mornings and afternoons are the times most in demand, with Thursdays being the next most popular and Mondays being the quietest. Some funeral directors make block bookings for the most popular times and hold them in reserve for their clients. So, if you are not using that funeral director, the times may be already booked so far as you are concerned. Early mornings are not in great demand and it is sometimes possible to obtain a reduced rate for these times.

Quite recently, exhibiting an enlightened approach to consumer demand, a few crematoria have been prepared to open on a Saturday morning, though a premium charge can be expected. At least one, newly opened and in private ownership, has a seven-day week cremation facility with service times at 45-minute intervals.

You may have the service conducted by a member of the clergy from your own church or one provided by the crematorium. You may commission an officiant from the British Humanist Association or some other organization or have a friend officiate. However, it will be a stressful time and it is usually best to have the experience of a professional to rely on (see Chapter 8).

On arrival at the crematorium for the funeral, you will be met by the supervisor or a member of staff who will liaise closely with the clergy, organists and funeral directors and who is responsible for ensuring that the service runs smoothly. If you are not using a funeral director, the crematorium staff should be available to advise and help.

Once the coffin has been brought into the auditorium and placed on the catafalque it passes from the funeral director's area of responsibility and into the control of the crematorium staff.

Music

It is highly recommended to have music playing as mourners move into the chapel before the ceremony and as they depart afterwards. Many crematoria have an organ and organist who will play the tunes you request; others will have facilities to play music tapes, records or CDs; some will have both. Do let them know what music you want and when. If you are bringing your own taped music, make sure it is wound and set to start at the right place in the soundtrack. And be sure it has been recorded at the same speed that it will be played back at.

Religious issues

If there is more than one chapel, there may be one that has Christian symbolism and one without. You should be able to have any Christian artefacts removed or screened off if this is desired. But do give the staff prior warning of any requests of this nature.

The committal

Crematoria have different arrangements for moving the coffin into the crematory after the service. Some transport it mechanically through a panel opening in a wall, others have it lowered on the catafalque through the floor. In some the coffin remains on the catafalque to be obscured by a motor-driven curtain. Alternatively, it may be left on view until after the mourners have left.

The facilities available will dictate some of the choices available but others you can decide: for example, is the curtain to stay open or to close? Is the coffin to be transported away while the mourners watch or is it to remain in place until you have all left?

The Cremation Process

The first official cremations in the UK, in the crematorium at Woking in 1885, took between one and one and a half hours. Today, even with the most modern machinery, the process takes the same amount of time. The early coke-fired furnaces were replaced by gas burners and nearly all of the UK's cremators are now fired by gas. A few electrically powered units have been commissioned in recent years.

Modern cremators cost approximately £150,000 each and most crematoria will have at least two and some twice that number. Each will complete 800–1,000 cremations a year. They are sophisticated machines with computerized controls and monitoring equipment to maximize efficient operation and ensure compliance with the requirements of the Environmental Protection Act 1990.

The chamber is designed to accommodate just one individual coffin. Some, indeed, cannot contain the largest of coffins, which has meant very big people having to be buried or transported to another crematorium where a more commodious model of cremator is available.

Before the coffin is put into the chamber, known as the charging process, the space will be preheated to 850 degrees Celsius. Using carefully controlled gas and air jets, temperatures in excess of 1,000 degrees Celsius will be attained during the cremation process. With the most modern cremators, microprocessors are installed and most of the controls are automatic. The aim is to maintain the most efficient temperatures as required at specific stages of the process and no emission of smoke.

The coffin may be manually pushed into the chamber off a bier (a trolley on wheels adjusted to the height of the cremator chamber door). More modern cremators have a mechanical charging system by which the coffin is placed on an extended platform and automatically moved into the chamber, the door to the furnace opening and closing with perfect timing and all without the physical intervention of an operator.

All that will remain at the end of the process, which takes about 1 hour 20 minutes, will be parts of the largest skeletal bones reduced to a calcified crumbly texture. These are then processed through a machine called a cremulator into a fine granular powder known technically as 'cremated remains' but generally called ashes.

There may be nails or staples from the coffin structure among the ashes and these are removed using a magnet. The ashes are then placed in a container and the identity card, which has followed right through the process, is placed with the remains and the name transferred to the identifying label on the container.

Identity Controls

An identity card is made out for each cremation at the start of the day from information provided on the cremation forms. At the end of each service the coffin is transferred directly from the catafalque into the crematory. The nameplate on the coffin is checked against the identity card and the coffin will be cremated only if the details are correct. Any differences are checked out and usually quickly resolved. The most common discrepancy to occur is when people use different names from those on the official forms, or nicknames that are not entered on the forms, and these 'unofficial' names are engraved on the coffin plate.

When the coffin enters the cremator, the identity card is removed from the coffin and fixed in a cardholder on the outside of the particular cremator. When the cremated remains are recovered at the end of the process, the card is removed from the holder and placed with the ashes. This obviates any risk of ashes being wrongly identified.

After the ashes have been collected, scattered or buried by the crematorium staff, according to your instructions, a note will be added to the identity card and this will be filed with the other cremation forms. A record will also be made in the cremation register that will include the location of the ashes if they have been placed within the crematorium grounds or cemetery.

If the ashes are to be taken away and placed in a churchyard, cemetery or crematorium grounds elsewhere, a cremation certificate may be required. This is evidence that the cremation was completed by whichever particular cremation authority. There may be a fee for this certificate.

Code of Cremation Practice

The Federation of British Cremation Authorities (FBCA) monitors and regulates the conduct of cremation throughout the United Kingdom. The FBCA began as a branch of the Cremation Society and eventually evolved into a separate entity. Together these organizations drew up a code of cremation practice that, since 1946, has provided the ethical standard by which crematoria are administered.

Ever mindful of public sensitivities concerning cremation, the code is very insistent about the admission of coffins for cremation. Rumours and suspicions still persist that coffins are not in fact burned during the cremation process but recovered and used again.

It is perhaps to avoid any misinterpretation of the passage of coffins on the premises that the code insists that coffins may only be accepted through the service chapel. They are very publicly viewed going into the crematory but never seen 'round the back'. This means that even if you are not having a committal service for the cremation, you still have to book a service period at the crematorium and have the coffin formally received and ushered through.

Another tenet of the code states that everything received on the catafalque has to be cremated. This has recently been redefined to permit use of 'cocoon' coffins, but still means that the 'proper' coffin and its contents – the body, clothing, mementoes, jewellery and so on – all go into the cremator.

Reusable cremation coffin

A new type of reusable coffin has recently been marketed in the UK that comprises a cardboard inner container housed in a substantial wooden outer shell that is intended for reuse. It is sometimes called a 'cocoon' coffin or casket. The whole ensemble is displayed on the catafalque for the ceremony but only the disposable inner box is destined for the cremator.

This provides for a better show and better security during transport than using a cardboard coffin for the entire journey. And it can result in a significant saving in costs if an expensive-looking coffin is required.

This harks back to the days of the parish coffin, when ordinary folk would be carried to their grave in a community coffin and then removed from it for burial wrapped in a shroud. The coffin was then retained for use for future parish burials.

Elaborate outer casket shells with plain and simple inner containers are widely available in the United States for both burials and cremation. But these are hired out for the ceremony rather than being 'on the parish'.

The innovative British version was at first banned under the conditions of the code. But the manufacturer appealed and, among considerable media publicity, the FBCA has condoned its use. They took the view that the use of an outer cover to encase a coffin was similar, in principle, to a flag or pall draping a coffin during a service and being removed before cremation. It did not therefore offend the code.

The FBCA is, however, to issue guidelines. Among particular points of concern is that the applicant for cremation should give written authority to the crematorium for the use of a coffin shell and for its subsequent removal. There should also be adequate identification of the deceased on both the outer shell and the inner container.

The decision on whether or not to accept 'cocoon' coffins is to be made by the individual crematorium and may be influenced by the layout of the buildings and the ability to remove the shell in a way that would not cause offence or concern to visitors.

If you intend to use a 'cocoon' you should check in advance with the crematorium and, if they can't accept, consider choosing a different site if using this type of coffin is important to you.

Same-day cremation

Another article of the code that is coming in for criticism insists that all bodies received at the crematorium must be cremated during that same working day. The method of operation of cremators is strictly controlled to limit the possible discharge of harmful chemicals and achieve compliance with the Environmental Protection Act 1990.

Each cremator has to be preheated in readiness for use. This consumes a considerable amount of gas, adding to the costs and creating emissions that could be avoided. The practice is to turn on the cremators in the morning, turn them off at the end of the working day and leave them to cool until the following morning. This also puts additional stress on the refractory linings. Logically, fewer cremators should be used for longer periods of time. But this would mean a change in the code of practice to allow cremations to take place over 24 hours rather than on the same working day that the funeral was conducted.

Essential Documentation

Statutory Forms

Since the earliest days of the cremation movement there has been anxiety about the possible destruction of a body that may have met death illegally. Unlike after burial, a body cannot be recovered for later examination if a crime or some other problem is suspected. Keen to avoid any criticism, the Cremation Society insisted on three conditions being observed before a body was accepted for cremation at Woking. These formed the basis for the statutory requirements that remain in force today.

It is sometimes possible to carry out a burial before registration of the death, on the authority of a disposal certificate, but cremation cannot take place until the death has been properly registered (see Chapter 3). Four statutory forms also have to be filled out. You can obtain them from the crematorium, the funeral director or the doctors who will have their own supply of the forms that concern them.

Form A, the application for cremation, is normally completed by the next of kin or the executor (one person may be both). If you are neither next of kin nor executor but you are the person taking responsibility for the funeral, you will have to explain why. For example, you may be a close relative or close friend. As an applicant you will make a declaration on the form that you have no reason to suppose the death was due to violence, poison, privation or neglect. A householder who knows you should countersign it, though many crematoria will accept the funeral director as a counter signatory.

Forms B, C and F have to be completed by doctors. Form B is filled out and signed by the doctor who attended the deceased during the last illness and it is this doctor who must examine the body. You may be asked questions about the deceased's medical history or if a pacemaker was fitted. Pacemakers have to be removed as they can cause an explosion during cremation.

Form C is a confirmatory certificate of cause of death and has to be completed by another doctor who was not attending the patient. This doctor also has to examine the body. Each doctor is entitled to a fee of £41 as fixed by the British Medical Association for 1999/2000. Form C is not required for some hospital deaths where a post mortem has been carried out and the doctor completing form B is aware of the results. This can save on the second doctor's fee.

Form F is completed by the medical referee at the crematorium and confirms that the particulars on forms B and C are satisfactory. The referee has the authority to prevent cremation taking place and order a post mortem but this is a very rare occurrence. The referee receives a fee, which is sometimes included in the crematorium's fee and sometimes included in the funeral director's disbursements.

Notice of Cremation

In addition to these statutory forms, the crematorium will require a Notice of Cremation. This form, supplied free, constitutes a binding contract for the payment of fees to the crematorium. If you sign it, you will be responsible for paying the bill and for what happens to the ashes. If the ashes are going to be kept and memorialized then this can mean a long-term responsibility for a memorial or columbarium niche.

Information you will need to fill in the form will be:

▋ name, address, age and occupation of the deceased;

▋ whether a coffin (tapered from shoulders to head and feet), casket (straight sided) or 'cocoon' (reusable outer shell with cardboard inner container) is being used;

■ date and time for which the service is booked;

■ details of the service including name of officiant or member of the clergy, order of service, religious artefacts desired or to be removed, music or other requests;

■ what you want done with the ashes (see Chapter 10).

Notice in advance

You should make a provisional booking at the crematorium in advance of the statutory forms being obtained. This will allow you to make a start on the arrangements straight away. Check first that the officiant or member of the clergy you want is available at the right time and day. The crematorium or funeral director will have contacts with these people if you don't know one already. Once that person's availability is confirmed you, or the funeral director, should contact the crematorium with the following information:

■ Date and time of the service. This is when the funeral cortège will arrive at the crematorium chapel and the coffin is transferred into the care of the crematorium staff. Normally at least three days' notice is given. Sometimes more time is needed to obtain the cremation medical certificates, death certificate from the registrar or coroner's order. Services may be booked at fixed times and may be of 20, 30 or 45 minutes' duration. The crematorium will have its own schedule. It may be possible to book extra time, most likely for an extra fee.

■ Name and address of the deceased.

■ Name, address and telephone number of the acting funeral director or the person arranging the funeral, who will be responsible for paying the crematorium's fees, usually before the cremation takes place.

The Cost of Cremation

The fees charged by crematoria for the use of their facilities are normally paid by the funeral director and passed on to you as disbursements. The crematorium fee will normally be inclusive of the use of the chapel, the process of cremation and container for ashes. The necessary fee paid to the doctor appointed as referee to sign the form F is sometimes, but not always, included in the basic fee. There may be extra charges for the provision of recorded music and the organist's fee.

The fees range widely from as low as £90 to more than £300 for a local inhabitant. Some authorities will charge a premium above the standard rate to cremate persons who lived outside their boundaries. However, in 1998 the majority of fees fell in the £150–£250 band.

Fees have been increasing at about three times the rate of inflation in recent years and may be expected to continue rising. The Chartered Institute of Public Finance and Accountancy has calculated that the cost to cremation authorities of compliance with the Environmental Protection Act 1990 will be well over £100 million.

There has been a minor flurry of building new, privately owned crematoria in the past two or three years and some municipal operations have been acquired by the private sector. This has resulted in a change of attitude towards service to the public and a wider choice of facilities and styles of presentation.

If you have more than one crematorium within reasonable travelling distance it will be worth making a comparison of costs and facilities available. There are increasing choices of memorialization being offered and some sites have nature reserves and wildlife areas that may be appealing.

Environmental Issues

Every cremation results in up to 2 kilograms of ashes – more than 1,000 tonnes a year in the UK.

The remains are calcified bone that has been heated to more than 1,000 degrees Celsius and then ground into a granulated material that may be described pragmatically as heat-treated bonemeal. In volume, the average body reduces to 3.5 litres (220 cubic inches) of remains. This material is biologically inert. Cremated remains, unlike a natural corpse, do not decompose and might not disperse when buried.

Sir Henry Thompson, campaigning for cremation in 1874, advanced as an economic-technical argument that the ashes might be used as a fertiliser. Bonemeal is tolerated by lawn grass when distributed at 100 grams to the square metre. A higher density causes 'burning' of the grass and the brown patches visible on the lawns at many crematoria.

The process of cremation uses up a lot of gas and releases carbon monoxide, the 'greenhouse gas', into the atmosphere. Burning coffins, mostly made from chipboard containing chemical glues, releases other gases and particles, some of which can be harmful.

Burning a body may also release harmful substances, such as mercury, into the environment. Or they can remain in the ashes with a risk of accumulating to an unacceptable concentration when cremated remains are scattered or buried in a high density.

The material from which coffins are made, whether wood or cardboard, results from the destruction of a tree, which some people consider undesirable. To burn it for a cremation is deemed even more unacceptable.

Cremationists argue that the process has released, 'for the living', thousands of acres of land that would otherwise have been used for burial. This is true of the UK, where the reuse of burial land was discontinued with the introduction of designated cemeteries in the mid-1800s. But it would not be so significant if a sustainable programme of reuse had been implemented such as is prevalent across most of mainland Europe.

The Essentials of Cremation

1. Crematoria are functional and busy. Their style may or may not suit your plans for the funeral.

2. You can have a ceremony elsewhere and/or at a different time.

3. The journey time to your nearest crematorium may be a deciding factor.

4. The cremation process is strictly controlled and you can be reassured that the ashes you receive are the right ones.

5. The cost of cremation varies from place to place but is generally less than burial.

6. It is possible to arrange a cremation without a funeral director.

7. If you are responsible for the funeral then you are also responsible for giving instructions about what happens to the ashes.

8. Memorialization after cremation can be arranged in a variety of ways.

Burial

The Choice of a Large Minority

No Standardized Regulations

Although 71 per cent of funerals within the UK ended in cremation in 1998, the level of 70 per cent had been reached in 1992, suggesting that 30 per cent is likely to be the size of population preferring burial for the foreseeable future. That is a substantial figure, accounting for nearly 177,000 burials in 1998, and there are reports from some parts of the country of a trend away from cremation.

There is very little statutory law surrounding burial. Rules and regulations have been drawn up locally within the framework of those Acts of Parliament affecting civil authorities and private operators, while churchyards come under ecclesiastical jurisdiction.

All burials were in churchyards until cemeteries were opened in the mid-1800s. There are fundamental differences between municipal cemeteries and churchyards that you should know about before acquiring a grave.

Most people imagine they will somehow come to possess their own personal two metres by one metre plot of land, pushing up daisies in a corner of God's Acre or the local cemetery; that they can grow plants and put whatever monument they like on it. Not so. The land always remains the property of the cemetery or church. They grant you the right to use it and possibly to erect a memorial upon it subject to a raft of terms and conditions and the payment of fees. The regulations and the fees vary a lot from place to place. They may even be different in certain parts of the same place and change over periods of time. Regulations concerning memorials are dealt with in Chapter 10.

You should make enquiries and look through the deceased's papers to see if there is already a grave in waiting. A new grave may have been purchased in advance, through a prepaid funeral plan perhaps, or by arrangement through a funeral director or directly with a cemetery. A plot in a churchyard may have been reserved, perhaps informally with a friendly vicar or by faculty (a formal permission from the bishop). There may be vacant space in a family grave in a churchyard or cemetery.

If you are to purchase the exclusive rights in a new plot, think carefully about how many people you should have it dug for. Depending on soil conditions, it may be possible to have four or more, though up to three is more normal. If the cost of a grave is allocated for several burials, it becomes much more economical. There may be a fee charged for the first and subsequent interments, plus the gravedigger's fee on each occasion and a fee for removing and replacing a headstone.

Grave rights can be passed on either through a will or as part of an estate.

Burial in a Churchyard

Rights of a Parishioner

Everyone with a fixed address has the right to be buried in the local parish churchyard. Increasingly, however, churchyards are being declared 'full' and closed for further burials. Traditionally, over the centuries, churchyards have been reused for burials. Any unearthed bones would be collected in the charnel house or reburied. Where this practice is continued, a churchyard should never be 'full'.

However, by having a churchyard officially closed, the responsibility and cost for care and maintenance of the land can be handed over to the local council. This is often the favoured option for the church authorities and the parish is left to make its own arrangements to provide a local cemetery or dispatch residents elsewhere.

If burials are still taking place in your local parish churchyard, even if you are not a churchgoer, nor a Christian, you may choose to be buried there. Exceptionally, people who are not inhabitants of the parish may also be buried in the churchyard, for example, those with a family grave or strong connections with the parish. You should contact the vicar or perhaps some other official such as a verger or sexton to make arrangements and ask about regulations.

While as a parishioner you may have the right to burial, you have no right to have a memorial. Permission to erect a memorial is granted as a favour and there will be conditions. Restrictions can be strict and if you have particular ideas about a monument, or think you may have some later on, find out about what you can't have before committing to a grave plot.

Most people having a burial in a churchyard will want a service in the church immediately before the interment, although the two events may be carried out on separate occasions. A church service is not compulsory. A service may be held at the graveside. It is possible to be buried in a churchyard with no service at all or with a Christian (non-Anglican) service conducted by a minister of another denomination.

Ashes may be buried in a churchyard and some that are closed for the burial of bodies will have space for ashes. Urns or caskets for cremated remains are usually not allowed in churchyard burials. Ashes are laid directly on to the soil. Regulations about memorials for ashes vary and can be strict, so make enquiries.

The Costs

The fees for services conducted by a member of the clergy in church, cemetery or crematorium, and for burials and monuments in churchyards, are set each year by the church commissioners. Part of this fee goes to the incumbent and is deducted from salary and part goes to the parochial church council (PCC).

As from 1 January 1999, the fees were as follows:

■ service in church (or cemetery or crematorium unless they have fixed, different charges) £64;

- burial in churchyard following on from a service in the church £115 (total £179);

- burial in churchyard on a separate occasion or with no church service £138;

- burial of ashes in churchyard on a separate occasion £58;

- funeral service in churchyard for burial of ashes £64 (total £122) (no fee for simple service of committal);

- burial certificate, if required, £8.

Gravediggers are a necessary extra. The parish may have its own gravedigger or expect the funeral director, or you, to supply one. Fees vary from about £60–£150 and are likely to increase. There may be other extra charges for heating and hire of the organ as well as for the organist, the bell-ringing and the services of the verger.

Nonconformist churches do not normally have graveyards, although some parts of the country differ.

Exclusive Rights

Paying the burial fee neither secures the exclusive rights of burial in the grave nor the right to erect a memorial on it. Without an exclusive right it is possible for somebody unknown to you to be buried in the same plot, though normally the incumbent will reserve spaces for members of the same family. Furthermore, you won't be able to select the location of the plot – it will be allocated by the incumbent.

Exclusive rights for a grave in a churchyard can be secured by obtaining a faculty. This is a form of licence issued by the bishop and obtained by petition to the chancellor of the diocese. It means filling in forms and paying a fee – the vicar will show you how. Legal niceties are involved and it can be expensive, depending on the amount of work that has to be done. Expect to pay at least £200. You will probably also be expected to make a donation towards the upkeep of the churchyard.

Processing a faculty can take at least six weeks. The petition has to be made by the petitioner so you can't make one on behalf of the deceased. However, you can apply for a faculty to reserve the same grave for future burials of other members of the family.

A faculty does not impart a right to a grave plot in perpetuity. The Faculty Jurisdiction Measure 1964 means that, unless the rights are renewed by faculty, they cease to exist 100 years after the passing of the measure. Extensions or new grants cease 100 years after the date they were granted. When a faculty is already in existence you will need to produce the document or other evidence as proof of the right to the grave.

Faculties for burial or a memorial inside a church are rarely granted and in urban areas burial in or under a church is prohibited. Cremated remains, however, may be placed within a building. Some churches have arrangements for them to be deposited under the floor or in a crypt or a columbarium in the basement.

Burial in a Cemetery

More Popular than Churchyards

Cemeteries and crematorium gardens have become much more popular than churchyards as a final resting place, according to the results of a survey published in 1999. Only 7 per cent of respondents said they would like their remains to be placed in a churchyard compared with 23 per cent who preferred a crematorium garden of remembrance or a cemetery. Scattering at sea was the chosen destiny for the ashes of 9 per cent and 7 per cent wanted their ashes placed in their home.

Other favourites were to be sprinkled in the Caribbean, Elvis's home at Gracelands, sent by rocket to the moon and scattered on Mitcham Common. Somewhat odder choices included the paddock at Silverstone, Alton Towers, the top of a mango tree and the bar at the local pub.

The national survey was carried out on behalf of SCI (UK), which owns more than 600 funeral homes, 21 crematoria and four cemeteries.

Choosing a Cemetery

There are thousands of cemeteries located throughout the United Kingdom and amounting to some 46,500 hectares of land in England alone. The Church of England is believed to be the largest single owner of burial grounds with 16,500 hectares among the same number of churches; 2,000 parish councils control some 10,000 hectares; 69 metropolitan and London borough councils, 275 county, district and borough councils and 14 unitary authorities control another 10,000 hectares at some 3,000 sites. Privately owned cemeteries account for another 10,000 hectares.

The styles vary enormously from a half-hectare in a village, cared for by local volunteers and grazed by sheep, to vast 'motor-mowed' swathes with regimented rows of headstones administered by town hall bureaucracies.

Most often the reason for choosing a particular cemetery is because it is closest to the home of the nearest and dearest. There may be other family members buried there or even space waiting in a family grave.

Communities are protective of their communal burial spaces. Both rural and large local authority councils may allocate grave plots only to local residents or charge premiums, sometimes double the price or more, to bury people from outside their boundaries. So, if you are thinking about burial in a place outside the district of the usual residence of the deceased, you should make enquiries about any extra charges. This can be confusing when a person dies in one district, perhaps in a nursing home, after living many years in another district.

The management of the burial procedure is generally according to a standard code of practice with local variations. The depth of soil on top of the coffin should be at least 66 centimetres but the depth of the grave may be decided according to how many coffins are to be buried in it, the nature of the soil, the excavation method and the equipment employed. Some dig graves by hand, others with earth-moving machinery.

Regulations about coffins are becoming more liberal, with increasing numbers of cemeteries permitting home-made, cardboard or wicker coffins, shrouds or body bags. Mourners are also being allowed to fill in the graves.

Style and landscape may influence your choice. Some cemeteries, it has to be said, are unkempt and over-grown and others, to some people's eyes, over-tended and formal. There will be regulations about closing and opening times, placing flowers and planting of grave spaces and the size, shape, material and even inscription on the memorial. Think about how you and the family will want to relate with the grave in the weeks and years to come, how it will be cared for and the ease and convenience of visiting. Can you take a car close to the gravesite? Is there adequate parking nearby or will there be a long walk? Is there shelter from the rain and toilet facilities?

The ecological movement is encouraging cemeteries to be managed in an environmentally friendly way. Grass is allowed to grow longer and wild flowers and trees planted, ponds introduced, bird boxes installed and areas for 'green' burials set out. There may be within the same cemetery a woodland burial area, a lawn memorial section, a traditional section and a cremated remains area.

Very few cemeteries are privately owned. Many that started in private hands went out of business when all the grave plots had been sold and ownership transferred to the local authority. Those that are privately owned are generally run along lines very similar to the municipal cemeteries. In some there may be a greater choice of grave styles and monuments.

Consecration

Cemetery land may or may not be consecrated or it may be in parts. When cemeteries were being built, there was dissent between the Church of England, Roman Catholic and non-conformist religions. Some cemeteries were strictly for one or the other and some strictly divided to the extent of having two chapels, as well as distinct sections for interment.

There remain sections in many cemeteries reserved for members of particular religions and faiths although, increasingly, new cemeteries and new extensions are inter-denominational. This both reflects modern society and makes for an easier administration for the management. Where desired, an individual grave may be consecrated at the time of burial.

Cemeteries and parts of cemeteries consecrated by the Church of England can fall within the influence of ecclesiastical law and be subject to faculty requirements, as described above.

Where religious ethnic populations have grown up, sections of cemeteries may be found dedicated almost exclusively to the dead of that community; for example, Irish, Polish, Italian and, more recently, Afro-Caribbean and Muslim. Traditional burial and commemorative customs still persist among these communities.

There are some single-denomination cemeteries exclusively for religions such as Roman Catholics, Jews and non-conformist churches.

Common Graves

You may be able to choose burial in a grave that is occupied in common with other bodies and not exclusively by one person or a group of family members. Called a common grave, this should be significantly less expensive than one providing an exclusive right of use.

The right to erect a monument on a common grave is not normally granted. As the grave will contain unrelated bodies, the names on a memorial and its ownership can lead to confusion and argument. Sometimes called a pauper's grave, there may be some stigma about a common grave but for anyone seeking a low-cost disposal, and not cremation, this little-publicized option could be suitable.

Rights of Use

You cannot own a grave in a cemetery. You may buy from the owner of the cemetery the right to use the grave for up to a specified number of bodies for a set number of years. You may also buy the right to erect a memorial on the grave within certain specifications.

The depth to which the grave is originally dug will govern the number of bodies permitted in the grave. Once a body is laid in a grave it may not be disturbed without an exhumation licence. A licence will not be granted for the purpose of digging the grave deeper.

Soil conditions, the method of excavation or equipment utilized may restrict the depth to which the grave may be dug. The cost of gravedigging may be included in the price of the plot or it may be an extra. It will cost more for a deeper grave. There will also be a charge for reopening the grave for subsequent interments, which may or may not include the gravedigging.

The number of years for which the right of use is sold is usually 75 years, sometimes 50 or 100 years. With the possible exception of private cemeteries, it cannot be for more than 100 years.

Check that all the essential information is included in the papers granting the right of use. It is important that anyone wanting to carry out a future burial in the plot can find out, and prove, exactly what can be done and what has to be paid for.

The person who pays for the grave should be the same person who signs the deed of grant of right to use. That signatory, or whoever inherits the grave rights from that person, will have to give permission for future burials, memorials or inscriptions on the memorial. Other relatives, spouses or partners have been known to make claims on burial space and memorials contrary to the interests of the original parties. That document and the signature on it may be critical in resolving a dispute in years to come.

It is a valuable document, particularly as the price of grave plots can be expected to increase in the future, so keep it in a safe place and keep a copy of it elsewhere.

The Costs

The price for a grave can vary enormously whether in a municipal or a private cemetery. It can vary from place to place in the same cemetery, between cemeteries in the same town and between town and country sites.

The graves themselves can vary not only in depth for number of interments but also in construction. Most, in fact, are simply holes in the ground that are back-filled with soil on top of the coffin. There are, exceptionally, stone- or brick-lined graves in which the coffin may be covered by a stone or concrete slab.

Continental-style pre-cast concrete chambers are being installed in a few British cemeteries. These are expensive initially but prevent subsidence and make reopenings easier. It is also possible in some cemeteries to be interred in a catacomb or mausoleum.

The location of a grave within a cemetery may affect the price as some sites may be more desirable that others. There may be a better view or some plots may be nearer a main driveway, entrance or car park. There may be expensive landscaping or planting in some areas. Larger memorials may be permitted in some areas.

Alternatively, as in some municipal cemeteries, graves may all be priced exactly the same and designed to be as nearly identical as possible, so that the under-privileged will not appear disadvantaged after death.

Comparative costs for a simple grave, including digging, may be £350 for 99 years in a country town or £1,200 for 50 years in a London suburb. Parish cemeteries in small villages often fix their prices according to the local church and are much cheaper: £138 in 1999 plus, say, £75 for a gravedigger. A plot in London's Highgate cemetery may cost more than £3,000. A walled grave on a prime London cemetery site can cost £10,000. A rough guide for a national average would be £400–£600 for 75 years for a two-person grave for a local resident.

Prices and conditions are usually displayed on a noticeboard at the municipal cemeteries and on leaflets available from the cemetery office.

Burial of Ashes

In recent years, cemeteries have been setting aside areas for the burial of cremated remains in a scaled-down replication of the spaces where bodies are interred. From the way they are proliferating, they are clearly meeting a need.

Customized gardens of remembrance utilizing concrete cubicles for the containment of ashes below the ground surface or in walls are also being constructed in cemeteries and crematoria grounds. Lease periods for the placement of ashes are usually much shorter than for graves and can be for as few as 5 years and rarely for more than 25 years. The cost may be £80–£300 (see Chapter 10).

Exhumation

If ashes have been buried underground, they come under the same regulations concerning their removal or movement as other human remains, which means that they should not be disturbed without first obtaining an exhumation licence from the Home Office.

A licence will only be granted if there are strong and compelling reasons for the remains to be moved. A licence will not be granted if the remains have been placed directly into the soil or buried in a biodegradable container. Not only cardboard but also aluminium and wood, especially chipboard, containers will degrade over a comparatively short time.

If the ashes are in an urn or casket on a shelf, in a niche or columbarium space above the floor level, no exhumation licence is required. You should, however, ask permission of the management at the cemetery or crematorium so that proper arrangements can be made and records amended. Like the Home Office, the management will have to be convinced that there are strong and compelling reasons for the remains to be removed.

Arranging a Burial

As soon as you have decided on burial and know there are no objections, a provisional booking with the cemetery can be made. The cemetery office should be open for bookings during normal office hours and sometimes over weekends. An increasing number of cemeteries are operating a phone-in computer booking system that allows bookings to be made 24 hours a day.

You will first have to confirm that the member of the clergy or officiant who will conduct the funeral ceremony is available for the desired date and time. Also, make sure you know the precise location of the cemetery – the office may have several within its control.

Fix the date and time for the funeral to arrive at the cemetery gates or, if it is to be used, at the cemetery chapel. This is where the funeral should be met by a cemetery official who will guide the proceedings. Normally at least two days' notice is required but be sure to allow sufficient time to register the death and obtain the necessary certificates. You will need to provide the name and address of the person being buried.

If there is already a grave in waiting, you should have a deed of rights showing how many burials are allowed and you should know that there is space remaining for at least one more. The deed will have a grave number, which will be asked for. If a new grave is required, you will need to decide on the type. Visit the cemetery if you can to select the style and place.

The cemetery office will also want the name and telephone number of the funeral director, or the person arranging the funeral, who will be required to pay the fees. Additional information, which may be provided later, will be the coffin or casket size, including the handles. Coffins have been known to stick while being lowered into the grave when, for example, the measurements have been wrong or when a tapered coffin shape has been dug and a large rectangular casket arrives.

The cemetery staff need to be advised about the type of funeral. Will you go straight to the grave or to the chapel first? There will be planks and boards for mourners to stand on and usually plastic grass mats round the grave. Not everyone likes the idea of plastic grass. Tell them if you do not want mats. Will you have a service at the chapel or at the graveside? (See Chapter 8.) Bearers will be needed to carry the coffin and lower it into the grave. Funeral directors will provide bearers and some cemeteries will also provide them, for a fee.

You will be asked the religion of the deceased and, if appropriate and available, whether a denominational plot is required. Knowing the religion helps cemetery staff estimate the style and length of service. They may also make dry earth available to sprinkle on the coffin if required.

Official Documents

An official form, supplied free, from the cemetery to the funeral director, or to you if you prefer, has to be filled in. This notice of burial, which confirms all the above details, is a binding contract and you will be liable to pay the fees even if the funeral is cancelled or transferred to another cemetery.

The registrar's certificate for burial or cremation (the green form) or a coroner's order for burial (white form 101) should accompany the notice of burial form. Normally a minimum of 24 hours' notice is required. Some authorities may accept the order or certificate when the funeral arrives but others will not. This can result in a funeral being delayed or cancelled.

Within 96 hours of a burial (or cremation) a detachable portion of the registrar's certificate or coroner's order has to be sent to the registrar noting the date and place of burial or cremation. However, the registrar does not keep a record of the place of burial. The cemetery office is the only place where any future matters concerning the burial or grave can be investigated.

The burial will be entered in the register of burials and in the index to these records. The allocation of a new grave will be entered in the register of graves, recording the sale of the right of burial and the period for which the right is granted. A deed of grant of right of burial will be prepared and dispatched. This grant should be made out in the name of the responsible person arranging the funeral, not in the name of the funeral director as sometimes happens. If it is sent to the funeral director, he or she may retain the deed until the bill, including the disbursement for the cost of the right of use, is paid. This practice is condoned by the funeral directors' trade associations.

New graves will be marked on the cemetery grave maps. Computer systems with facilities for mapping and recording graves and after-cremation plots are being adopted and adapted at an increasing number of cemeteries and crematoria since legal acceptance of computer records was given in 1986. These records are available to the public and for research and have to be maintained forever.

Environmental Issues

The most commonly quoted reason against burial is that the land could be better used for the living than for the dead. Cemeteries are intended as much for the living – as a focus for grief and for community remembrance. This was the intention of the Victorians when they were built. Today, in fact, they are lost to the living by being considered virtually sacrosanct when in reality they are deserted, derelict spaces.

But these spaces can be given back to the living. Burial and memorial grounds can be evolved to contribute to wealth creation through the multiplicity of cross-industry occupations involved and at the same time enhance the quality of life for future generations.

The reuse of graves, once common in Britain and always normal in Continental Europe, provides for the sustainable use of burial land. Cemeteries can also be a natural reserve for plants and wildlife, a lung in inner cities, a haven unharmed by agrochemicals.

The burgeoning interest in woodland burials ('green' burials) indicates increasing public awareness of the link between burial and nature (see Chapter 15). Concern is often expressed about the toxic glues in chipboard coffins and the chemicals used in embalming, which leach into the ground of burial sites. There is also increasing concern about the use of plastics and synthetic materials, which do not biodegrade. The felling of trees for the manufacture of wooden coffins is also unpopular with environmentalists, who may prefer to see recycled wood or alternative materials being used instead.

Grave Reuse

The reuse of graves in UK cemeteries is virtually prohibited by the Burial Act 1857, which requires that human remains, once buried, must not be disturbed. This Act does not apply to churchyards.

The church generally has no legal objection to burial in a grave that has already been used. *The Churchyards Handbook* says, 'It is usual for a gap of at least 50 years to elapse between burial and re-burial'. In years past, unearthed bones would be stored in a charnel house, a sort of underground burial chamber. Nowadays, they are re-interred at a greater depth.

Where grave space is becoming very scarce, as in some inner city cemeteries, a way round the difficulty has been found by digging to a restricted depth, which leaves previous burials undisturbed. This practice is resorted to only where graves have been abandoned for 100 years or more and attempts to trace relatives have been unsuccessful. Areas of common graves, where no memorials were ever erected and no rights of exclusive use granted, are considered suitable for reuse for single-depth graves in certain circumstances.

The Burial Acts of 1852 and 1853 permitted the sale of exclusive rights, either for fixed periods or in perpetuity. Those sold in perpetuity had become a major problem for cemetery authorities by the mid-1960s when thousands of graves, with decrepit memorials, had been abandoned and the owners of the rights were untraceable. Another Act was passed in 1977 that redefined perpetuity as no more than 100 years, dated retrospectively. This enabled cemeteries to begin clearing old sections of monuments and lay the grounds for potential reuse. However, there still exists a general feeling of a taboo against disturbing the dead in the UK and the practice of reuse is likely to be slow in gaining ground.

The Essentials of Burial

1. Churchyards are not the same as cemeteries.

2. You cannot own a grave. What you do with it will be regulated.

3. Every parishioner has the right to be buried in the parish churchyard.

4. If you are responsible for the funeral, you may have long-term authority over the grave and memorial rights.

Two thirds of the world's blindness is preventable

Photo by: Colin Jones

With your help

Imagine you have a nine year old grand-daughter who is blind.

One day you discover that in a country far away, there is a miraculous cure that will bring her sight back. But you can't afford it.

Sadly, for millions of families the world over, this is reality. Two thirds of the world's 38 million blind need never have lost their sight or could be cured. Human beings have the technology and the drugs. All that is lacking is money.

Will you help?

The British Council for the Prevention of Blindness is a charity (also known as Save Eyes Everywhere) which funds research in the UK into every cause of blindness: from childhood injury, to glaucoma to improvements in the treatment of diabetic retinopathy. In many developing countries, we support practical work such as eye camps to repair cataract and the treatment of river blindness.

Please help us with a donation, a deed of covenant or a legacy.

8 *Ceremony and Ritual*

Recognizing Death has Occurred and a Life has been Lived

There are two main elements to the ceremony surrounding the leave-taking from the departed. There is a celebration and a committal. This applies whether the service is religious, with a belief in an afterlife, or secular, with no belief in life after death.

The celebration will normally take the form of a thanksgiving and a tribute to a lifetime's achievements. The committal may mean simply the act of putting the coffin into the grave or into the flames or, for the religious, the commendation of the deceased to the mercy of God: the last farewell of the community to a departed member.

The committal may take place at the crematorium or at the graveside. At most crematoria it will conclude with a curtain closing to shut off from the mourners the view of the coffin on the catafalque. A few close a lattice gate. In others, the coffin is lowered or left in the auditorium until the mourners have departed and a small number of crematoria have the coffin disappear through a hatch-door in the wall. Some crematoria have different methods in different chapels. Where there is a curtain, you may choose to leave it open while the mourners depart.

Most people are quite happy to follow the usual routine and find it quite acceptable. If you would like to make some changes then tell the crematorium staff well in advance, when you make the booking if possible. If there are crosses or other Christian artefacts, you can ask for them to be screened off or removed.

The Coffin as the Focal Point

The coffin is the focal point of the service. In many crematoria, the catafalque, on which the coffin is intended to stand, is in a corner of the chapel, against the far wall or in a nave. This allows convenient removal of the coffin to the committal room or the crematory but keeps the centre of attention remote from the mourners. You may prefer to have the coffin on a bier, closer to the mourners and more in view. If the seating allows, you could have chairs arranged in a circle or a semicircle with the coffin in the centre. As people leave, you may like them to be able to touch or kiss the coffin or leave a flower or token on it.

The method of taking leave of the coffin, the finale to the service, is very important. It is the last memory you will take away. Walking away from the coffin marks the conclusion of the funeral, the final severing of the links between you and the deceased. Where there is a choice it is worth thinking carefully about how it should be completed.

Unlike burial, where the service of committal has long been practised, new conventions are evolving around cremation services. The lack of a sense of finality or of completion when a coffin is left at a crematorium is often commented on. This is rarely the case after an earth burial.

Service at the Graveside

Machines used to dig graves make a straight-sided hole, whereas a grave dug by hand can be made to taper at the top and bottom to neatly accept a traditional coffin shape. And a person is also less likely to damage the surrounds. You may be able to hire a person to dig the grave, even if machines are usually used.

In readiness for the funeral, planks will be placed round the grave for bearers and mourners to stand on. Artificial grass mats will probably be laid over the edge of the grave and surroundings and over the soil removed from the grave.

The hearse, guided by cemetery staff, member of the clergy or officiant, will take the coffin as near as possible to the correct grave. It will be carried or perhaps wheeled on a bier for the final distance and placed on two wooden spars spanning the grave.

The coffin handles are not usually intended to carry the weight of the coffin but as well as being decorative they serve a useful function in guiding the webbing tapes that are wrapped round the coffin. The ends of the tapes are held by each of the four or six bearers. At a given moment, the bearers lift the coffin so that the wooden spars can be removed and the coffin lowered into the grave.

The coffin-handling procedure varies from place to place. Sometimes it is laid beside the grave rather than on spars across it and it is lifted sideways when the moment for lowering arrives. There may be other regional differences in practice.

The Christian ceremony of committal calls for soil to be sprinkled on the coffin and cemetery staff may provide a container of dry soil for this purpose. Mourners may also like to sprinkle soil or drop flowers on to the coffin.

Some mourners will want to throw shovelfuls of soil into the grave and some cemeteries will allow them to fill in a token amount or help with the back-filling. The soil should be compacted at six-inch levels to minimize settling. This is achieved by treading-in, which can make the task somewhat unsuitable for mourners.

Choice of Places

A Christian or any other service of committal may be held at the graveside or in the crematorium chapel. (Alternatively, there may be no service at all.) A longer service to include committal and a celebratory thanksgiving or tribute may also be held at these locations. The celebration may be held at a different place, a church or hall or at home for instance, and followed by a second service for the committal at the crematorium or graveside. If the ashes are to be buried, the Christian service of committal may be performed during their burial.

Memorial Service

A memorial service may be held after the cremation or burial, at a church or elsewhere but rarely in a crematorium chapel.

However, some crematoria chapels are now being designed for use for weddings and naming ceremonies as well as cremation services. They may be prepared to let you use it for a memorial service.

There will, of course, be no coffin at a memorial service but if there was a cremation then perhaps the ashes in an urn may be on view. Then the memorial service may be followed by the committal of the ashes. Some churches and crematoria hold annual memorial services.

Crematorium Chapel

When there is to be a cremation it is unusual nowadays for a service to be held anywhere other than in the crematorium chapel. This may be because fewer people are churchgoers, although many prefer to fall back on the comfort of the well-known ceremonies at the time of grief. The additional journey time between locations can be stressful and will probably add to the cost. Having the service at the crematorium is undoubtedly the most convenient arrangement.

Gathering the mourners and ushering them into the chapel or to the graveside is the first part of the event management. The chief mourners usually travel in one or more limousines behind the hearse. Others may follow in their own cars or wait at the chapel entrance or cemetery gate for the cortège to arrive.

When the bearers carry the coffin into the chapel or to the graveside, the mourners will line up behind the next of kin and follow the coffin. Alternatively, the mourners may take their seats in the chapel and wait for the coffin to be carried in. This is an arrangement better suited to our cold, wet weather.

There may be several funerals following each other so you may have to wait for a previous service to be completed and the mourners to leave before you can move into the chapel. It is important to keep to a close timetable, which is another reason why having services in different locations can be problematical.

Music

Music is strongly recommended for the times when people are

entering and leaving the chapel. Facilities for playing tapes and CDs are often available as well as organs. Many crematoria will have a music library with the most-requested tunes.

The most popular music for funerals varies from year to year and in different parts of the country. The Federation of British Cremation Authorities and some funeral directors' groups carry out surveys. Perennials among the funeral hymns chosen at churches and crematoria are: 'The Lord's My Shepherd', 'Abide With Me', 'The Day Thou Gavest Lord Is Ended' ,'In Heavenly Love Abiding' and 'The Old Rugged Cross'.

Non-sacred popular songs at cremations include: 'My Way' by Frank Sinatra, 'Candle In The Wind' by Elton John, 'I Will Always Love You' by Whitney Houston, 'Unchained Melody' by the Righteous Brothers and 'Wind Beneath My Wings' by Bette Midler.

Make your wishes known and deliver special tapes or records well in advance to the funeral director or crematorium management. If you are supplying your own tapes, make sure they are set to start at the right place.

The Order of Service

The churches' group on funeral services at cemeteries and crematoria have drawn up suitable services with forms of words and prayers that have been adopted by most cemeteries and crematoria. Handbooks are published and available in the same way as prayer books and hymnbooks in churches.

Typically, a service will begin with the officiant or member of the clergy welcoming the mourners and explaining the purpose of the gathering. Prayers may be said, followed by a period of meditation when a favourite piece of music may be played or a hymn sung.

There will be a time for readings, either from the Bible or of poems or other texts. Perhaps family members or friends or colleagues of the deceased would like to read something personal and appropriate.

Readings may be followed by the tribute, which may be delivered by the officiant or someone (or more than one) who knew the deceased. This should last no more than 10 minutes.

Then it will be time for the words of the committal, probably best said by the officiant. The words may be from the official, authorized service or an alternative humanist version. They may be amended to be suitable for a burial, a cremation or a cremation followed by burial of the ashes. The purpose is to remind us that death is a natural part of life. Probably the best-known phrases from the passages most often used are: 'Man born of a woman has but a short time to live. Like a flower we blossom and then wither' and 'ashes to ashes, dust to dust'.

If the coffin is to move or be curtained off, it happens now. The officiant will probably have to press a button on the lectern. If an inexperienced person is taking the service, knowing about that button is important. So is arranging how to cue the organist or music-deck operator.

There may be a final meditation or prayer and the invitation for the mourners to 'leave in peace'. At a busy crematorium they may have to leave by a different door. This is to avoid mingling with incoming mourners for the next service.

It is helpful for mourners to have an order of service, a printed programme setting out the sequence of events and perhaps including the text of poems, readings and a tribute – even a photograph of the deceased. Most funeral directors will be equipped to produce this for you, either with their own desktop publishing package or through an arrangement with a printer.

Appointing the Officiant

If neither the deceased nor the family have any affiliation to a church but would like a member of the clergy to officiate, the funeral director, crematorium or cemetery staff will be able to help. The funeral director will have regular contact with the local ministers and know those who will be happy to conduct the type of service you require. Some will even conduct non-Christian services.

However, incumbents with a busy parish to look after may not have the time for funeral services for people they don't know at a crematorium or cemetery miles away from their parish. Or it may not be possible to make contact with them at the time a booking is about to be made.

Many crematoria operate a rota system with a contact list of ministers ready and able to conduct funerals at specific times. While effective and convenient, this can be criticized as impersonal. Sometimes, for example, the deceased has been referred to during a service by a formal name when known to everyone by a nickname. You can help ensure the service is personalized by making sure the officiant is given full and detailed information beforehand; the funeral director should ask you for such details and pass them on.

Non-Christian or Minority-group Funerals

While most funerals follow the Christian and Church of England formula, in today's multi-ethnic and agnostic society a significant number of people do not conform to these conventions. Where there are concentrations of national/religious groups in certain areas, specific funeral directors may be contracted to serve them. In places such as Southall, the East End of London, Birmingham and Bradford, funeral directors serving exclusively Asian, Muslim and Afro-Caribbean communities are operating.

Specific bereavement support groups are listed in the 'Useful Addresses' section at the back of this book.

A Humanist Service

You may want to have an elegant, meaningful funeral service but, because the deceased had nothing to do with churches or Christianity, feel it would be hypocritical to call on a member of the clergy to officiate. You could do it yourself (see Chapter 15) or you could turn to the British Humanist Association.

Humanists do not believe in God either explaining or being concerned in human conduct. They aim to be caring humanitarians and have members experienced in conducting funeral ceremonies in most parts of the country. They prefer to celebrate a person's life and encourage support and help for the bereaved rather than look on the funeral as a service to God.

Contact details for the British Humanist Association are given on page 250.

Jewish Funerals

Orthodox Jews will have only burial while Reform Jews may be buried or cremated. Members of the synagogue will organize the funeral, usually through a Jewish funeral agency such as United Synagogues. Alternatively, the local community will arrange a contract with a Gentile funeral home. Orthodox Jews bury their dead within 24 hours. A Reform Jewish funeral is not necessarily so swift and may take place after two or three days. Some Jewish authorities have their own cemeteries attached to their synagogues. If not, a section of a cemetery will be set aside for their use.

Muslim Funerals

Muslims are always buried. The community will appoint one of their members to represent them in arranging funerals. One funeral director will be appointed and instructed to provide facilities for their strict rituals. Embalming is not done unless the body is to be transported over a long distance. The family will lay out the body for ritual washing and preparation for burial.

There are many variations of Muslim funeral rites. Generally in the UK the body is wrapped in a sheet and buried within 24 hours without a coffin and with the face turned towards Mecca. There is no law that says a coffin must be used for a burial but some cemeteries insist the body be carried to the graveside in a coffin.

The orientation of the graves is important: north-east south-west with the head at the south-west end. The surface of the grave is raised some four to twelve inches above ground level and must not be walked over or stood on. These requirements don't fit in with most cemeteries' procedures, where graves are quickly levelled, mown over and aligned with roadways. Some authorities provide special areas for Muslim burials and many Muslim communities acquire large family plots in private cemeteries.

Hindu Funerals

Hindus are always cremated, unless death was a result of suicide. Rites and customs vary hugely, there is no central authority and funeral directors do not have to be approved. The body may be laid out and embalmed by a funeral director and arranged for visiting either at the funeral director's or at a private residence. Hindu women pay their respects with open mourning and weeping but some castes forbid them to go to the crematorium. The ashes are scattered over water in a river or lake or taken to India for similar dispersal. There are funeral directors specializing in providing Hindu services who may also arrange transportation of a body for cremation by the Ganges.

Sikh Funerals

Sikhs, like the Hindus, insist on cremation. The body will be washed and dressed by the family and visited at home before being taken to the religious centre, the gurdwara, for the main funeral service or direct to the crematorium. The eldest son or a senior member of the family will want to press the button to ignite the flames in the cremator or at least witness the coffin going into the cremator. The ashes will be retained for scattering over water or taken to India.

Cult Funerals

The many divergent Christian groups have their own variations for funeral services. The churches' group on funerals at cemeteries and crematoria has gone a long way to codifying a common ceremony for non-conformist and Church of England funerals that are not held in their own respective churches. Here, differences are cherished. Some, for example, have the coffin longways down the aisle, others sideways in front of the congregation. Salvationists, members of the Salvation Army, don't die but are 'promoted to glory'. Cremation is forbidden among strict Baptists.

New liturgies are written, tested and either discarded or

accepted. The funeral of Princess Diana is expected to bring about some changes to long-held assumptions of what may or may not be proper ritual or behaviour.

There are westernized versions of Hinduism, such as Hare Krishna and Bahai, which generally follow Hindu funeral rites.

New Age culture is a mix of eastern mysticism and northern paganism and ritual may veer from Hinduism to earth, wind, fire and water rituals.

Natural funerals are evolving alongside the work of the Natural Death Centre and do-it-yourself audience-participation ceremonies are being created. The emphasis on providing a service of which the deceased would have approved is giving way to something more centred on satisfying the bereaved.

A non-conventional funeral is likely to require more than a 20-minute crematorium time frame to be appreciated and it may not be possible to arrange this through a traditional funeral director. A specially choreographed memorial service may be the solution (see Chapter 15).

The Essentials of Ceremony and Ritual

1. The funeral ceremony aims to pay respect to the deceased, celebrate a life and comfort the bereaved.

2. New conventions are evolving for cremations, for secular services and in Christian liturgy.

3. The more you can 'personalize' the service, the greater the therapeutic benefit for the bereaved.

4. The service can be in a variety of places and at different times.

9 Dress Code and Conduct

The Ages of Mourning

Early Christians

Early Christians wore white and danced and sang at funerals. Their brother or sister had gone to a better place and it was a time for celebration. Of course, there was also sorrow, but a funeral was a time for joy because the soul had gone to heaven and for reassurance and comfort of those left behind.

Purgatory put an end to the celebrations. The dominant doctrine of the church from the 6th to the 16th century was that the soul did not go straight to heaven but lingered in limbo until cleansed of sins. The joyful thought of going straight to glory was replaced with gloom and apprehension. Black cloaks and hoods were worn by the mourners and all and sundry were asked to offer prayers to release the soul from purgatory. Funeral processions led by a priest or sexton, with bell ringing to invoke prayers, became customary. A funerary trade emerged, making and hiring black cloaks, hoods and large and elaborate palls to cover the coffin and supplying uniformed pall-bearers to carry the corners of the pall.

Puritans

Then came the Civil War in 1642 and Parliament swept away all customs of praying, reading and singing in procession to the church or at the graveside. The Prayer Book was replaced in 1644 by the Directory of Public Worship, which stated: 'When any person departeth this life, let the dead body, upon the day of burial, be decently attended from the house to the place appointed for public burial, and there immediately interred, without any ceremony'. It was almost the death of the funeral. But the phrase 'decently attended' enabled the forerunners of funeral directors to continue in business, albeit with toned-down pomp and ceremony.

A common Puritan funeral is illustrated in an engraving published in 1641. In his book *The English Way of Death*, Julian Litten describes it:

> *A short-palled coffin is carried towards a churchyard on the shoulders of four bearers, neither a priest, clerk nor beadle heading the procession. Behind follow the mourners, first six men in day dress with short cloaks and flat hats, then a group of women in Puritan dress. Each is shown holding a sprig of rosemary, as well as a nosegay; these sprigs were cast into the grave at the close of the ceremony – this was especially useful where intramural burial was concerned, as the herb's sweetness helped to mask the odour of decay. Simple as they were, these processions had a certain dignity.*

After the restoration of the monarchy in 1660 the *Prayer Book* was revised and reissued as the *Book of Common Prayer* in 1662. The Order for the Burial of the Dead was extended with psalms and the choice of a graveside or church service. This formed the pattern for the service still in use today.

Public restraint prevented a return to excessive pomp and ceremony but a middle-class funeral could still require black hatbands, scarves, gloves, full suits of mourning for pall-bearers and as many mutes, feathers, plumes, carriages and candles as you cared to hire.

Victorians

The Victorians are often cited as the inventors of the modern 'traditional' funeral but many of the trappings and much of the ceremony has an older heritage. Cemeteries began to open in the

1830s, enabling the undertakers to extend their involvement with a second procession from church to cemetery as well as from home to church. This also brought about the introduction of the glass-sided horse-drawn carriage for the coffin.

Queen Victoria's protracted mourning for Prince Albert led to a fashionable interest in black. Ladies would be swathed in black crêpe and bombazine, veils and jet jewellery. The conventional day dress for men in the 19th century was a complementary black suit which, for a funeral, would be supplemented by the display of a white handkerchief and a crape hat-band. The striped trousers and black swallow-tail coat, which set the style still favoured by the traditional funeral conductor, was an Edwardian innovation.

Lavish display was seen as an important mark of respect by the working classes, whereas the upper and middle classes adopted a more restrained approach. It was the First World War that profoundly simplified the British way of death. Workers and workhorses went to war and, with soldiers dying and being buried in foreign fields, costly funeral displays at home were viewed with disfavour.

The Second World War reinforced this attitude and cremation has brought in even simpler services in terms of both logistics and ceremony. Perhaps things have become too bland for we are now witnessing a revival of horse-drawn hearses and passenger carriages at one extreme and personalized ceremony at the other.

What to Wear

Modern funerals continue as dignified and fairly formal affairs. They are a time to pay respect to the deceased and to show respect, understanding and sympathy to the bereaved. Clothes should reflect this respect and as much care be taken about dress as at a wedding, naming ceremony or any other important, formal occasion. Everyone should be turned out in what would once have been called 'Sunday best'.

The degree of formality will be set by the family and should be explained to mourners in the press notice about the funeral or when you are inviting them to attend. Strict codes for mourning behaviour are no longer de rigueur. People will be looking to you for guidance. For a traditional funeral, a simple 'Please wear black' or 'Black will be worn' should be sufficient to set the tone. If the funeral is to be more a celebration of a life there may be a specific request not to wear black or to wear some bright colour. A natural death or New Age-style funeral may even request smart casual dress. The important thing is for mourners to respond as best they can to the style decided for the event and conform to the majority.

More often than not at a traditional funeral the next of kin and close family and friends will favour black. If you don't have a black outfit and don't want to buy one then select something in a dark blue, grey or other sombre colour. A touch of black with a tie, pocket-handkerchief or scarf would be respectful. Black armbands are traditional in some parts of the country but are generally becoming outmoded. Ladies should make the effort to wear a hat, dark in colour and sober in style.

Take notice of the weather and dress accordingly. Churches and many crematoria chapels are not well heated, and you may spend some time standing out in the open. Wear appropriate clothes under a dark coat that will be a layer you can take off if it should be too warm.

Dark glasses may sound a cliché but can be a comfort at emotional moments. And don't forget hankies and tissues. If in any doubt about what should be worn, settle for the safe option of a sober outfit and something black.

Perhaps most important, as a mourner, you should feel comfortable that you are wearing what you consider appropriate. A request for smart casual wear or something bright is open to interpretation. What you wear is an expression of your feelings at the time and about the dead person, which may not be so bright or casual as may be expected by the person organizing the funeral. You are making a statement by what you wear. Be confident it is what you really mean to say and will not be misunderstood.

Where to Sit

The 'best seats' should be reserved for the immediate family. Funerary etiquette, originally for church services, has established that they sit in the front on the south side of the building, with other relatives sitting in the pews behind them. The widow or widower will be seated in the front row immediately next to the aisle. If friends or relatives are to carry the coffin out of the church, they should be seated at the front on the south side and next to the aisle.

At funerals of people of note, any official representatives, those of the Crown, the county, the town or of societies with which the deceased was connected, sit on the north side. The more important people go to the front and other general friends of the deceased take the seats or pews behind them.

The auditoria at crematoria do not necessarily follow a similar or standard layout. Whatever the seating arrangement, there is usually a central aisle and the officiant, at a lectern, will be to one side of this aisle. If there is a small gathering in relation to the size of the auditorium, fill up the seats closest to the lectern. The chief mourners should be in the front row of the block of seats facing the lectern.

Encourage people to sit close together rather than scattered about the room so that the officiant can have a crowd to address, even if it is a small one. If more people than expected arrive, and there are not enough seats, then give priority to the elderly and infirm. Most chapels and churches have facilities for wheelchairs but try to keep them within the gathering, not isolated to one side or at the back.

If the coffin has been left in the church or chapel overnight, as is frequently the case in Catholic churches, then the family and congregation take their seats in good time for the service. Alternatively, if the coffin is to be brought in at the start of the service, the congregation will be seated at first but will then stand as the family enter in procession behind the coffin. The officiant will then direct the congregation to be seated or to remain standing for the first part of the ceremony.

Similarly, at a crematorium, you may be able to arrange for most of the mourners to be seated before the coffin is brought in, with only the chief mourners walking behind the coffin and then going to their reserved seats. This avoids mourners having to wait outside in possibly inclement weather. The audience stands as the coffin is brought in. At a busy crematorium this may not be possible as there could be another service taking place a few minutes in front of yours.

It may be possible to have the coffin wheeled into place on a bier and so do away with the need for bearers. This may be done, before mourners arrive if required, by crematorium staff (if the coffin has been held in their chapel of rest prior to the service) or by the funeral director's chauffeur and attendant.

In some regions, and at some crematoria, it is the custom for wheeled biers to be used but this is not a necessity and you can arrange for the coffin to be shouldered for the processions. However, there are some crematoria where a wheeled bier is required to transfer the coffin from the auditorium to the crematory.

Funerary etiquette directs that the immediate family are the first to follow the coffin out of the church and only then can the other guests follow. At a crematorium, the same etiquette is maintained although, of course, the coffin remains in the auditorium.

How to Participate

Making yourself part of the gathering, wearing the style of clothing as requested and simply joining in is an obvious way of contributing to the service. You may suggest mourners take a final leave of the coffin by touching it or laying a flower or token on it as they depart.

At a burial, you may suggest that mourners drop a flower or petals on to the coffin, sprinkle soil or take a hand in filling the grave.

Just as mourners should respect any requests regarding dress, so they should follow the wishes of the family regarding floral tributes or donations to charity or a memorial fund.

The bereaved may draw comfort from a simple gesture, a handclasp or a word of condolence. Simply saying 'I am sorry' can mean a lot. Writing a note or a few words on a card with the flowers that can be re-read may help the family in times to come.

While there are greetings cards for almost every occasion, cards expressing sympathy about a bereavement can be hard to find. Some shops have a few with biblical quotations. Illustrated cards with no printed message can be suitable.

Children at Funerals

It is generally a good thing for children to attend the funeral of someone they knew and loved. Just as for adults, it is an opportunity for them to come to terms with the realization that the deceased has actually died and to participate in a solemn ritual of farewell and thanksgiving. They should be included as part of the gathering in as adult a manner as possible in consideration of their age.

A full explanation of what is going to happen at the funeral should be given to the child in advance and plenty of time made available to answer questions both before and after the service. But, and this is most important, no child should attend a funeral if any element of persuasion is required.

Do not expect a child to respond to a death in the same way that you do. Their perspective of the deceased is bound to be different from yours.

The Essentials of Dress Code and Conduct

1. Conform to the requests of the family regarding dress and behaviour and flowers/charity donations. Messages of condolence can help.

2. Dress also with regard to the weather and conditions and to feel comfortable and confident. You are 'on parade'.

3. The chief mourners take precedence.

4. Be punctual and participate in the ceremony.

Memorialization

Tangible Commemoration of a Lifetime

Rights and Responsibilities

When you pay your money for a memorial, of the kind that is a tangible marker of the place where a body or ashes are deposited, you become the outright owner of that artefact or structure. But you are never the owner of the grave plot or niche to which the memorial is attached.

In a cemetery or churchyard, the freehold of the plots stays in the ownership of the landowners. Only a right of use, a sort of lease, can be purchased for a fixed number of years. This is never more than 100 years and may be as few as 5 for a niche for ashes or 25, 50 or 75 years for a body. The right may be in common, to be shared with others, or exclusive, for the use of members of one family or their heirs at law (see Chapter 7). You are unlikely to be allowed to erect a memorial or even place an inscribed vase on a common grave.

Having been granted an exclusive right of burial, you should be able to secure an additional right to erect a memorial on the plot. Very often both deeds of grant are issued at the same time. There will be a fee for the right and restrictions placed on the kind of monument you will be allowed to erect.

The cemetery or churchyard is a public place where your property will be held by the landowners, technically exercising custody in possession. Overall responsibility for the safety of visitors, even those intent on vandalism or other mischief, rests with the landowners. They have ultimate control of what goes on to the land and how it is kept. They draw up the regulations and issue or sell the rights of use.

The landowners will be concerned about the effect your memorial will have on the overall appearance of the landscape and environment and that your memorial will not cause offence to other people. You are unlikely to be allowed to erect it yourself but will have to retain the services of a recognized monumental mason, who is most likely to be the one who sells you the monument. The landowners may insist you employ a mason who is one of a number they have approved and who is properly insured. It is as well to check that your mason is cleared to work in the cemetery or churchyard of your choice before you commission the work. And obtain approval for the design, type of stone and the wording to go on the memorial before authorizing the start of any work on it.

The monument remains your property and you or your heirs at law are responsible for keeping it in a safe condition throughout the period of tenure of the grave. If the monument falls and injures someone, you could be held responsible. The landowner has a general responsibility for the safety of the public using the cemetery or churchyard and may find it necessary to remove or lay down a memorial should it become unsafe.

The monumental mason or contractor you employ has a duty of professional care to carry out the installation in a fit and proper manner and in accordance with the regulations. You may be provided with a guarantee for the work. But the guarantee will not be for the number of years that the memorial may be expected to stand.

It will be your responsibility, and that of people who may inherit rights to the grave in future years, to maintain the integrity and inherent safety of the memorial in good condition. It is possible to obtain insurance cover against damage and many monumental masons, specialist firms and sometimes the cemetery management can provide memorial – and grave – maintenance contracts. If you have rights or an interest in a grave, you should notify the cemetery or incumbent if you change address or if the rights pass to someone else.

The Time to Set a Memorial

Many people like to see a memorial above a grave right from the beginning. This is understandable. You want ownership of the grave to be clearly demonstrated and your lovingly selected and individually inscribed stone in place at the time when you most need to visit and relate to the grave space. For most people this is immediately after the burial.

Conflicting advice is given about how long you should wait before erecting a memorial. You may be told to wait for months or even a year 'so that the ground will have time to settle'. More likely than not, the real reason is that the stonemasons would rather complete your order in their own good time, or when the weather improves, or that there is long or unreliable shipping time for the material to be supplied from overseas.

A memorial should not be erected on top of the back-fill soil in a grave. If it were, waiting six months would not resolve the problem of settlement for this might recur over a number of years. A strip of unexcavated ground should be saved at the head of the grave and be wide enough to carry the foundation slab of a plinth and plate memorial with no risk of subsidence.

When a traditional upright headstone is to be installed, of the kind with a couple of feet going straight into the ground, this can be put in place while the back-filling is carried out providing good firm tamping is applied.

A modern version of this setting, thought to be borrowed from the methodology of war graves, is to dig a hole about one foot deep and set the upright headstone on a foundation slab at that level. A concrete-cast foundation shoe, with a slot into which the headstone fits, may be used rather than a foundation slab. The appearance is indistinguishable from that of a traditional stone setting.

If a ledger stone or kerb set is to cover the full grave space, the foundation slab should span the freshly dug area and rest on firm ground on all four sides.

There are bound to be exceptions. Some churchyards, which may have been dug over for centuries, will be hard put to find firm ground. And ground in some places is naturally liable to settling. Advice from knowledgeable people in the locality should be sought.

Traditionally, especially in rural areas, memorial masons have taken a proprietary interest in the churchyards and cemeteries where they regularly work. When they notice a memorial they have erected is tilting, they are naturally inclined to put it straight. This old-fashioned attitude is dying out and modern businesses are likely to seek a fee for resetting a memorial.

Subsidence is not the only cause of memorial instability. Other factors may be tree roots or burrowing animals, weedkiller chemicals that can make soil friable, storm damage, vandalism, accidental damage during ground maintenance, weathering and lack of maintenance over long periods, inadequate joints between component parts, poor workmanship and inferior materials.

Some cemeteries, in an effort to overcome the inherent instability of plinth and plate memorials, have laid strips of concrete between the rows of plots, which the memorials stand upon. Clearly in such situations settlement can be no reason for delay in installing the memorial.

Continental-style, pre-cast concrete burial chambers are being introduced in some cemeteries. With these the headstone can be safely installed even before the funeral takes place.

Suggested rules for the introduction of memorials into churchyards published in *The Churchyards Handbook* include this injunction: 'A minimum period of six months must elapse between the date of death of a person to be commemorated and the approval of a memorial by the incumbent'.

Many churchyards are adopting these suggested rules. The delay, according to the clergy, is to give the bereaved relatives time to calmly consider the type of memorial they really want – and can afford – and to plan the wording they should have upon it. Some psychologists, who have found that headstones can be useful therapy for some people in the time immediately after a death, would not agree. The bereaved consumer may see an enforced waiting period as interference in their freedom to make a personal decision.

There is perhaps more justification for this clerical attitude than for the 'settlement' excuse sometimes used by the trade to cover up the inadequate customer services they provide. Like funeral directors, monumental masons are protected from market forces by the mysteries of their trade and the disinclination of the public to seek to be better informed about a subject allied to death.

Memorialization in a Churchyard

Long History of Change

Memorials in churchyards have been subject to many changes over the years. Burials around churchyards have been confirmed since AD 750 but until the late 16th century graveyards were virtually empty of monuments. Those who could afford a memorial were buried inside the church. The churchyards were open spaces used for community activities such as archery practice, weapons inspections, fairs and bleaching linen and drying hides.

The Puritans put a stop to burials and monuments inside churches and the titled and wealthy moved their tombs outside. The Reformation, however, meant that every person, being equal in death, had the right to a plot and, gradually, ordinary people set up family graves marked with both a headstone and a footstone. The idea developed that the headstone could be made into an interesting memorial and local stonemasons embarked on a new line of business. The idea caught on and during the 17th century ornamental headstones began to crowd out activities in churchyards.

These memorials were highly individual and personalized with symbols saying something about the deceased's lifestyle, trade and reminders of mortality such as hourglasses and death's heads. They used mostly local stone, which was easily accessible. Base stone in some regions would be painted white and lettering and ornamentation brightly coloured.

At first, sandstone, limestone and slate were the main materials but by 1840 white marble was being imported in quantity from Italy and proved very popular. However, it does not react well to acid rain and atmospheric pollution and is less in use nowadays.

Machine tools made working granite more economic and

gradually this has become the most common material for the majority of headstones. It polishes to a highly reflective surface, resists weathering and when coloured black it sets off the gold paint or gilded letters that appeal to many people.

Various types of recumbent stones, ledgers or body slabs have been used to cover the space between footstone and headstone. More recently, kerbs have been fitted to surround the grave plot and the enclosed space planted with flowers or covered in stone or glass chippings.

Wood was often used in the form of a headstone or the now neglected 'leaping board'. These boards became popular in the 1750s. They comprised a long narrow board running the length of the grave and supported on posts at each end. They were inscribed like a memorial with name and date carved and painted.

Most 18th-century headstones were in one piece; one third of it buried as an anchor to keep it in the ground. This has been the means of retaining a great many of them safely in place for up to 300 years. The 19th-century two-part memorial with monument mounted on a pedestal base becomes insecure when the cement weathers and many have been pushed over by vandals or blown down by the wind. Cast iron memorials were popular in some areas from the beginning of the 19th century.

After 1918 there was a trend to small uniform headstones, emulating war grave architecture. Cemeteries and, to a lesser extent, churchyards began to fill with rank upon rank of them.

Upkeep of this mixed collection of stonework became a problem for many churches. As scythes gave way to motor mowers, obstructions to the progress of the machines were removed. Footstones were probably the first to go, then kerbs and then wholesale clearances of tombstones to create an open-lawn freeway for the mowers.

This was too much for conservationists and historians and in the 1960s a movement to protect the heritage of memorials in churchyards gathered in strength. Some sort of regulation was called for.

A Special Significance

There are around 16,500 Church of England churches in England alone. Each incumbent is the freeholder of the churchyard and views it as a personal garden. However, churchyards are subject to planning regulations, that is, faculty controls vested in the bishop and applied by the chancellor of the diocese. There are 44 dioceses, each with its own chancellor.

Regional practices have evolved and it would be a pity to lose local customs under nationwide standardization. A valuable guide and resource of 'advice on the history and significance of churchyards, their care, improvement and maintenance' – *The Churchyards Handbook* – was published in 1962. Subsequent revisions have appeared in 1976 and 1988. This handbook has set the standard framework within which most contemporary churchyards regulate their memorialization policies.

An ideal is envisaged in which the church itself, unarguably the dominant feature, is complemented by a surrounding landscape of harmonizing monuments. Churches are generally made of mellow stone or brick and memorials should be sympathetic. White marble, black granite and highly polished surfaces are generally considered inappropriate.

The size of the memorial is also an important factor. Against the scale of the church building, mature trees and established older stones, small memorials can give the impression of a pets' cemetery.

Safety Put at Risk by Two-part Headstones

The introduction in the 1950s of machinery that mass-produces small stereotyped two-part memorials put memorialization on to the trail of dismal banality that so many cemeteries, and modern sections of churchyards, present today.

Many thousands of these plinth-and-plate headstones have been found unsafe within a few years of erection and areas of cemeteries have been cordoned off while repairs are carried out. In response to health and safety measures, the memorial masonry trade has devised a system of extended dowel pins to tie the structures into the earth. This is intended to avoid the danger of 'catastrophic collapse', which has caused injuries and even deaths.

Some churchyards – and most memorial sculptors – are returning to the well-tried and tested 18th-century practice of one-piece headstones set straight into the ground. Not only are these intrinsically safe but they also seem to bond directly with the earth, as if growing out of it, in a reassuring and aesthetically pleasing fashion.

The Christian Factor

You need not be a Christian to be buried in a churchyard. Providing you qualify as a resident of the parish, you have a right to be buried there. But the regulations will most likely be written to ensure that your memorial will not offend Christian sensibilities.

Monuments were not made in the form of crosses until the 19th century, when machinery made such shapes practically viable. Neither was the cross used as a carved emblem as it was considered a papist symbol. Many churchyards today prohibit the use of crosses. Too frequent a repetition of the ultimate Christian symbol, it is said, will devalue its relevance.

Unconventional shapes and ornamentation, in addition to crosses, are not allowed by most churchyard regulations. Heart-shapes are not admitted, neither are Bibles, nor upward pointing fingers, which may be seen as presumptuous. Animals are not allowed because of the Christian dislike of idolatry, although birds, bees and butterflies are OK.

Bereaved parents who would have liked a teddy bear, a Bugs Bunny or a Mickey Mouse on their child's grave puzzle about the presence of angel statues and engravings. 'Angels are not of this earth; they are not real so they cannot have effigies,' the parents are told. But the same argument doesn't get them permission to have a Teletubby tombstone.

Wording on Tombstones

Inscriptions, both what they say and how they are applied to the stone, are also liable to be carefully scrutinized before acceptance in a churchyard.

The Churchyards Handbook says 'our burial grounds are becoming deserts of verbal, as well as visual, banality. The consecrated ground of a churchyard, like a church itself, should be a reverenced place, where everything should, as much as possible, enhance the spirit.'

It goes on to spell out at considerable length what should and should not be inscribed on gravestones in churchyards, down to such detail as to insist that names are inscribed in full (no initials and no missing out a name that may have been so hated and avoided in life). Expressions such as 'fell asleep' are to be avoided and so are nicknames or pet names. In particular, 'Mum', 'Dad' and 'Ginger' are mentioned as not to be allowed. Mum and Dad, though not so much Ginger, have resulted in considerable furore when arguments about their inclusion have arisen.

The authority of the handbook's recommendations was tested when, in 1994, a consistory court upheld a vicar's ruling that the use of what he called pet phrases ('Dad and Grandad') should be banned from a headstone. Later, on the grounds that they had been 'unintentionally misled' by the Church of England, another consistory court gave the family permission to move their grandfather's body to a municipal cemetery where the desired wording could be used.

The family argued that other gravestones in the Freckleton, Lancashire, parish churchyard used similar words and they had not known of the vicar's relatively new ruling until they went to order the headstone.

Regulations May Change

Clearly you should not rely on looking round the churchyard to see what sort of memorial you may erect. Not only may the regulations be changed but also the interpretation of the regulations can be different. A new vicar may have other ideas or an incumbent may suddenly decide that the churchyard should in future aspire to a more mellow uniformity.

A leaflet, clearly setting out the regulations, should be available and you should ask for a copy of this and insist on a discussion with the relevant cleric so that everyone is clear about the type of memorial and inscription you may have – before the burial takes place.

The Handbook includes an appendix that details 'suggested rules to govern the introduction of churchyard memorials'. This is increasingly being taken as the template for drafting regulations. However, there are likely to be local variations and some will allow the vicar more scope to exercise personal judgement than others.

Essential Faculties

Anything to be erected in a churchyard requires a faculty licence. This is a form of planning permission issued under ecclesiastical law by the chancellor of the diocese acting for the bishop. Many chancellors grant an overall faculty for simple upright headstones and delegate authority to incumbents for them to allow memorials within the scope of these regulations.

Local memorial masons are normally familiar with these regulations, and also the vicar's interpretation and attitude towards them, and probably have a stock of suitable 'blank' headstones awaiting the addition of a name and date. These cosy arrangements rather encourage the proliferation of standard look-a-like simple headstones in churchyards. Even though, if you really want something more unusual than is permitted under the standard regulations, you can insist on applying directly to the chancellor, this can cost quite a lot more money (see Chapter 7).

You will require a faculty for the exclusive right of use of the grave and another faculty for an out-of-the-ordinary memorial. There will be a fee for submitting your petition for a faculty, which can range between £70 and £200. You will probably be expected to make a donation towards the upkeep of the churchyard, perhaps on an annual basis. Filling in the forms and submitting a drawing and details of the inscription could mean extra work for the mason, who may ask for more money.

Every application to erect a memorial, place anything on a grave, bury ashes in a grave or do any works in a churchyard should be made in writing to the incumbent. There will be a form available from the incumbent. Be sure you have the proper permission before entering into a contract or accepting an estimate for a memorial.

The Extent of Regulations

The suggested rules cover such details as the dimensions of an acceptable upright headstone, which will aim to set an appropriate scale in relationship to existing ancient headstones, setting out minimum as well as maximum sizes. They are not intended to set standard proportions but that tends to be the result.

Specifications for foundations will be laid down and in the light of health and safety developments outlined above, current specifications may be expected to undergo some revision.

The type of stone and finish will be recommended. There will probably be predominant local stones used in traditional buildings, including the church, and stones similar to them in colour and texture will be preferred. Stones that 'stand out like a sore thumb', which are therefore not permitted, will also be listed and will probably include black, red and other coloured granites, white marble and any polished surfaces.

Curved tops are generally preferred but heart shapes and animal silhouettes are generally banned. Expect kerbs or railings, chippings and photoplaques to be banned.

Bronze, leaded or plastic lettering is normally banned in favour of carved inscriptions. Wording will have to be simple and reverent and a long list of handbook dos and don'ts may be applied.

Even flower vases are subject to faculty permission and, unless built into the headstone, will probably have to be sunk completely into the ground. Some churchyards ban artificial flowers and withered flowers will be expected to be removed. Churchyards are often less restrictive about bulb and flower planting than cemeteries and may have a conservation plan you can take part in.

Commemoration After Cremation

You are unlikely to find arrays of mini-headstones on reduced graves for ashes in a churchyard, although they are popular in many cemeteries.

Some churchyards have areas set aside for flat inscribed stone slabs let into the turf, which will eventually engulf them. Paths are sometimes widened by inscribed paving slabs with ashes beneath. There are innovative gardens of remembrance with inscribed boulders and even tubular ash vaults beneath paved or gravelled areas.

A system favoured by many incumbents is to have one or a number of memorials carved with the names of all the people whose ashes are strewn or buried in the churchyard. These are sometimes called recordia panels or recordia tablets.

Columbaria, named after the Roman word for a dovecote as they resemble a collection of pigeonholes, are niches in which ash urns can be stored. Some are left open so the urns can be admired while others are sealed with a stone plaque that can be inscribed.

There are spaces inside some churches that are suitable for columbaria and some crypts and basements have them installed. They may also harmonize with other monuments in a churchyard by taking the form of a chest or box tomb.

Inscribed plaques, similar to the enclosures of columbaria niches but with no space behind them, may be mounted on walls specially built for the purpose or on the boundary walls of the churchyard.

A form of memorial that seems eminently suitable for commemorating the interment of a number of people's cremated remains would be the leaping board grave marker described previously. This would be particularly suitable for the shorter lease term of commemoration most often provided after cremation. I have yet to discover a churchyard currently offering this form of memorialization.

Costs

The church commissioners issue a table of fees for various services provided by the church including monuments in churchyards (see Chapter 7). These are revised every year. From January 1999, the fees for monuments in churchyards are as follows.

The fees relate to monuments, including original inscription, erected in churchyards with the consent of the incumbent under the chancellor's general directions. For the purpose of definition, take monuments to include headstone, cross, kerb, border, vase, chain, railing, tablet, flat stone, tombstone or monument or tomb of any other kind:

- Small wooden cross £12.

- Small vase not exceeding 305 mm x 203 mm x 203 mm £24.

- Tablet commemorating person cremated, erected horizontally or vertically and not exceeding 533 mm x 533 mm £42.

- Any other monument £98.

- Additional inscription on existing monument £23.

- The fee for an additional inscription on a small wooden cross, a small vase or tablet not exceeding 533 mm x 533 mm shall not exceed the current fee payable to the incumbent for the erection of such a monument.

Memorialization in a Cemetery
A Variety of Entombment Options

The history of cemeteries begins only 150 years ago. Unlike churchyards, the burial land in cemeteries has not been reused nor the place vandalized by reformists, so their monumental heritage remains largely in place. Plots were sold in perpetuity and impressive monumental structures were erected on the early privately owned sites. Eminent architects entered competitions to win the commission to design the cemeteries as grand memorial parks.

A variety of entombment options was available. There were mausoleums, aboveground structures in which encoffined bodies are placed, which were usually reserved for members of the same family. Larger models may have a walk-in facility with coffins on tiered shelves.

Then there were catacombs, which provide a similar arrangement for encoffined bodies to be stored without burial but in a larger communal space shared with other citizens. Another option was privately owned brick- or stone-lined and even tiled underground vaults, ranging in size to accommodate between 2 and 20 coffins.

The majority of plots, however, were like the traditional churchyard graves with a single headstone, though sometimes dug deep enough for several generations.

The first grand cemeteries of the 1830s and 1840s were privately owned. Liverpool led the way with the Necropolis in 1825, quickly followed by St James's Cemetery. Glasgow's Necropolis (1832) was praised by Queen Victoria and Prince Albert. Kensal Green, also opened in 1832, was the first of the famous London cemeteries including Highgate, Nunhead and Abney Park. Leeds's private General Cemetery Company laid out St George's Fields at Woodhouse in 1835.

Burial Boards Set Up

A series of Acts of Parliament passed in the 1850s made it compulsory for towns and parishes to set up burial boards and municipal cemeteries. Since 1860, most cemeteries have been run by local authorities that at first emulated the private entrepreneurs in architectural planning and elaborate memorials, which were sometimes built by public subscription.

Those who could not afford expensive cemetery plots were permitted modest memorialization in the municipal cemeteries. But, with the tenet that all should be equal in death, the dimensions of memorials were strictly restricted.

Some cemeteries had expanses of 'guinea graves', identified by rows of headstones each covered front and back with the names of people who could just afford to avoid the paupers' burial plots. And great efforts were made to keep out of those paupers' graves. Cemetery records reveal that superintendents in some boroughs competed to bury the greatest possible number in a single grave. As many as 32 adults and 55 children was achieved in Leeds Corporation's Burmantofts cemetery in 1881.

Many of the private cemeteries went into liquidation when all the plots had been sold and local authorities were then forced to take over responsibility for their upkeep. As they experienced the problems of maintaining the remnants of a free market in entombment, councillors resolved to avoid a similar future in public cemeteries. Easy-care plans were introduced and enforced on a malleable public easily directed in matters of death. Gradually, the original grand vision has given way to the bland uniformity of contemporary lawn-sectioned monumental monotony.

Lawn Memorial Sections

The lawn-type system of headstones and grave maintenance was introduced to cemeteries throughout the country in the early 1950s. The objective is to have a stretch of grass over which a motor mower can be driven without hindrance. Uniform-sized headstones are lined in rows on either side of the mower's path and at the head of graves. The spaces between the headstones and a strip in front and behind are left unturfed as these are not easily accessed by the mowing machine. Shrubs may be planted between the headstones or gravel laid and weeds kept down in these strips by spraying herbicide.

Concrete strips are sometimes installed along the heads of the graves and the headstones are mounted on to these. No surrounds are permitted on the graves, or planting or vases or the laying of flowers, except perhaps on the strip in front of the stone.

The maximum size of memorial allowed varies slightly from place to place but is generally around 91 x 76 centimetres (3 ft x 2 ft 6 in) and sometimes thickness is also specified at 5–7.5 centimetres (2–3 in) on a base/plinth of 69 x 38 centimetres (2 ft 3 in x 1 ft 3 in). Some masons and cemeteries have not adapted to metric measurements, so be careful if translating. Cemetery superintendents have been known to insist on a metre being cut down to three feet to fit the local regulation. The maximum permitted sizes are often not attained with the majority of memorials fitting into a factory standard that is smaller and easier to handle.

The lawn sections, introduced by cemetery managements to make the job of grass cutting easier, coincided with memorial manufacturers introducing the complementary lawn memorial. This is a 'doorstep' plinth with an upright flat slab plate fixed to it and often with one or two vase holes. They are mass-produced with a standard range of shaped tops and they are almost inevitably in black granite polished to a reflective surface and with sandblasted gold-coloured lettering.

The lawn section-style is copied from the Commonwealth War Graves cemeteries, where members of the armed forces killed on active service are commemorated. Here, identical headstones are used and the regimented uniformity is appropriate to the circumstances.

In civilian cemeteries, lawn sections have been the death knell of the individuality of memorial shape and design. Park landscapes and sculptured ornaments are replaced by rows of burial lots and grave markers in the pursuit of easy maintenance. There are, however, signs that cemeteries are becoming more aware of their responsibilities to the public and sections with more freedom of choice are being introduced.

Traditional Memorial Sections

At the height of the enthusiasm for creating mowing fields for graves, lawn sections were made retrospectively by removing the kerbstones, chippings or body slabs from the older graves, which had been installed at a time when these had been permitted. Only the headstones were left in position and grass was cultivated where masonry, wrought iron and chain link fences had once marked out the individual grave spaces.

The gang mower could now motor between the ancient headstones with impunity. Sometimes the headstones, designed to rely on the kerbs for integral support, became unsafe and they too had to be removed.

This plot conversion procedure is not so often implemented nowadays and older cemeteries, and some churchyards, have space left in the sections where these full-size graves have been retained. In such places it should still be possible to surround the entire grave plot with a kerb or fence, set a stone slab over the surface of the grave, plant flowers or lay chippings. However, there may still be some restrictions laid down by an arbiter of good taste or in the pursuit of easy care, so do look carefully at the regulations before making any decisions. Height restrictions are often imposed.

Traditional memorial sections where these more elaborate types of monuments are allowed are going to be more expensive than a plot in the lawn section. This, plus an interest in providing a wider choice for the public, is encouraging some cemeteries to open new sections where full-size kerb memorials may be installed.

No Way Round Regulations

Money won't buy a better monument in a civic cemetery. There is no machinery to apply for special permission to install a memorial outside the limits set out in the regulations. Your only chance of getting something different is to bring about a change in the regulations. This will involve due democratic process, committee meetings, votes and decisions in council.

There is no national standard for regulating memorials in cemeteries. Each authority decides what they want to allow and the personal opinions and prejudices of committee members can sometimes become enshrined in the doctrine. These frequently amount to restrictions on choice written into the regulations because one or two committee members didn't like the look of something and the others didn't care one way or the other.

Some insist that only gold or black may be used to colour lettering on headstones. With many different colours and textures of memorial stones, a sensitive sculptor will want to select a colour for the lettering that will best complement the medium. But there is no chance of this happening if the book says 'only black or gold'. Photoplaques, for example, are an important commemorative artefact for some nationalities – few memorials are without them in Italy – but they are often banned in UK cemeteries.

Modern techniques of engraving make it possible to etch a picture on to a granite memorial and then paint it in rainbow colours. Regulations, drafted in years when such technology did not exist, can thoughtlessly be phrased so that such ornamentation is not permitted.

Modern machinery has made it possible to cut outlines of cartoon figures or teddy bears out of granite and these are obviously popular with parents whose child has died. If you would like this sort of memorial first check that they are permitted.

Height limitations are strictly enforced in most cemeteries. No headstone is allowed to stand out above the masses. But there is unlikely to be a lower-level limit such as is imposed in churchyards. Cemeteries normally allow very small memorials, right down to kerbstone-size wedges or just a vase. Councillors are cost conscious and sympathetic towards low-income residents. Large ostentatious monuments are thought to make those who cannot afford such a show of wealth feel inferior in their grieving.

Floral Tributes and Grave Gardens

Except for the first few days after the burial, before the grave is turfed over, you will not be allowed to place flowers on top of a grave in a lawn section. Floral tributes, wreaths and artificial flowers are particularly unwanted because bits of wire can get caught up in the mowing machine.

The person riding on the mower does not want to keep stopping to move vases, wreaths, picket fences or other tributes from out of the way of the machine. Flowers will be restricted to the space close to the headstone or perhaps just to the flowerpot holders in or on the plinth. Planting flowers in a lawn section grave is definitely not a good idea for the same reason – the mower will mow them down.

The same does not apply to traditional graves where you can, within reason, place tributes over the entire surface. However, flowers and floral arrangements may be beautiful when they are fresh but they become unpleasant when withered and can spoil the scenery for people visiting other graves.

Cemetery gardeners may be expected to clear away old flowers, perhaps on a weekly basis, if you do not keep the grave freshly tended yourself. If you are thinking of planting flowers or shrubs on a traditional grave, avoid anything that is very vigorous or intrusive and may spread to other plots. And beware of small shrubs and trees that can deceptively grow to a size unsuitable for a grave garden.

Planting schemes especially designed for grave gardens have been produced. They aim to be low maintenance with a basic ground cover and a specimen plant selected to be at its best at the time of a special anniversary.

Some cemeteries, for a fee, will plant out a grave and maintain it for you within the overall gardening maintenance plan. It is also possible in some areas to retain the services of a grave gardening company that will tend the plants and the memorial if you are unable to visit it often enough yourself.

Removal of a Memorial

The 1977 Act (Local Authorities Cemetery Order, Article 10) effectively redefined perpetuity as it applied to an exclusive right to a place of burial to mean no more than 100 years. This means that headstones, when they reach this age, may be removed and the land released for new burials. Private cemeteries may have different rules.

Before a memorial is removed, the cemetery authorities are required to take a number of steps to notify the owner, who will be the heir at law of the original purchaser. That person can then take possession of the memorial and take it away or purchase a new period of ownership of the grave space. If the owner cannot be found then the owners of the cemetery or churchyard will decide what to do with it. If it has a historical or artistic worth, they may decide to keep it.

If it is not going to be kept, it should be broken up and rendered unrecognizable. Sometimes pieces of old memorial stones are used to build pathways, walls or rockeries.

A memorial may have to be removed temporarily while a grave is reopened, another dug nearby, for an additional inscription to be carved or if it becomes unsafe. The owner should be notified if any of these things happen. It is important to remember to tell the cemetery owners if the owner of the grave rights changes address.

Costs

In addition to the cost of the memorial itself, you will have to purchase the exclusive right to burial in the grave plot. This will be for a set number of years, not more than 100, and should be renewable (see Chapter 7). The right to burial may also include the right to erect a memorial but this may be sold as an additional right. As with burial rights, the costs vary greatly from, say, £70 to several hundred pounds. There may be another charge for a permit to erect the memorial and you may have to pay for a foundation supplied by the cemetery.

The price of the memorial itself depends entirely upon what you choose – the material, size, shape, amount of lettering and ornamentation (see Chapters 11 and 12). A typical lawn-style headstone may be about £850 and it is quite easy to spend £1,200–£3,000.

Memorialization After Cremation

At a Crematorium

Grave monuments are not considered compatible with cremation. With the idea being to 'save the land for the living', crematoria built since 1945 have, as a rule, allowed for no form of stone or permanent structured memorial. Many provide only a book of remembrance. Earlier crematoria included elaborate buildings for the display of funerary urns containing the ashes and miniature landscaped gardens for the interment of ashes beneath Lilliputian monuments. Recent years have seen the development of a wide variety of memorial options following cremation (see Chapter 12).

In a Cemetery

Until the mid-1980s, only a very small number, around 12 per cent, of cremated remains were taken away from crematoria, where they were mostly scattered or interred with no monument.

Quite a number of crematoria were situated within or next to an established cemetery. So, being already surrounded by grave memorials, some of them accepted the principal that a monument after cremation could be acceptable. Full-size grave plots were and are sold for interment of cremated remains and the usual regulations for headstones and full memorials apply.

Gradually, the practice of selling half-size grave plots in lawn memorial-type sections began to spread. The headstones, usually of the plate-and-plinth variety, are also reduced in size. Some have evolved into miniature traditional memorial sections, with tiny grave gardens and kerb surrounds lined up on concrete rafts. When massed together they amplify the banalities of full-size lawn sections but serve to satisfy many people.

These cremated remains sections are now to be found in most modern cemeteries. The number of cremated remains taken away from crematoria, many presumably to be deposited in cemetery plots such as these, had risen from 12 per cent in 1970 to 44 per cent in 1997.

Costs

As with a full burial, you will have to purchase an exclusive right for deposit of cremated remains, for a specified number of years, if you want a grave and memorial stone in a cremated remains section in a cemetery. The price will vary from place to place but generally it will be a bit more than half the price of a full-sized grave plot. It may be for a much shorter time than for a full burial – and correspondingly less expensive. Local authorities may double the price for people outside their district.

You can expect to pay at least £150 in a town or urban cemetery for, say, 25 years. There may also be a permit fee to erect a memorial of around £30. Additional interments will most likely be allowed during the period of tenancy, for a fee of £50–£70. In a small rural cemetery, the prices will be a lot less, probably in line with those charged by the church. Costs may be higher in a city where grave space is in short supply.

There is also the cost of the memorial itself, which will depend on how simple or grand it is. There is almost certain to be a height

limit, maybe as low as 66 centimetres. A typical memorial cost
will be around £500 (see Chapter 11).

The Essentials of Memorialization

1. Although the memorial may be yours, you cannot own the
    site it occupies.

2. You, or your heirs at law, will be responsible throughout the
    lifetime of the memorial for its structural integrity and safety.

3. The landowners are responsible for the safety of the public
    visiting the site and may have your monument removed for
    reasons of safety.

4. Your memorial will have to conform to regulations. Be aware
    of these before selecting a site or commissioning any work.

CPRE *working to protect England's countryside*

The English countryside has been the delight of countless generations - yet this very heart of our national heritage is constantly under threat from damaging development.

Working at a national and local level for over 70 years, CPRE has played a major part in the creation and protection of National Parks, the provision of Green Belts around cities, and in establishing firm planning controls. CPRE also campaigns for stronger woodland and hedgerow protection and more benign agricultural, forestry, water and transport policies. CPRE's success is based on careful research, constructive ideas and reasoned argument.

CPRE is ever vigilant but its work as a small but cost-effective charity is almost totally dependent on public support.

By making a bequest to CPRE, you can help ensure that England's countryside is enjoyed by future generations. Remember, a legacy to CPRE is exempt from Inheritance Tax.

President Prunella Scales CBE   *Patron HM The Queen*
Registered Charity No 233179
Council for the Protection of Rural England

If you would like further information on how you can provide for CPRE in your will, please contact Stephen White at

CPRE
Freepost SW 3524, London SW1W 0BR.

Tel: 0171 976 6433
Fax: 0171 976 6373

CPRE

Your countryside
Your voice

Stone Memorials

Where to Buy

Memorials are still one of those few remaining products that can be bought directly from the workshop of the craftsperson who makes them. Monumental masonry businesses can still be found with stone sawing and polishing facilities, grit-blasting machinery and hand carvers' bankers (work benches) and a yard or shop window displaying unlettered memorials, all together on the same site. Many are family owned firms, often representing several generations working in the same trade.

Increasingly, few actually saw, shape and polish monuments, preferring to buy them ready-made from a factory. They can be brought in ready lettered, leaving the local mason with the task of simply erecting them in the cemetery or churchyard. Some firms operate a halfway house, buying in finished blanks and adding the inscription and perhaps ornamentation on their own premises.

Unlike most trades, there is no real distinction between the manufacturing and retailing function. Shopping for a memorial can be a dusty if educational experience.

Funeral directors sometimes include memorials among the services they provide. Some actually own a memorial masonry operation as part of their business. The Co-op has one of the largest memorial-manufacturing businesses in the country as well as a quarter of the funerals market.

Other funeral directors work on a commission basis with a local memorial mason while some prefer not to get involved with memorials at all. There are some centralized manufacturing organizations that market memorials from catalogues, either through funeral directors or by advertising in the national press, local newspapers and magazines. Trade-made memorials, although personalized with a chosen assembly of motif, lettering, shape and wording, work from pre-planned patterns and machine-cut lettering fonts.

For a special, custom-made memorial you may go to a sculptor or letter-carver who will work with you to create a unique work of art. The local church will probably be able to introduce you to a sculptor in your area or you can contact one through Memorials by Artists at Snape Priory, Saxmundham, Suffolk IP17 ISA (tel: 01728 688934).

Type and Quality of Stone

Stone can be cut and shaped into many forms: flat tablets, three-dimensional geometric shapes or sculptured effigies, rough-hewn, polished or painted. There are various colours and textures of stone from the soft white of marble to the mellow yellow, red or grey grittiness of sandstone. There is the gentler texture and creamy off-white, pinks and blues of limestone, the smooth hardness of grey or green slate and the tough, many-coloured granites that range from pink to blue, grey to black and mottled hues in between.

Other stones with their own special qualities are also used for memorials. Stones such as Nabresina, a pale grey-beige with small fossil markings, the tough gold-tinged York stone and pale brown Purbeck with clearly identifiable fossils on the surface. There are other regional varieties with their own special characteristics.

Stone for memorials comes from the lower beds of quarries and is harder and denser than stone suitable for building or other construction purposes. A memorial is, after all, exposed on five sides to the weather and has the sixth planted in or on the damp earth. It must also be of a quality to accept the small and intricate detail involved in inscribing letters or ornamentation on a memorial.

Standing upright as intended, headstones will withstand weathering and the inscriptions remain legible for many years;

but lying flat, in the open, many quickly deteriorate. Old stones found lying flat in churchyards would most likely have been originally upright or inside the church.

The recently introduced practice of laying flat plaques over cremated remains not only speeds up deterioration but allows the grave markers to be lost under rain puddles, snow falls, leaves and even turf. Gold leaf or paint on the lettering of a flat slab can be damaged in a matter of months because rain cannot run off the surface.

Granite is the most popular stone used for memorials today. It is very hard but modern machinery makes it possible to shape it and cut deep clean-edged letters. It takes a high polish but can have a smooth dull finish, be 'rough hewn' or have a contrasting combination of finishes. It stays looking smart for many years, resisting weather, algae and lichen growth.

Some granite is still quarried in this country, in Scotland, Cumbria, Devon, Cornwall and Ireland, and it is also imported from Africa, India, Scandinavia and EU countries.

White marble is the next most popular stone. It first began appearing in our cemeteries and churchyards in the mid-19th century, imported from Italy. It is comparatively soft and easy to carve into shapes like angels or doves but does not weather well in some parts of Britain.

Nabresina is a recently introduced alternative to white marble. Being darker in colour it is more acceptable in churchyards.

Slate is a 'home-grown' material, quarried in Devon, Wales and Westmoreland. It takes extremely fine and detailed carving on its matt surface and withstands the UK climate very well. Colours range from black or blue-grey to a subtle dark green.

Sandstone and limestone are the other types generally used for memorials. There are many regional varieties but the best-known are Portland (limestone) and York (sandstone). They vary in hardness and ability to take detailed carving and withstand the climate but none are as hard as granite or slate. These materials demand a robust style of carving. They have attractive mellow colours, natural in the countryside, and will gradually age, harmonizing with the environment in a way that many people find appealing. They can provide a comfortable home for lichens and moss.

If a memorial is to be erected in a churchyard, it is as well to consider that the type of stone should harmonize with other stones that have collected over many years and with the church building itself. The incumbent will probably have strong views about materials and designs and it is advisable to discuss this with the cleric concerned before ordering a memorial.

Cemeteries rarely worry about the type of stone used but most have regulations about size and shape (see Chapter 10). You should be able to obtain a leaflet setting out the rules and regulations. Your local mason will be familiar with them and has a duty of professional care to supply and erect a memorial for you in accordance with the stipulated regulations. Some stones may react badly with minerals in the soil, airborne pollutants and local weather conditions. Your local mason will be able to give advice.

Most of the stone used for modern memorials is imported because quarries in the UK cannot supply enough of the quality and variety of stone required. It arrives in rough-hewn blocks or slabs to be cut, shaped and finished in UK-based factories. Alternatively, the stone may arrive already made into the basic memorial shape and polished.

Techniques for Inscribing

Various techniques are used today for inscribing the lettering or emblem. Different types of lettering as well as different styles are available, varying just as they do in print, from simple block letters to roman, gothic or elaborate scripts.

The type or method of lettering can be incised (cut into the stone), relief (with the background cut away and the letter standing proud of the surface) or leaded (with lead beaten into the cut-away stone and shaped to give either raised or smoothed-flat letters). Incised or relief letters can be overlaid with gold leaf or painted to enhance legibility and for decorative effect.

Carvings may be made using a mallet and chisel, a letter-cutting machine, which grinds out the stone in the required shapes, or by a sandblasting technique, which etches away the stone not protected by a vinyl stencil with a bombardment of grit particles under high pressure. In the hands of a skilled craftsman all these techniques can result in a neatly cut and attractively displayed inscription.

Stone shapes and decorative or symbolic motifs, such as flowers or religious or craft emblems, can be selected from catalogues or samples on display. Computer technology enables exclusive designs for grit-blasting masks to be produced and some masons will provide one-off designs.

Long-term Care

Anyone comparing the condition of stones in a cemetery will quickly conclude that highly polished granite stays looking new longer than other stones and finishes. That's enough for those house-proud people who have spent a lifetime keeping the home spick and span and want to continue the habit for their partner's headstone. Polished granite is far and away the most popular material for headstones. It looks better longer.

Mud splashes, rain stains or bird droppings can normally be simply wiped off the surface with a damp cloth. Scrubbing bushes, scouring powder, strong detergents or chemicals should never be used. Even washing-up liquid is best avoided.

If an accumulation of dirt has to be removed, use a block of wood with a cloth wrapped round it and plain clean water – and don't rub any harder than necessary. Take special care over the lettering. If it is gilded or painted, the gold leaf or paint may lift off if you attempt to clean inside the letters – another good reason for not using bristles to scrub the surface.

Gilding or paint can't be expected to last indefinitely, any more than the paint on your door and window frames at home. Your monumental mason will be able to repaint or gild lettering if required after a few years. Inscriptions in softer stones may lose their definition after years of weathering and these can be re-cut.

With a pale-coloured stone such as marble, Nabresina or a limestone, an accumulation of lichen or algae inside the lettering can create a contrast with the surface and make it easier to read.

The blurring of the outline of lettering and the edges of cut stone, plus the patina of lichen, algae, moss or pollution are desirable attributes of memorials to some people who prefer them to exhibit marks of the passage of time. This mellowing is particularly sought after in country churchyards and the reason why polished granites are often banned from them.

Staining can be stubborn to remove from grainy stones like marble and sandstone. Scouring powder, which is to be avoided on polished surfaces, may be required for rougher textured surfaces.

A way to remove a stubborn growth of lichen and other organisms is to completely cover the memorial in a black plastic bag. By depriving the plants of sunlight for a number of days they will loosen their grip on the stone and be easier to rub off.

Vulnerable Joins

If you have a plinth-and-plate memorial, a two-part headstone with an upright slab fixed to a 'doorstep', you should keep a weather eye on the joins. There should be dowels (metal pins) sticking up from the plinth and into the base of the plate and a skim of cement where the plinth and plate come together. The dowels will be sunk into plugs of cement dabbed into holes drilled into the granite or stone.

You won't be able to see the dowels but the cement around them, and between the plinth and slab, is vulnerable to moisture penetration and freeze-and-thaw action. Over time the cement can become loose and the headstone unstable.

There is another join between the plinth and whatever form of foundation is supplied. This is unlikely to have dowels and may become loose when the cement dries out.

The third join may be where the foundation slab connects with the soil. In trials at the University of Newcastle, with newly cemented joins, the entire plate, plinth and foundation slab was found to topple over when a force of 30 kilograms was applied. Wind can gust at up to a force of 50 kilograms. Metal spikes, which in effect extend the dowels into the soil, can prevent a sudden collapse of this nature and some cemeteries insist that such ground anchors be installed.

The application of a mastic sealant round the joins above ground level can help preserve the cement. The recommendation from the University of Newcastle was that chemical fixatives should be used in preference to cement. They also recommend the seal be replaced every 20 years or whenever the base and headstone are temporarily separated.

Bearing in mind that you may be held responsible for any damage or injury caused by a falling memorial, part of your long-term care should be focused on those joins and fixings.

Choosing Your Stone

A high level of standardization has evolved within the memorial industry, largely in reaction to the rules and regulations imposed by lawned cemeteries. Although these generally set maximum height and width sizes, and don't intend to standardize, the effect has been for the trade to adapt a basic pattern within the parameters laid down and offer only these to their customers.

Headstone proportions take the general grave-size norm of 75 centimetres high by 60 centimetres wide, though sizes can vary a little. There are half a dozen top shapes: ogee, oval, flat, centre or off-centre mitre or peon. Then there are the special shapes such as hearts and books and children's memorials featuring cartoon characters and animals.

Granite is the most popular material. It is available in many colours and shades from a very dark grey, which when polished is recognized as black, to blue pearl, pinks, reds, light greys and coloured cloud and wave effects. White and dove-grey marble are the next most popular choices followed by 'churchyard' stones in Nabresina, York, Portland and matt-finished grey granite.

Normally only granite will be finished to a high polish, but granite and other stones can have a rough-hewn, punched, pecked or rustic chiselled finish to contrast with a smooth eggshell surface prepared to accept the lettering. Sometimes a riven surface is achieved by leaving a natural finish where the stone, usually slate, has been split along its grain.

Lettering choice is standardized down to three basic styles: block, roman or Olde English. Motifs such as roses, religious figures, crosses, church windows and shepherds may be applied with relief carving or sandblasting. Most come from the same pattern books or computer-cut stencils.

Personalization can be achieved with pictures of people or places etched into the stone or granite to represent, for example, a favourite hobby, holiday place or occupation. Photographs can be reproduced on ceramic plaques and fixed to the memorial. Traditionally, photographs have been fired into the plaque using a technique perfected in Italy and resistant to fading in sunlight. There are some modern systems that don't always have the same lasting qualities.

Statues and figurines carved in marble, reconstituted marble or bronze can be supplied to represent, for example, religious figures, doves, cherubs, teddy bears and many others. Bronze and plastic lettering, symbols and motifs can also be applied to the memorial.

Influencing Factors

Your choice of stone is likely to be influenced by a variety of factors. Probably first will be personal preference for something that will look clean and shiny for a long time, or else a material and finish that will age and mellow and be host to lichens and other organisms.

If the memorial is to go in a churchyard then that choice may be made for you by the regulations, which will go against the clean and shiny look. Granite and marble may be banned altogether because the clergy envisaged only polished black granite and 'glaring' white marble. But granite may be a dull-grey colour with a rough and matt finish and marble can also be grey. After a few years of exposure to weather and organic growth, such granite and marble will blend happily with other types of stones. The easy-carving quality of marble or the hardness of granite, which enables it to hold an inscription, may then be utilized without offending the mellowness of the churchyard. But you may have difficulty in overcoming those regulations and obtaining a faculty.

Some cemeteries go the other way and won't admit sandstone and limestone because this can suffer from water penetration and frost damage. The management then has to cope with complaints from families who expected the stone to keep its pristine looks for longer.

Geography will be a factor because of the weather and pollution. Sandstone and limestone, which will weather fairly well in the south, may not last many hard winters in the north. Marble in some districts erodes much faster than in others. York sandstone can be blackened by urban pollution but can do well in a country environment. And, of course, in churchyards and rural cemeteries, the geography can show in the dominance of local quarried materials with which you may want to harmonize. Do you want the memorial to stand out from those around it, to make a different statement, or blend into the scenery by taking on the uniformity of the majority of materials and designs?

The personality of the person you are commemorating may also influence your choice of stone. Marble, because of the purity of its colour, is often chosen for children. The brighter granite colours may reflect another person's preferences or lifestyle. Someone's origins may be considered and a regional stone such as Scottish granite or Welsh slate selected for that reason.

The wording, ornamentation and amount of lettering to go on the stone will also be a factor. Rough textured grainy stone needs to have big letters and robust carving. Slate can carry fine detail and small letters. Granite can have a mirror finish and surface etching.

Stones such as polished granite, slate and hard limestone show a different colour inside the cut letter, which contrasts with the smooth surface. Others keep the same colour and rely on shadows to be read. Sometimes the lettering is painted in a darker shade or another colour or gilded.

Names and Epitaphs

The inscription on a memorial serves a variety of purposes. It identifies the resting place of a particular person or persons; it provides a public record of the person's life; it stands as a tribute to that life and as a comfort to the living.

In the past, an inscription and the style of monument have boasted of the deceased's wealth and family connections. Many carried a reminder of our mortality in the shape of an hourglass, a scythe, a skull and crossed bones or even a brief sermon.

Nowadays, the majority of inscriptions have only the basic message of the person's name and dates of birth and death. This is the most important part of an inscription and should take the central position and the largest, most dominant typestyle.

In smaller size, above the name, there may be a standard phrase, such as 'In Loving Memory of' or 'Sacred to the Memory of'. Rather than the old-time reminders of mortality, modern epitaphs often seem to deny death with such phrases as 'Passed Away' or 'Gone to Sleep'.

There is often a family's tribute like 'Beloved Father and Grandad' or 'Dear Wife and Mother'. More interesting are brief tags that say something about the deceased's activities like 'musician' or 'churchwarden'.

A quote from the scriptures or a verse may follow beneath the name and occupation. Masons will have a collection of standard verses and quotations but you may prefer to compose something original.

Symbols can impart something of a person's achievements and may be found in the sandblast stencil cutter's computer file or mason's pattern book. A scroll and quill pen for a writer or poet, masks of comedy and tragedy for an actor, military insignia, shepherd, rose, teddy bear, cartoon characters and many more can all be reproduced. Classic cars, motor bikes, caravans, coloured soccer strips or country scenes can all be etched and painted or carved on to stone memorials.

The mason or funeral director will probably have some standard patterns and catalogues to help you make a selection. By picking and mixing features from various illustrations and examples you should be able to come up with a combination that suits your requirements.

Always insist on seeing a drawing of the inscription, with lettering and motif included, before commissioning any work. Where a computer stencil is to be cut, you should also see a printout of the design and lettering. If it is to be cut straight into the stone, you should be able to see it drawn on the stone before the chiselling begins. Always check as many stages as you can before the work is actually 'cast in stone'. If there is a mistake, or you want to change your mind, it is most likely to be impossible to make alterations once the stone has been carved. A new stone would have to be worked on and this will obviously be costly.

You should be able to have some say in the design and positioning of the lettering and motifs although some masons prefer you to leave the sizing and positioning to their craftspeople. If you go to a sculptor you will most likely work together to produce a design you are both pleased with.

Costs

The cost of a memorial is controlled by the quality and rarity of the material it is made from, the amount of material used, the complexity of the shaping and cutting, the amount of polishing or other finishing carried out, the ornamentation and colouring, the lettering and the transportation and setting of the memorial and foundations. There may be additional charges for such things as figurines, bronze embellishments, flower vases and photoplaques.

The most popular type of memorial is an all-polished black granite lawn-style with an ogee curved top, size 75 centimetres high by 60 centimetres wide by 10 centimetres thick. This is the type most often advertised in the press at less than £500. You need to be careful to compare like with like when comparing prices. The sizes may differ slightly and in particular the thickness of the material can vary by several centimetres. It may be polished only on the front or the front and sides; polishing is a slow process and quite costly. Lettering is sometimes included, up to a certain number of letters, in the basic quoted price. Otherwise lettering, or additional lettering, can cost around £1 per letter.

You should plan for a cost of around £850 for a reasonably interesting lawn-style memorial, £1,200 for a full-size with kerb surround and up to £3,000 or more for really impressive memorialization.

The Essentials of Having a Stone Memorial

1. The site, cemetery or churchyard may restrict the type of stone, the design, size, shape and inscription.

2. Be aware of all regulations before commissioning any work.

3. Many styles of lettering, ornamentation and finish are available using traditional craft methods or modern technology.

4. The stone for memorials can be in a variety of colours and textures with different weathering and wearing qualities.

5. The design and personalization of the memorial can be therapeutic.

Other Memorials

Not Necessarily Stone or Granite

Stone has a natural appeal as a material for memorials. Mankind has been using stone to make its mark on the world since time immemorial. Examples of stone being moved, erected, painted or carved exist all over the world and from prehistoric times. Cut from mother earth, no other material seems to satisfy the criteria of natural quality, longevity, beauty and essential mystery that are inherent in stone.

There are, of course, alternatives, though after looking round modern cemeteries and churchyards in the UK it can appear that no other material is suitable. The standard book of rules and regulations is responsible for the lack of innovative materials as much as for the uniformity of size and shape in our cemeteries. Model guidelines produced by the clergy and trade masons have been adapted lock, stock and barrel by incumbents and superintendents and applied to the letter.

The Churchyards Handbook's suggested rules say 'all materials should be made of natural stone with no reflecting finish, or of hardwood'.

Included in listed criteria for the choice of material in the masons' guide is: 'must be a natural quarried, not reconstituted material'. It goes on to say: 'the whole of the memorial must be of the best natural quarried material. Soft stone, fireclay, composite materials, wood or metal (with the exception of bronze) will not be permitted to be fixed'.

Wood, however, has a long tradition of memorial use in churchyards. Examples of 18th-century 'leaping boards' can be found as well as ancient wooden headboards and crosses. There are a few modern interpretations of letter cutting and carving in wood in churchyards but rarely in cemeteries.

Iron and chain link railings were also once popular in tombstone design in Britain. Cast-iron memorials came into vogue with the development of the industry in Shropshire and some quite elaborate ornamental versions can be found, as well as simple grave markers, quite often in the Midlands but also in other parts of the UK. Memorial artists are beginning to work in cast iron once more and both wood and iron memorials are welcomed in some churchyards.

Sculptors work in glass, fibreglass, Perspex and other modern materials as well as metal, ceramics, *pâte verre* and mosaics and some exemplary memorials in these materials can be found overseas. Serviceable, low-cost memorials made from synthetic materials are also available for low-income families in other countries. But anything outside traditional masonry is normally banned under the rules and regulations followed in UK cemeteries.

Innovation for After-cremation Memorials

Cremation, however, is beginning to make a difference. Many crematoria sell small cast-bronze plaques for fixing to walls, round path edges, on to small boulders or for staking under commemorative rose plants, shrubs or trees. Name and dates embossed on a bookmark-size strip of leather and filed in a wall rack are another form of alternative memorial offered at crematoria.

Inscriptions on granite, however, remain a popular choice where crematoria offer this facility. These may be plaques that are displayed on a wall of a building, a perimeter boundary or constructed as part of a garden of remembrance.

Concrete and reconstituted stone products are also appearing for after-cremation memorialization. They may be in the shape of a pre-cast wall unit for plaque mounting, a flower planter or a path- or lawn-edge unit designed to display an array of inscribed granite plaques.

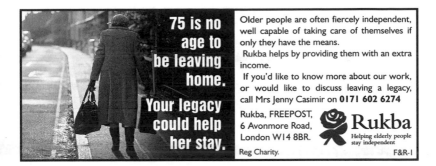
Columbaria, which are collections of niches to contain ash urns; and vaults for the deposit of cremated remains are also frequently made from concrete or reconstituted stone. The enclosures or lids of these structures are usually granite and suitable for inscription.

An example of a modern product designed with a new material to meet the particular requirements of after-cremation memorialization can be found in a unit called an 'UrnKerb'. Finely powdered quarried material is mixed with resins and poured into a mould to make a hollow kerb that serves as an edging for paths, lawns or flowerbeds. Lids set into the kerb carry an inscription and enclose a space that can contain ashes or urns. The material is as durable as granite, can have a matt or polished surface and can replicate virtually any type of stone or colour.

Urns for ashes can in themselves be significant memorials. Columbaria at the earlier crematoria, Golders Green being a fine example, may contain and display a wonderful collection of urns, many of which are individual works of art.

Most crematoria today deliver ashes in a bland plastic jar or a cardboard box. Funeral directors offer a miniature wooden coffin/casket and little else. Slightly more elegant, but still basic, is a spun-aluminium container. However, beautiful urns are in demand in other countries and imported urns of style and quality can be found at an increasing number of crematoria and funeral directors.

In Germany, ashes have to be buried. But graves are reused, so the urns must be biodegradable. They must also be attractive because a service is held before the burial, with the urn being the focus of attention on a catafalque. As a result, urns have been developed that are highly decorative, look and feel like metal or ceramics but have rapid oxidising characteristics.

Italy, Germany, Holland, France, Sweden and the United States all make and market urns in bronze, granite, turned wood, ceramics and terracotta to suit a wide variety of aesthetics. They may be buried, installed in a sealed niche, put on display in an open-fronted columbarium or take pride of place as a decorative work of art in the home.

A Living Memorial

Roses are offered as memorials at many crematoria. These will be planted in a flowerbed and looked after for you for a set period of time. You may be able to bury the ashes under the bush although, contrary to popular belief, this can be harmful to plant life. You will probably be able to place a nameplate, either plastic, inscribed metal or cast bronze, next to the bush.

Where there is space, some crematoria will allow you to plant or dedicate an existing tree to the memory of a loved one. You may also be able to purchase a memorial bench which may have a name and dedication carved into it or a commemorative plate fitted. Some crematoria have accumulated more benches than they have room for and so may allocate them for a fixed period or simply remove them when they start to age.

You may be able to contribute to a bulb or wild flower planting scheme or to a wildlife project such as the siting of nesting boxes in the trees around the crematorium. The Woodland Trust charity will plant a tree as a memorial in a person's name as part of a national tree-planting programme. You won't have an exact location of where that tree is but the name goes into a register. For more information, write to: The Woodland Trust, Ref. 1744 Freepost, Grantham, Lincs NG31 6BR (see Chapter 15).

One of the companies offering prepaid funeral plans, Golden Charter, promises to plant a tree for every funeral plan it sells (see Chapter 17).

Book of Remembrance, Also in Cyberspace

All crematoria, plus an increasing number of churches, provide books of remembrance. Invariably these are large, hand made and leather bound books in which the name and dates of birth and death are inscribed in calligraphy. You may also have a few lines for a dedication, an illuminated initial letter or an illustration such as a flower or insignia.

As with an inscription on a monument, what is written becomes a public record and the authority may refuse to permit an entry that they consider improper or undesirable. The book will normally be kept in a display cabinet in a chapel of remembrance and open at an appropriate page each day. An attendant will open the book to the page you require should you visit on a day other than the anniversary of the death (or other date you have chosen for the entry).

Information technology is being introduced to improve access to books of remembrance at a few crematoria. Pages are scanned into the computer files so that visitors can more easily call up their particular entry and view it on the computer screen.

There is also a system for creating an entry using computer graphics, photographs and scenes or other appropriate images. Pioneered at Emstry Crematorium in Shrewsbury, the electronic pages are stored in a memory bank from where they can be called up for viewing on a computer screen in the crematorium's chapel of remembrance.

It is possible to place a memorial dedication, even a family history, on specific sites on the Internet. At the University of Newcastle, the computer department set up a page on the Internet to record obituaries of famous people. It attracted entries from people with no claim to fame and grew into a virtual memorial garden for ordinary browsers.

An international computer library in Canada allows you to place in cyberspace a digital death notice incorporating text, drawings, photographs and even sound, for example a voice recording.

Based in the United States are Angels Online and the World Wide Cemetery, where you can file memorial pages made up with photographs, emblems and eulogies. There is even a movement to archive people's Web sites after they have died and keep them available on the net to be accessed by future generations (visit www.afterlife.com).

Entombment Above Ground

Mausoleums, houses for the deceased which characterize the older Victorian sections of cemeteries, are being built again after being out of vogue for many years. These provide an above-ground resting place for coffins. Some are like a small house with a door allowing entrance to a space where one or several coffins may be stored. Others are low structures that can just enclose one or two coffins. A number have been constructed, mainly for Italian families, at Kensal Green cemetery in West London. Traditionally, mausolea in the UK have been for the members of individual families. In Mediterranean countries and some parts of the USA and Canada, large mausoleum structures have been built providing a complex of spaces for the containment of hundreds of coffins.

In Streatham, South London, a similar community mausoleum structure, built into and around a crematorium chapel, was completed in 1998 with accommodation for 260 bodies. The prices for a single interment range from £8,000–£10,000, which includes a standard inscription, plus a vase and lamp, on the polished granite slab enclosing the coffin space.

The company behind the venture, Texas-based Service Corporation International, is already planning more in Birmingham and Leatherhead.

Charitable Donations and Endowments

You may want to have a memorial that is 'useful'. Memorial windows in churches and public buildings are a traditional example. So too are donations to charities and building funds for hospitals, theatres or schools.

But be aware that memorials that are part of everyday life can bring you face to face with your grieving at an unexpected moment. You can be prepared and composed when visiting a place set aside for commemoration but a sudden reminder in a theatre foyer or by catching sight of a Sunshine Coach in the High Street can be quite unsettling.

There are hundreds of charities and worthy causes that rely on donations, which can range from a collection taken in place of flowers for the funeral to a substantial bequest. There are ways in which charities can enjoy tax benefits if a donation is carefully planned. And consider carefully if there are conditions to be attached to a bequest. Insisting that a home be used only as a cattery, for example, may be unhelpful if the property is unsuitable or in the wrong location.

Costs

Prices vary considerably from place to place and can increase over the years. Types of contract also vary. You may be able to get a contract that allows a memorial and space to be renewed at a pre-determined price after a set period. Some people have been dismayed to find the cost to renew a period for a niche or rose can have increased much more than inflation over 5 or 10 years. Local authorities, the church and private companies have all been ratchetting up their charges to attain a level more in line with the true costs of running the service after generations of a perceived free or low-cost 'on the rates' provision of burial and cremation.

Very few crematoria or cemeteries sell the actual memorial artefact for after-burial commemoration in a lawn or traditional monument section, though they will charge for use of the space (see Chapter 10). However, for other types of after-cremation memorial, many do charge for use of the space and also sell the only permitted product.

An entry in the book of remembrance or computerized retrieval system at a crematorium chapel costs, on average, £50–£60 but can vary between £30 and more than £100. Some entries can be more ornamented than others and this, in addition to the locality, will make a difference to the price.

A plaque or wall tablet is likely to cost around £200–£300 but can be as much as £500. The number of letters and extent of ornamentation is restricted by the small size of the plaques but, as with entries in the books of remembrance, added motifs or photoplaques will increase the cost. Rental periods may be fixed at 75 or 80 years but are being reduced with an option to renew.

A rose bush, planted and tended in a garden of remembrance and normally with a name plaque, is about the same price as the wall tablets or other plaques: £200–£300 for, say, 10 years.

A niche in a columbarium, large enough to contain two urns or caskets and with an inscribed enclosure plaque, can be from around £500–£1,500, depending on the site and type of inscription.

A memorial bench would be typically £1,000–£1,500, depending on the site.

The Essentials of Other Memorials

1. Stone is not the only medium for making memorials, though many cemeteries and churchyards insist it is.

2. Living memorials, such as trees, rose bushes, shrubs and flowers, are an alternative.

3. A book of remembrance is ubiquitous for after cremation; now also available in cyberspace.

4. Practical memorials, such as benches, windows, scholarships or libraries, appeal to some people.

5. Many charities and worthy causes depend on memorial donations and bequests.

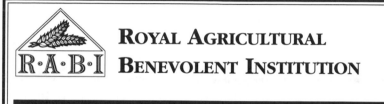

A lasting gift of hope...

Darren has Muscular Dystrophy. After struggling to cope in a mainstream school, his life was completely turned around by the care he received from a Shaftesbury specialist school. He is now a happy, confident student, with every hope of gaining good qualifications and having a successful career.

But we can only give gifts of hope like this with the help of our supporters. People like Hilary, who was born with a disability at the turn of the century. As a child, she joined in one of Shaftesbury's holidays for disadvantaged children - and went on to lead an active, fulfilling life.

She was always keen to help people in need and was a committed supporter of Shaftesbury's work. Through leaving a legacy to Shaftesbury, she has continued to give hope and encouragement to others after her death - and her brother celebrates her life by making a yearly donation to Shaftesbury in her memory.

Could you give hope to the many people with disabilities or living on low incomes that Shaftesbury seeks to serve? We rely heavily on donations and legacies to finance our work. For more information about ways of supporting Shaftesbury or any aspect of our work, please contact us at the address below.

- >✂- -

Please send me more information

Title: _____ Name: _____

Address: _____

_____

_____ Postcode: _____

Return to: The Shaftesbury Society, FREEPOST, 16 Kingston Road, London SW19 1BR

Tel 0181 239 5555 or Fax 0181 239 5580

Registered Charity No 221948 Registered in England no 38751

 **Shaftesbury**
150 years of Christian care in action

...your gift can help transform lives.

U770-DTFR

13 Exceptional Events

A Funeral Away from the Place of Death

People move around to different places to work and live, holiday, retire and eventually die; and they often express the wish to be buried 'back home'. Sometimes family and friends are concentrated in and around the town where the deceased was born and brought up and would rather have the funeral and memorial close to where they are living rather than where the death occurred.

A body may be transported anywhere in the country, or overseas, and it is quite possible to arrange a funeral at long-range. There are certain procedures to observe and it can be expensive, certainly more so than a local funeral.

Local authority crematoria and cemeteries often charge double, and sometimes more, for services for people from outside their locality. A funeral director will most likely insist on embalming if the body is to be carried some distance in a hearse and will charge extra for mileage and staff time. A funeral conductor will probably accompany the driver and have arrangements made for a local funeral director to provide bearers and any facilities needed at the other end. Funeral directors have even been known to claim a fee for crossing county boundaries although this kind of toll tax died out long ago.

It is quite feasible for you or a friend to drive an encoffined body yourself, in a van or estate car, from the hospital to a funeral director's in the town where the service is to take place or even direct to the crematorium or cemetery (see Chapter 15).

Registration has to be lodged in the district where the person died, not where the distant funeral is to take place, although it is possible to have the information transferred between district registrars' offices (see Chapter 3). A coffin in transit in the UK must be accompanied by all the necessary documentation for a funeral (see Chapter 3). If going abroad, further documentation is required.

If someone who has died in England or Wales is to be taken for burial or cremation to Scotland, Northern Ireland or the Channel Isles, or any other country for that matter, you must first get permission from the local coroner. Notice of your intention to remove the body from England or Wales should be given to the coroner by filling out a form, which the registrar or funeral director will provide.

The usual certificate for burial or cremation, the green form, will not be issued if the registrar knows the body is to leave the country. If a green form has already been issued then it must be sent to the coroner together with the out of England/Wales application form. Allow four days to receive the coroner's permission on a removal notice (form 104). A personal visit may speed up the process. It may be delayed further if there is any doubt about the cause of death.

Air and train transport regulations make embalming a requirement, as well as a metal lining, sealing and hessian wrapping round the coffin. The coffin then has to be packed in a wooden crate. All this obviously adds to the size, weight and therefore the cost.

By far the easiest way of travelling 'back home' is after the cremation. The ashes should be carried as hand luggage and you should have documentation to explain what they are, in the local language, in case the container is suspected of containing any suspicious substances.

Death Abroad, in Scotland or Northern Ireland

Registration

Regulations and customs for recording a death in other countries can be quite different from those in the UK. There are even differences in forms and procedures within different parts of the UK (see Chapter 14). If you are on a package holiday, your tour operator will know what to do. If travelling independently, local police, doctors or funeral directors, even hotel managers, will be able to tell you what has to be done if you have no friends or contacts nearby. If you have taken out insurance, or have cover through a credit card plan, try the emergency helpline.

You must register the death according to local regulations and get a death certificate. You should also register the death with the British Consul; this will result in a record of the death being kept in the UK. You will, at a later date, be able to get a certified copy of the death certificate from the consulate or from the General Register Office, Overseas Registration Section, Smedley Hydro, Trafalgar Road, Birkdale, Southport PR8 2HH.

If there are any suspicious circumstances surrounding the death, any reason to believe it may not have been from natural causes or the required information is incomplete then this must be reported to the coroner in the same way as if the death was in England or Wales.

Death at Sea

A death counts as a death abroad if it occurs on a foreign ship. It will be recorded in the ship's log and the authorities at the port where the ship is registered will be responsible for registering the death. The port superintendent where the body is taken ashore will make formal enquiries into the cause of death. The local consular authorities will have their own regulations and the procedure for arranging a funeral will be the same as if the death had occurred in that country.

On a UK ship, a death is recorded in the ship's log and the particulars are dispatched to the Registry of Shipping and Seamen on arrival at any port within or outside the UK. If the body is taken ashore at a foreign port, it will come under the regulations of that country and funeral arrangements will be the same as for a death abroad.

The coroner takes charge of a body brought into a UK port and may order an enquiry if not satisfied as to the cause of death. A death certificate or copy of the entry in the ship's log needs to be provided for the registrar in the district where the funeral is to take place. A certificate of no liability to register will then be issued.

Copies of log entries can be obtained from the shipping company or port superintendent where the body was brought ashore. Copies of the death certificate can be obtained from The Registry of Shipping and Seamen, PO Box 165, Cardiff CF4 5FU.

Death in the Air

In aircraft, a death must be registered in the country to which the aircraft belongs. The captain will notify local police at the first landing after the death and also notify the appropriate registration authority, which may not be in the same country. What happens to the body depends on local regulations but, for relatives, the procedure is the same as for a death that occurs abroad.

Funeral Abroad

You can arrange for the deceased to be cremated or buried in the country where the death occurred. This avoids the expenses of transporting the body back to the UK. The death should be registered with the British Consul in that country, who will send a record back to the UK where it will be kept at the General Register Office. You will eventually be able to get certified copies of the entry in the register in the same way as if you had registered the death in the UK.

Funeral Back Home

You may be able to bring the body back to the UK, although in some unusual circumstances this is not practicable. Most funeral directors will be able to advise you about the particular case and the costs involved.

The process of repatriating a body is complicated and expensive and can amount to several thousand pounds. It is as well to make sure that any holiday or travel insurance you take out covers repatriation – and always remember that emergency telephone number.

To permit removal of the body from the country where the

death occurred, you would need the death certificate, issued in the place where the person died. Should a death certificate be unobtainable, you will need an authorization from the coroner or equivalent person.

In order to arrange the funeral in England or Wales of a person who died abroad, you will need an English translation of the foreign death certificate. This must show the cause of death.

You will also need a certificate of no liability to register, issued by the registrar in England or Wales in whose sub-district the body is to be buried or cremated (see Chapter 3). This certificate is not required if a coroner has been involved and has issued an order for burial or a certificate for cremation.

Cremation Back in England or Wales

If the funeral of a person who has died abroad is to end in cremation in England or Wales, you will need a cremation order from the Home Office or a form E from the coroner. You will not, however, need the doctors' cremation certificates B and C, which can save £82.

To get the cremation order from the Home Office you will have to show them the application for cremation (form A, obtainable from your funeral director or crematorium) and the original official documents from the country where the death occurred that clearly state the cause of death. Translations from foreign languages may be required.

You should send these forms to The Home Office, Coroners Section, Constitutional Policy Directorate, Room 972, 50 Queen Anne's Gate, London SW1H 9AT (tel: 020 7273 2888/3574). Mark your envelope 'Cremation Urgent'.

If the death was not due to natural causes and a coroner is involved, there must be a coroner's inquest in the UK. In most cases, the coroner will issue form E for cremation on opening the inquest.

Getting these forms processed is going to take some time and you should make allowances for this when planning the funeral.

Sending a Body Abroad

The Repatriation Process from the UK

Transporting the body or the cremated remains of someone who has died in the UK to a foreign country can be very complicated. After the requirements of notifying the relevant UK authorities have been met, you then have to cope with the regulations of the country of destination. There are funeral directors that specialize in arranging transport of bodies overseas, which is known as repatriation. Your local funeral directors may refer you to a specialist firm or undertake the task for you. Doing it yourself is possible but not to be recommended.

There are no legal restrictions about taking cremated remains out of the UK; but taking them into a foreign country can be tricky. For example, Italy treats ashes in the same way as a body: permission to import is required from the prefect of police in the local area to which the ashes are being sent and the container must have been hermetically sealed in the presence of a representative of the consul in the UK. France also requires consular sealing and an engraved plate, displaying the particulars of the deceased, fixed to the casket. Greece treats ashes like an exhumed body and won't let them in until one year after the death. Regulations vary enormously and change from time to time. Enquiries should be made at the appropriate embassy or consulate.

Permission has to be obtained from the coroner to remove a body from England or Wales. Application should be made at least four days before the body is to travel so that any necessary enquiries may be completed. You will be given a removal notice, form 104, part of which has to be sent to the registrar after the funeral.

Almost always, the body has to be embalmed and sealed in a metal-lined coffin, which is then covered in hessian and crated. Freight documents have to be complete and accompanied by a death certificate for UK customs clearance. Bodies usually travel by air and the airlines can charge more than their usual freight rates. Some of the smaller airlines that fly to countries where repatriation is quite frequent – for example, Jamaica, India and

Ireland – are accustomed to the traffic and often less expensive than the major national airlines.

Consular regulations for the destination country have to be complied with and documents translated, sometimes into several languages. Consular requirements can be changed, so it is essential to check with the local consulate or embassy of the appropriate country.

Generally, consular requirements include:

▌ a copy of the entry in the registry of deaths, ie the death certificate, suitably translated;

▌ an official certificate stating the cause of death;

▌ a freedom from infection certificate;

▌ certification of a consul representative's attendance at the sealing of the coffin;

▌ a declaration that sanitary arrangements for transporting the body will be met;

▌ a declaration that the coffin contains only the body, clothing and packing;

▌ details of route, flight number and date of departure;

▌ in the case of exhumed bodies, a certificate of exhumation and copy of the Home Office licence.

Satisfactory arrangements for the reception and disposal of the body in the country of destination will need to have been made prior to departure.

Child and Infant Deaths

Having become much more a rarity than in the past, the deaths of children and infants, plus neonatal, stillborn and foetal losses, are gaining in significance with regard to funerals and commemoration. The death of a child or young person has traditionally been a cause for special grief and mourning but baby and infant deaths were, until recently, demoted and parents urged to forget the 'unfortunate event'.

Now it is recognized that mourning by parents over the loss of a baby can be as intense and more protracted than that of a widow or widower. Establishing an identity and memories of the baby are important. Parents are encouraged to hold and photograph the baby, perhaps take hand and foot prints or a lock of hair. Some hospitals will be able to arrange these mementoes. If not, your funeral director should be able to assist, though some of the old brigade may try to persuade you otherwise.

A naming ceremony may be appropriate and a memorial with a name carved upon it can provide important and comforting proof of the significance of the short life. The Stillbirth and Neonatal Death Society, a bereaved parents' group, has been campaigning for sympathetic burial, cremation and memorials for babies with considerable success in recent years. Community baby memorial areas are appearing in cemeteries, crematoria and hospital grounds and cemeteries are increasingly setting up children's burial and memorialization sections.

Ideally, these sections are enclosed in room-size proportions and formal restrictions lifted. Memorials in baby-related designs, such as teddy bears, cartoon characters, hearts and angels, and wording of a colloquial nature are admitted. Toys and dolls and whirring plastic windmills often appear among the flowers. With the inclusion of benches, these areas can become centres for therapeutic meetings of bereaved parents.

Small white coffins, either painted or cloth covered, are generally provided for children's funerals. Many funeral directors will not charge for the funeral of a baby or small child. Making the arrangements, services of staff, use of the chapel of rest, a coffin and a hearse or estate car are normally provided free. A charge would be made for more elaborate requirements such as a more expensive coffin and additional vehicles.

Many hospitals have contracted funeral arrangements with a specific funeral director and cemetery, which are made available at no cost. The hospital makes the arrangements and agrees a time for the funeral with the family, who are invited to attend.

You will be provided with a right of use of the grave, plus a right to erect a memorial upon it for a set period of time. Many cemeteries make no charge for the use of children's graves.

In some areas where burial space is restricted, hospital arrangements for stillbirth and other baby deaths only allow for cremation. All the foetal deaths and stillborn babies may be taken to the crematorium at the same time, perhaps each month. The parents will be invited for a service, after which each cremation takes place individually.

You should be aware that, after the cremation of a small child, there might be no remains available. This is because, as no large bones have developed, the skeleton is entirely cremated and no residue is left.

The period of time for which a grave or memorial use is granted needs to be carefully considered by the family. While 10 or 25 years may be adequate for a grieving widow or widower, parents may cherish memories of a child for many more years. The longest possible term and a fixed-price renewable option should be considered.

Parents should also consider a long-term renewable right of use for an adult plot in which the child may be buried. If a full-size grave is excavated to the proper depth, the parents will have the use of it in years to come.

Coroner's Inquest

Coroners are doctors or solicitors responsible for investigating all sudden or unexpected deaths that occur within the curtilage of their sub-district. They are assisted by coroners' officers, usually police officers, who provide the point of contact with the public. The coroner's office is financed by the local authority but is independent of both local and central government and responsible only to the Crown.

Deaths have to be investigated by the coroner if they occurred in the following circumstances:

■ the deceased had not been visited by a doctor during the last illness or had not been seen by a doctor either after death or 14 days before death;

■ the death was violent or unnatural or occurred under suspicious circumstances;

■ there is any doubt about the cause of death;

■ the death occurred during an operation or failing to recover from the anaesthetic;

■ death was caused by an industrial disease;

■ the death occurred in prison or police custody.

If you believe there may be some contributory cause of death such as an old war wound, injury or industrial disease where compensation may be involved, you can ask for the coroner to investigate and confirm the cause by a post mortem examination. It is usually the doctor who reports a death to the coroner – sometimes the police.

More often than not, the coroner is satisfied that the cause of death was in fact natural and the death can be registered in the usual way with the doctor's certificate. The registrar then receives a formal notification (pink form 100) from the coroner and the qualified person completes the registration (see Chapter 3).

The coroner may, however, arrange for a post mortem examination of the body. The consent of relatives is not needed but they are entitled to be represented at the examination by a doctor. If the result of the post mortem is that the death was from natural causes then the pink form 100 is sent to the registrar and arrangements for the funeral can commence.

But if the cause of death is still uncertain after the post mortem – or was unnatural, violent, caused by an industrial disease or occurred in prison or police custody – the coroner will hold an inquest. This is a court of law set up to establish the medical cause and circumstances of a death. It is held in public and there may or may not be a jury. The coroner's court has the power to summon witnesses and jurors and to deal with contempt.

If there is to be an inquest, the coroner must inform the married partner of the deceased, the nearest relative and the personal representative. Anyone with a proper interest in the case may question witnesses at an inquest and may be legally represented. People with an interest may include, for example, relatives, insurers, beneficiaries of a life policy, anyone involved in the death, government inspectors, trade union officials or police. If there are any circumstances that could lead to a claim for compensation, such as a road accident or injury at work, it may be important for you to have a lawyer at the inquest.

There is a minimal amount of ceremony. The coroner questions witnesses and then the witnesses can be questioned by anyone with a proper interest. But questions may only be about the medical causes and circumstances of the death. You should tell the coroner's officer before the inquest if you want to give evidence or ask questions so that you can be invited to participate at the right time.

There is no prosecution versus defence and no final speeches. After the witnesses have been heard the coroner sums up, for the jury if there is one, or gives the verdict. This is, in essence, the conclusion that has been reached in regard to deciding the category of death. Possible verdicts are obviously wide ranging and can include, for example, an open verdict, suicide, misadventure, industrial disease or natural causes. An inquest does not determine liability.

The Cost

There should be no cost charged to the family for an inquest or post mortem. The coroner will pay for the body to be taken to the mortuary and all the other costs. If you decide to be represented by a lawyer at the inquest then this will be an expense that you have to bear – there is no legal aid.

The Essentials of Exceptional Events

1. Transporting a body over long distances in the UK is expensive if done by funeral directors; but you can do it yourself.

2. Repatriation of a body to or from a foreign country is complicated and expensive. Insurance cover when travelling abroad is advisable. It is much easier to bring back cremated remains but documentation is important.

3. Child and infant deaths, now more a rarity than in the past, are gaining in significance for funerals and commemoration.

4. A coroner's inquest is to decide the category of a death where there is any doubt, not to determine liability.

"Caring Cancer Trust"
RAISING FUNDS FOR CANCER RESEARCH

An inspiration to us all
Leukaemia sufferer Gemma has been helped
on several occasions by:

"Caring Cancer Trust"

The Charity only supports research that is not carried out on any animal - into the causes, treatment and cure of cancer. These humane alternatives include cell culture, clinical tests, laser imaging and fluorescent in situ hybridisation, as we believe this type of 'kind' research to be morally acceptable, and the results to be more accurate. The Charity is currently sponsoring research into Breast Cancer at Kings College in London.

Caring Cancer Trust also provides: amenities, equipment and facilities in order that cancer sufferers' conditions of life may be improved.

For more details on the Charity's work, or to make a donation - perhaps in lieu of flowers or in remembrance - please contact our *Head Office at: 14 Newnham Lane, Ryde, I.O.W. PO33 4ED*
Tel: 01983 810 375

Thank you for your consideration

14 Funeral Law and Tradition in Scotland

Differences and Similarities

Burial Customs

Scotland is a place to which many expatriates like to return for a final resting. Graves are called lairs and have often been excavated to accommodate 12 or more coffins. Unlike in England, where it is not unusual for purchased grave space to be abandoned by families who have moved away or forgotten about it, Scots cling to their inheritance and minor feuds have been known to break out over who is entitled to the last remaining lair in the family plot.

A Scottish burial custom, perhaps originally a precaution due to the depth of the lairs, is for a number of mourners to be invited to hold courtesy cords and take the strain of lowering the coffin along with the bearers. In country areas the cords still take the weight, though elsewhere the silk-tasselled variety are merely symbolic.

A cushioning mattress or padding may be put on top of the coffin after an old custom of laying straw or grass to dull the thud of soil landing upon it. By tradition, women did not follow the coffin into the graveyard after the church service, though this practice has largely been discontinued.

In Scotland, an exclusive right of burial in a lair in a kirkyard (churchyard) or cemetery, a lair certificate, can be purchased for a limited period or for perpetuity. Kirkyards are administered by the appropriate local district, or islands, council.

Registration in Scotland

A Death

The registrar of births, deaths and marriages must register deaths within eight days. As in England (see Chapter 3), the person qualified to be the informant has to attend in person to give information to the registrar by way of a question-and-answer interview. A medical certificate of cause of death should be taken to the interview. If one is not available, you should have the name and address of a doctor who can be asked to provide one. Normally, the doctor who attended the deceased during the last illness will give you a certificate.

The other information you need to take is similar to that required in England and Wales, except you will also be asked the time of death, the name and occupation of the deceased's father, the name and maiden name of the mother and whether the parents are alive. If the person had been married more than once then details of previous spouses will also be required. The registration may take place in the district where the death occurred or where the deceased normally resided, provided this was also in Scotland.

After the information has been checked, entered in the register and signed off, the registrar is able to supply you with certified copies of the entry, known as the death certificate. In England, all copies have to be purchased; in Scotland, you will be given one free of charge but this can be used only for National Insurance claims. There is no Scottish equivalent to the certificate for burial or cremation, the green form used in England and Wales. Instead, a free certificate of registration of death, form 14, is issued, which is to be given to the funeral director, crematorium or burial authority so that the funeral can go ahead. A death must be registered before a cremation takes place.

Additional copies will cost £7 if applied for within one month or, if later, £10 for a personal application or £12 for a postal application. Death certificates can always be obtained from the office where the death was registered. After about 12–18 months they are also obtainable from the General Register Office (Scotland).

Registering a Stillbirth

A stillbirth must be registered within 21 days in Scotland, either in the district where it took place or in the district (in Scotland) where the mother was usually resident. The informant should have a certificate of stillbirth issued by a doctor or midwife. If this is not possible, a declaration has to be made on a special form (form 7) which can be obtained from a registrar's office. All such cases, and where there is any doubt about whether the baby was alive, are reported to the procurator fiscal who notifies the Registrar General.

The informant must produce a doctor's or midwife's certificate or form 7 and give the same information as in England (see Chapter 3) and also the time of the stillbirth and, if appropriate, the place of the parents' marriage.

If the body is to be cremated, the stillbirth must have been registered with a certificate of stillbirth issued by the doctor who attended the confinement or who carried out the post mortem.

The Procurator Fiscal

The duties of a coroner are, in Scotland, carried out by a procurator fiscal, a full-time law officer under the authority of the Lord Advocate. Among many functions, the procurator fiscal is responsible for investigating unexpected, violent and suspicious deaths. If satisfied with the doctor's medical certificate and other evidence, no further action may be taken. If a further medical report is considered necessary then a medical practitioner, often a police surgeon, will give an opinion on the cause of death. If a post mortem is thought necessary, permission to do this is sought from the sheriff.

Public Enquiry

In Scotland, a public enquiry, known as a fatal accident enquiry, takes the place of an inquest (see Chapter 13). Cases are reported by the procurator fiscal to the Crown Office and the Lord

Advocate then makes the final decision about applying to the sheriff, the chief local law officer, for a public enquiry to be held. The procurator fiscal will interview relatives and witnesses in a private investigation, called a precognition, before deciding whether to take the matter further. Where public interest is involved, for example to prevent a recurrence of a fatal incident or when a third party is involved such as in a road accident, the case may be sent to be considered by the Crown Office for either criminal proceedings or a public enquiry. Cases involving death while in police custody, prison or as a result of an industrial injury must go before a fatal accident enquiry.

Public enquiries are held in the local sheriff's court. After the procurator fiscal has questioned the witnesses it is the sheriff who issues the verdict as to the cause of death.

In Scotland, a death can be registered even if a medical certificate is not available, for example, when the circumstances of the death are being investigated. In such a case the registrar will notify the procurator fiscal, who will then take possession of the body. When the results of the inquiry are known, the procurator fiscal will notify the registrar so that the entry may be changed, if necessary, or entered.

Sending a Body out of Scotland

No formal permission has to be sought to take a body or cremated remains out of Scotland. This is unlike England and Wales where the coroner must be notified four days in advance of a body being removed. In Scotland, the procurator fiscal does not have to be informed.

If the body is to be buried or cremated in England or Wales, the authorities there will want the certificate of registration, form 14, or the standard death certificate.

Bringing a Body into Scotland

The registrar in Scotland does not require evidence of the death having taken place in another country when a body is brought into Scotland for burial or cremation. If the body were removed from England or Wales, the cremation or burial authorities in Scotland would require the coroner's form 104, which permitted the body to be removed.

When a body is brought into Scotland for cremation, the Secretary of State for Scotland must give authority for the cremation to be carried out. Application with supporting papers, such as a properly translated foreign death certificate, would need to be made to the Scottish Office Department of Health. Cremated remains brought into Scotland need a certificate from the crematorium.

The Essentials of Differences of Funeral Law in Scotland

1.   Procedures for registration and certification differ in some respects from those in England and Wales.

2.   There is no coroner in Scotland. The procurator fiscal carries out similar duties.

3.   A public enquiry takes the place of an inquest.

Alternative Funerals

People Seeking Something Different

Most people are quite content with the routine ritual of cremation and to have a funeral director manage the entire event. A traditional burial service is perfectly acceptable for those who don't want cremation and the bereaved family will nearly always leave the arrangements to the professionals.

There are, however, exceptions and for various reasons an increasing number of people are seeking to have something different. Horse-drawn hearses and mourners' carriages are enjoying a revival. About 100 woodland burial grounds have been set up in the past five years and cardboard coffins and shrouds have come on to the market.

Cremation has made it possible for unusual and even bizarre send-offs. Ashes have been sent heavenwards as fireworks and rockets, blasted from shotguns, sprinkled from hot air balloons, boats and planes and even launched into space.

Celestis Inc, a company based in Houston, Texas, inaugurated its Earthview Service in 1997 when it launched the cremated remains of Gene Roddenberry, Timothy Leary and 22 others into Earth's orbit. A second mission was launched in 1998 and will stay in orbit for approximately 240 years. The spacecraft will eventually re-enter earth's atmosphere where they will harmlessly vaporize, like a shooting star.

In addition to the 'now routine' Earthview Service, Celestis has expanded its service options to include lunar missions and a trip into deep space where the plan is to go by Jupiter on a trajectory out of the solar system.

Information technology has made it possible to have a

memorial, complete with obituary, photograph and floral tribute, committed to cyberspace.

Environmental Issues

Air and Soil Pollution

Cremation was originally promoted as a clean hygienic way for disposal of a body; one which 'saved the land for the living'. Today's environmentalists take a different view. Cremation burns up a lot of fuel, usually natural gas in the UK although a few electric cremators are now in use. Some 400,000 coffins made mostly from chipboard are burned each year as part of the process that pollutes the atmosphere with dioxins, hydrochloric acid, hydrofluoric acid, sulphur dioxide, carbon dioxide and even mercury released from teeth fillings.

The industry has imposed regulations on the types of chipboard, veneers and plastics that may be used in the manufacture of coffins for cremation and also the clothing, footwear and other items that may be sealed in coffins. Some synthetic materials can produce undesirable emissions when burned.

Burial locks the carbon underground so does not add to the greenhouse effect. Cemeteries and churchyards can become a nature reserve for wildlife and plants, a place for peaceful recreation, so burial can save the land for the living more effectively than cremation.

Some people do not like the idea of a tree being cut down in order to make a coffin that is to be burned or buried. Even chipboard is unacceptable as the resin glues can release chemicals into the atmosphere or leach them into the ground. So the green movement has encouraged the development and marketing of coffins made from cardboard, wickerwork, recycled timber and other environmentally friendly materials. Woollen shrouds, complete with board support and cords, are also now available though not permitted in all cemeteries.

Embalming

Embalming is another issue of concern to environmentalists who believe the quantity of formaldehyde injected into the body can be harmful as it leaches into the soil or is consumed in the cremator. Embalming, or hygienic treatment as it is practised today, involves removing the blood, some eight pints, from the circulatory system in the body and replacing it with eight pints of chemical fluid. What exactly is this about? The national general secretary of the British Institute of Embalmers, Peter J Ball, explains in an article published in the _Funeral Services Journal_ in November 1994:

> _The addition of embalming fluid to body tissue brings about a chemical reaction which forms an inert and chemically different substance. The most widely used preservative chemical in embalming fluids is formaldehyde (also present in some plants), which is a toxic substance. However, the amount in concentrated arterial injection fluid varies from about 18 per cent to 30 per cent by volume, the most widely purchased chemical being 26 per cent by volume._
>
> _This is used in diluted form of about 1.6 per cent formaldehyde by volume, for injection into the circulatory system. As 80 per cent of the human body is water, therefore a further dilution of the formaldehyde takes place following injection; it then combines with the cell protoplasm to form the inert substances referred to._
>
> _At these high levels of dilution, any degree of toxicity remaining would be at an extremely low level, and would indeed be lower than substances produced in the normal body. A concentrated cavity fluid is injected into the hollow organs with a higher level of formaldehyde concentration. This is quickly absorbed into the tissues, effecting the chemical changes referred to._

The official line is that the level of pollutants emitted by both cremation and inhumation is so low as to be insignificant. But being green is about being seen to be green; having a cardboard coffin, no embalming and a woodland burial is a way to make a clear green statement.

Woodland Burial

The green credentials of the woodland burial schemes, which are being marketed with much enthusiasm as the fastest growing sector of the environmental movement, don't bear much scrutiny. Like the Victorian cemeterians who sold plots in perpetuity, they are laying down problems for the future. When all are sold there is no source of further income; but the land is expected to emerge as a nature reserve needing care and management, which will not be forthcoming without finance.

Some green burial sites are addressing this problem by making arrangements with local wildlife trusts to take over and manage the area as a nature reserve when it is closed for further burials. Oakfield Wood burial ground in Essex, for example, is close to nature reserves managed by the RSPB and Essex Wildlife Trust and these organizations will hold the land and grave plots in permanent trust.

An environmental imperative is for sustainable development. The problems caused by cemetery graves being vested in perpetuity were overcome by a 1977 Act defining perpetuity as less than 100 years. This opens the way to the reuse of cemetery land as had always been the case in churchyards (see Chapter 7).

Covering graves with a wooded nature reserve is a 'double whammy' towards permanent removal of the land from the burial resource. Once the wood is fully planted there can be no further interments, no sustainability through reuse of graves, no further income towards upkeep.

Trees are not suited to having holes excavated round their root structures. Second interments, which are normally expected for a spouse or partner, necessitate roots being disturbed or even cut away and perhaps killing the tree.

The public perception is that 'their' grave would be surmounted by 'their' tree. Indeed, many woodland burial schemes advertise that a tree will be planted on every grave. These would be too close for growth as they matured and would have to be thinned out. Graves would be disturbed and distress caused to those relatives whose memorial trees were removed.

A hectare of land, for example, could contain 800–1,000 grave plots but would support only 200 mature English oak trees. Drastic thinning would have to take place after 10 years. Ground upheaval caused by the uprooting of trees in gales is another hazard too fearsome to contemplate.

A more practical response to green requirements for burial is a wild flower meadow. Graves could be marked, if required, with headstones of the kind traditionally erected in churchyards or with wooden memorials. Trees planted as part of a landscaping scheme would be at a safe distance from the burials.

You can get particulars about nature reserve burial grounds from The Natural Death Centre.

The Woodland Trust

If the desire is to have a commemorative tree or to create a wood then this can be achieved with the Woodland Trust. This charity provides the opportunity for trees to be planted and for areas of mature trees to be dedicated as memorials.

Individual trees are not marked but groves can be dedicated with an engraved stainless steel plaque fixed to an oak post. Trees can be dedicated in any county or Scottish region. Gates, stiles and rustic seats can also be bought and marked with a plaque. Prices are: £10 for one tree or £25 for two or more; £250 for a stile; £475 for a seat and £1,000 for a grove.

Whichever form of memorial you choose, a personalized certificate of dedication will be sent, which tells you the name of the wood, and a record entered in a book of remembrance lodged at the Trust's head office in Grantham, Lincolnshire. You and your family and friends are welcome to visit the wood at any time.

Interments are not undertaken in Trust woodlands although discreet placement of cremated remains is welcomed. Digging around roots is not.

Special memorial funds can be set up by the Trust to co-ordinate donations requested in lieu of flowers at funerals. All donations sent directly to the Trust are acknowledged and when all contributions are received a dedication is arranged according to the wishes of the bereaved family.

Do-it-yourself

Rights Being Recognized

With death happening mostly in hospitals or care homes and the body routinely released to the funeral director and crematorium carousel, the bereaved can feel left out and marginalized. As a reaction, more people are taking personal control of funeral arrangements.

Few go to the full extreme of laying out the body, making the coffin, conducting the funeral and digging and filling in the grave. However, increasing numbers are getting involved in some practical stages and many take a keen interest in organizing rituals and arrangements (see Chapter 8).

Paying last respects to the deceased in the chapel of rest, helping to carry the coffin and planning or taking part in the service are the most usual areas of participation. But it is possible to carry out the complete funeral without a funeral director. Mortuary, crematoria and cemetery staff are slowly coming round to the idea.

The Charter for the Bereaved, promoted by the Institute of Burial and Cremation Administration (IBCA) and published in 1996, identifies:

∎ the right (of members of the public) to organize a funeral without the use of a funeral director;

∎ the right of an executor or next of kin to be given the body by a mortuary, hospital etc in order to carry out a funeral;

∎ the right to be given a leaflet by your Charter member describing how to arrange an independent funeral;

∎ the right to obtain a coffin (biodegradable type) via your Charter member.

Laying Out

If you are going to keep the body at home until the time for the funeral, you will first have to organize the laying out. Pennies on the eyes to help keep them closed and propping up the chin with a pillow or bandage round the head is tradition. Washing the body may be an act of devotion. Plugging orifices to prevent seepage and draining the bladder calls for skills as well as devotion. Help from a nurse or other experienced person is advised.

Pacemakers and similar devices must be removed if there is to be a cremation. Your doctor or funeral director can arrange for the operation, which costs £63 in 1999/2000.

When dressing the body, avoid nylon and other synthetic fabrics, plastics and composite materials for boots or shoes. Such materials are not permitted for cremation. If you are intending a green burial, and natural biodegrading, these materials will delay the process.

The materials used in making coffins for cremation are also controlled. Your crematorium will give you details and will probably ask you to sign a declaration that the regulations have been met. Check this out if you are planning to make your own coffin. And remember, the container must be strong and robust enough to bear the weight of the body (and being carried and handled into the cremator or lowered into the grave) without mishap.

Not all funeral directors will supply you with a coffin if they are not arranging the funeral, though increasingly they are beginning to do this. And more funeral directors will co-operate in providing a partial funeral support service than was the case 5 or 10 years ago. You should be able to get help in obtaining a coffin, even if only a cardboard one, from your crematorium or cemetery office. Remind them about the IBCA Charter for the Bereaved if need be.

If you do buy a coffin, be aware that the handles fitted to it are usually only for decoration or guiding the lowering tapes, not for lifting!

Keeping the Body

Some hospital and municipal mortuaries will keep the body for you until it is time to collect it for the funeral. A few cemeteries and crematoria have chapels of rest where bodies can be kept. A funeral director with facilities may help. You may be charged a fee.

When you go to collect the body, take someone with you to help lifting. Mortuary attendants may or may not be available to help encoffin the body.

At home, the body should be in the coldest room you have or even in the basement. Keep windows open and a fan rotating. Portable air conditioning units can be hired by the day – look in your local directories for equipment suppliers. If necessary, you may put ice packs or dry ice into the coffin.

Transport

The coffin may be taken to the crematorium or cemetery in any suitably sized vehicle, though some degree of decorum should be maintained. Commercial vans may be discouraged as unseemly and high-sided vehicles may not fit under the porte cochére. Large estate cars and Range Rovers seem suitable. You may be able to hire a hearse from a funeral director or direct from a carriagemaster, a vehicle hire company specializing in funerary cars.

Burial at Home

Permissions

You don't have to be buried in a proper cemetery or churchyard or consecrated ground. Planning permission is not required for burial on private land unless there are going to be more than two or three burials, which would constitute a change of use of the land from garden or orchard or whatever into a working cemetery. You don't need to notify the local environmental health officers.

However, the health officers do have powers to prevent any 'deposit' which might be 'prejudicial to health or a nuisance'. The Environment Agency (formerly the National Rivers Authority) takes an interest in burials and suggests that a grave should not be within 250 metres of any well or borehole, at least 10 metres from any standing or running water and 1.5 metres from underground cables or pipes. It is advisable to check with your local office of the Environment Agency to satisfy yourself as to the whereabouts of any wells or springs. They are unlikely to object providing the grave is more than 10 metres away from a water source.

A suitable grave should be deep enough to allow 60 centimetres of soil on top of the coffin lid, 1 metre of subsoil beneath the coffin and have no water in the bottom when first dug.

Documentation

You must send to the registrar of births and deaths, within 96 hours of any burial in England or Wales, the completed tear-off slip from the burial authorization, giving the date and place of burial (see Chapter 3).

It would seem that to comply with the 1864 Registration of Burials Act you are required to maintain a land burial register, even for just one grave in a garden. This register should be durable and record, in columns, the entry number, date of burial, names in full, age, address, date of birth, plan reference number and officiating minister. Each entry is to be separated by a printed line. The register is to be stored in a specially protected steel cupboard.

However, the Local Authorities' Cemeteries (Amendment) Order 1986 permits the register of burials to be maintained in a computer. This should contain the same information as if the burial had been recorded in a book. The 1986 order added an article, 11A, which provides the criteria for the recording, production, storage and operation of a computer in connection with the requirements of the order. The disposal of cremated remains in your garden or private land should also be recorded in the register.

It is difficult to understand how this law can be applied to individual burials in a garden. Only if non-compliance is 'wilful' can a prosecution take place. It would seem prudent to record the information required for a burial register, plus a detailed plan showing where the body is buried, and store a copy of this with your house deeds and another copy with other valuable documents.

Think very carefully before making a grave on your property. It is easier to bury a body than to exhume one. Exhumation without a Home Office licence is a criminal offence. The licence costs nothing but the exhumation, transport and re-interment is likely to be expensive and distressing.

Neighbours or relatives may be offended by the proximity of the grave and the value of the property affected, though views differ as to whether the price would go up or down if, for example, the grave is that of a famous person.

A more practical solution may be to have the body cremated and keep the ashes in the garden.

Private Disposal of Ashes

There is very little regulation about the placement of cremated remains except that once buried you will require an exhumation licence from the Home Office to dig them up again. Ashes can freely be moved unless they have been buried below ground.

Cremated remains consist of granulated calcified bone. They are biologically inert and do not encourage plant growth. If sprinkled thickly they will cause grass to turn brown and die. The roots of rose bushes grow away from any ashes buried near them.

You should get permission from the landowner to place them in or on private land. Avoid causing distress or nuisance to other members of the public. If scattering ashes, take due note of the wind direction; be sure it is blowing away from you and any bystanders.

Strewing is an alternative to burial or scattering and comprises lifting an area of turf, distributing the ashes on the exposed soil and replacing the turf on top.

Burial at Sea

Possible But Not Encouraged

People with strong associations with the sea may like the idea of resting on the seabed. This is possible to arrange but only at two sites around the coast of Great Britain: one near Newhaven in East Sussex and the other at the Needles Spoil Ground to the west of the Isle of Wight. Local coastal funeral directors will provide advice and make arrangements or your neighbourhood funeral director will probably be able to liaise with a colleague near your chosen site. A company that specializes in sea burials is The Britannia Shipping Company, Newton Poppleford, Nr Sidmouth, Devon EX10 0EF.

If you are planning a sea burial you should tell the registrar when registering the death and fill out a form to notify the coroner of the intention to remove a body out of England or Wales. This form, together with the appropriate authority for disposal, must be given to the coroner at least four days before the body is to be removed. You will be given a removal notice, form 104, part of which is sent to the registrar after the funeral. You will also need a certificate of freedom from infection, obtainable from your doctor, and the death certificate, which, together with the form 104, have to be submitted to the Marine Environmental Protection department at the Ministry of Agriculture, Fisheries and Food (MAFF) with a request for a licence to carry out the sea burial. Or you may submit the papers direct to the district fisheries office in Poole, Dorset, or Newhaven, East Sussex, which can issue the licence.

Various conditions are made that are intended to provide identification and ensure that the coffin will sink quickly, stay down on the seabed and biodegrade. Coffins of oak are not allowed but rather chipboard or softwood. The coffin has to be weighted with 200 kilograms of iron or concrete and drilled with holes to prevent buoyancy.

The body must not be embalmed but preferably wrapped in a biodegradable cotton or paper sheet, not canvas, bound in chains and have two plastic tags carrying the deceased's name, date of burial and the telephone number of the funeral director or a solicitor.

Lowering a heavy coffin over the side of a boat demands special seafaring skills and it would be prudent to hire a craft and crew with experience. The MAFF inspector will insist on a qualified skipper and a vessel with accurate positioning equipment.

Ashes at Sea

No special documentation is required for disposing of ashes at sea but sensible precautions should be taken. If the ashes are to be sprinkled on to the surface of the waves then take due notice of the wind direction.

If the cremated remains are to be deposited into the sea in an urn or any container then this should be treated like a coffin for sea burial. Make sure the container is heavily weighted and has holes to let water in and air out.

It should be biodegradable to avoid any risk of being trawled up or washed ashore by tide and sand movement. Chipboard or softwood will degrade quite quickly if weighted on the seabed. There is a special patented urn for sea burial that is heavy and substantial but made from a composite material of sand and salt. It is heavy enough to sink quickly to the bottom but gradually dissolves and allows the ashes to disperse. Called the Neptune urn, it is available in the UK from Regale Memorials in London.

Medical Research and Organ Donation

You will have to act quickly if organs are to be donated for transplants or the body for medical teaching purposes. Relatives are normally asked for consent even if a donor card is carried and the name entered in the NHS organ donor register or a proper oral declaration made.

Authorization is required from the person lawfully in possession of the body. This could be a close relative, the person owning the house where the death occurred or the coroner. A hospital is legally in possession of a dead patient until the body is claimed – and so in a position to authorize the operation.

Some organs can only be useful for transplants if removed while blood is kept circulating by mechanical means; others within 24 or 36 hours after the heart stops. The doctor will advise you of procedures. The body will be released after organs have been removed and you can then continue with funeral arrangements.

Bodies are not always accepted for medical research. It will depend on the condition of the body at the time of death and the demand from local medical schools. If accepted, the body may be kept for up to three years before being released for a funeral. The school will advise relatives when they are going to arrange and pay for a funeral; or they may release the body for the family to complete funeral arrangements.

The Essentials of Alternative Funerals

1. Cremation is not now considered to be so environmentally friendly.

2. Woodland burials with a tree planted on every grave are not best practice for tree husbandry.

3. Preparation and organization for a funeral calls for more than do-it-yourself devotion.

4. Burial at home is feasible but not without problems.

16 *Planning in Advance*

Discuss With Those Who Will be Concerned

Exactly whose funeral is it? If you are making all the arrangements for the funeral, perhaps even paying for it, you will have a proprietary control over the event. You may feel you are arranging it on behalf of the deceased but that person is not there to share in the grieving and derive comfort from the ritual.

People often say, 'I don't care what happens to me after I'm dead; don't waste money on a funeral or memorial.' Those same people care very much about what happens to the loved ones they leave behind. It is for them, for the bereaved, that a meaningful ceremony and the tribute of a lasting memorial can be so important.

Bear this in mind when planning for a funeral, whether or not you will be in the coffin. The family members, the bereaved, have to make major adjustments to the changed circumstances initiated by the death, both practical and psychological. The amount of therapeutic benefit derived by the bereaved from the funeral can be related to the amount of involvement they have in the planning and the ceremony.

A Funeral for Yourself

If you can, discuss with members of the family the key factors for your funeral while you are hale and hearty. Make your own preferences known but encourage ideas from others about how they would like to express their feelings and memories and make a farewell gesture. And leave the plan open-ended so that final touches can be added according to prevailing circumstances.

Some families think it morbid to have such group discussions and here the best that can be done by way of pre-planning is to drop heavy hints. While family can draw some comfort from arranging a funeral it will help them if they have information about your wishes, if only for the most essential matters. Whether to be cremated or buried is a choice that must be made and your preference, if known, can be quite influential, especially if based on religious beliefs. Removing just that one element of doubt can be helpful to those arranging the funeral.

If frank and open discussion is not an option then written instructions may be the best alternative. Even after discussion, writing down a record of the plan would be a good idea. But don't just leave it with your will. This may not be found until after the funeral. Tell somebody what you have done and where the plan is kept.

The Funeral Guardian

You may like to appoint a 'funeral guardian'. Just as your next of kin or the executor of your will takes responsibility for your estate, this is someone who takes charge of your funeral arrangements. The funeral guardian would be aware of your wishes and keep close contact with your family to make sure their interests are taken into account with regard to the funeral arrangements (see chapters 2 and 3).

You should tell your next of kin and/or executor who the funeral guardian is (name, address and telephone number) and make arrangements for access to funds that will be required to pay for the funeral, perhaps before probate is completed (see Chapter 17).

The guardian, who may or may not be a member of your close family, will co-operate with the family in finalizing plans and making arrangements for your funeral. Among the tasks that have to be undertaken, which could be the responsibility of the funeral guardian, are:

- registration of the death;

- contact/select and brief the minister or officiant;

I liaise with the chosen funeral director *or*

I obtain written estimates and appoint a funeral director *or*

I assume the role of event manager if no funeral director is to be retained;

I arrange/agree dates and places for funeral ceremonies;

I notify mourners;

I plan order of service;

I arrange for the laying out/viewing of the body;

I organize floral tributes or donations;

I write text for press notices, obituary and funeral address;

I arrange transport, hospitality and reception;

I plan rehearsal for ceremony if required;

I arrange memorialization and/or placement of ashes.

The National Funerals College supports the idea of a funeral guardian in its publication of the 'rights' which, it says, everyone preparing for death is entitled to. You can obtain a copy of *The Dead Citizens Charter* from the National Funerals College, The University of Bristol, 3 Priory Road, Bristol BS8 1TX (tel: 0117 928 9024).

Make a Will and Appoint Executors

Select Someone Sympathetic

Only one in three people in the UK have made a will. They are not expensive. A simple will can be less than £50. Some people think that the making of wills is avoided because it focuses on mortality. However, a will makes continuing life much easier for the bereaved.

Some will forms include the statement, 'I wish my body to be cremated', which would have to be deleted if you wish to be buried. But it is best to make your wishes about funeral matters known elsewhere. The will may not be read until later.

The executor you appoint in your will has responsibility for your funeral and what happens to your body and need not comply with your wishes in respect of cremation or burial or any other funeral matters. The cost of the funeral is normally paid out of the estate. The executor is responsible to the other people who have an interest in the estate and is therefore expected to pay only a reasonable amount towards the cost of the funeral. What a reasonable amount is may depend on your lifestyle as well as how much is left in your estate. If you leave no will or appoint no executor, a responsible person is found from among your relatives who has to discharge these duties.

The executors are liable to pay out of the deceased's estate the expenses incurred in arranging a funeral suitable to the deceased's circumstances and position in life.

There are numerous instances to illustrate that executors are not allowed to incur unnecessary funeral costs at the expense of creditors. For example, in the case of *Hancock* v *Padmore*, concerning an army captain who was on half-pay at the time of death, the court held that £79 was too much and suggested that £20 would have been reasonable.

At the same time, the person who actually contracts with the funeral director is liable for all the expenses. Even if the estate is insolvent, the person responsible for the funeral may not be able to recover expenses from the DSS, which sets out very stringent regulations (see Chapter 5).

If you have strong feelings about how your funeral should be conducted, it behoves you to appoint an executor who is sympathetic to your wishes. Be aware that appointing a solicitor or a bank to be your executor is like writing them a blank cheque. It is as well to appoint at least two people you really trust and a third as reserve in case your first choices, for whatever reason, cannot discharge the duties.

There are various firms specializing in providing will-writing services and, of course, most solicitors will organize this for you.

Do-it-yourself wills can generate more work (income) for solicitors as they are often required to sort them out. Using the services of a solicitor in the first place can often represent a considerable saving in the long run. Get professional help.

Reserve a Grave

Costs are Rising

If there is a particular cemetery where you would like to be buried, or a special place within a cemetery, you may be able to purchase the rights of burial there in advance of need. This may even prove to be a bargain.

The cost of grave plots is likely to rise quite steeply. Local authorities, which have subsidized and depressed the prices for many years, are beginning to charge realistic fees in an effort to raise funds to plough back into better services. In some towns where grave space is running out the laws of supply and demand are driving prices up and there may be no plots left when the time comes for you to need one. Remember, some authorities charge a premium to people from outside their district. Some authorities will not sell rights in their graves unless there is to be an immediate use – but many will.

Reserving a plot in a churchyard is problematical and will depend on whether you live in the parish and have the support of the vicar in making your application. But churchyards are filling up in some areas and being closed for further burials. If a churchyard is part of your plan, it is as well to make enquiries about taking out a faculty for a plot (see Chapter 7).

If you do reserve a grave then be sure to notify your next of kin and funeral guardian and keep securely among your papers the deed of grant (if in a cemetery) or faculty (if in a churchyard).

The Essentials of Planning in Advance

1. A funeral is just as much for the bereaved as for the deceased – perhaps more so. Discuss your ideas for your funeral with

your family. Let them be involved in the planning, the organizing and the ceremony/ritual itself.

2. Appointing a funeral guardian can be pivotal to a funeral plan.

3. If a burial is in the plan, reserve a grave space, if you can, as soon as may be appropriate.

I put the laundry in my washing machine

Mum put hers in the oven

Dementia is not only a tragic condition in itself, it can also bring real physical dangers.

We need your help to provide more specialist dementia care facilities for older people, irrespective of their beliefs or background. A place where they can lead a comfortable and dignified life in a loving caring environment.

When you're writing your Will please don't forget those who can no longer remember for themselves.

For your free, no obligation copy of our comprehensive **METHODIST** Guide to making and changing your Will write to us or **HOMES** call 01332 296200, Mon-Fri 9am-5pm. *for the Aged*

Registered as a Charity - No 218504

Methodist Homes for the Aged Epworth House Stuart Street Derby DE1 2EQ

WE NEED MORE FRIENDS TO STAND UP TO MUSCULAR DYSTROPHY

Tom and James are brothers, typical young lads, blooming nuisances sometimes, but adorable ... most of the time. Two normal boys of their age, except that one has Duchenne muscular dystrophy.

A boy with Duchenne md is likely to need a wheelchair by the age of 10 as his muscles progressively weaken. He is unlikely to survive beyond 20. Don't you sometimes wish time would stand still?

Their mum does

Muscular dystrophy progressively wastes muscles, restricting a person's ability to live independently. Some forms also take young lives.

At the Muscular Dystrophy Campaign we have a vision of a day when muscular dystrophy can no longer blight and end lives. You could help make that vision reality, by helping to fund vital research that will find cures. Please contact Ivan Clarke at:

THE MUSCULAR DYSTROPHY CAMPAIGN FREEPOST LON314 SW4 6BS
Tel 0171 819 1823 or visit our Web site www.muscular-dystrophy.org

Planning for Funeral Finance

Pay Before You Go

Savings, Insurance or Pre-purchase

There is a lot of advertising in magazines, on television and through the letterbox for packaged funeral plans that you can buy in advance of need. This is a novel development in the UK where advertising funeral services on radio and TV was not allowed until recently and even now, at the beginning of the new millennium, funerals as such are rarely advertised. When funeral directors were approached to advertise in Sainsburys, their trade association wrote to the company complaining they believed it to be in poor taste.

Prepaid funeral plans, however, are being heavily promoted with glossy leaflets and inducements such as free clocks and gift vouchers. They offer peace of mind and a chance to buy a funeral at today's prices and hence save against the likely higher cost in a few years' time. But handing your savings to a funeral director may not be your best plan.

Paying in advance for a funeral is not a new development. Funeral directors in days gone by would collect contributions from future clients 'not yet dead'. Communities operated their own funeral clubs, some of which evolved into friendly societies still in existence. Funeral insurance plans with local agents making door-to-door collections were commonplace in a generation fearful of a pauper's funeral that could end with the body being used for medical dissection.

The death grant and subsequently payments from social security benefit schemes rendered private funeral savings plans unnecessary. More recent regulating of the finance market has forced the winding up of other informal schemes. The Teapot Club in the village of Flash in Staffordshire was, for generations, a means of putting away small, regular amounts of money towards funeral costs. Each summer, members led a procession through the village. But in 1995, unable to meet the requirements of financial regulators, the club was wound up.

Though funeral clubs may be no more, there are various ways you can set aside some money for your funeral, thus ensuring that relatives won't be faced with a large bill at such a time of stress.

Friendly Societies

The Manchester Unity Friendly Society persists with a keen interest in funerals. As well as providing cash help towards funeral costs for members (among many other benefits and a 'great social life') the society carries out regular and detailed surveys of funeral costs and services throughout the UK.

Several of the mutually owned friendly society lending companies can trace their beginnings to funeral clubs and they still offer insurance schemes that pay out a lump sum on the death of the member. The sum can be fixed at a level calculated to pay for all or most of a funeral's basic costs and be topped up with bonuses added on over the years.

Insurance Schemes

There are variations with insurance schemes. Many do not pay bonuses. Some companies will pay out only a small amount if the death occurs during the first one or two years of a plan; indeed, they may just refund the premiums. However, premiums may cease after 10 years, with cover lasting thereafter until death. Your age and state of health are obvious factors although quite a few schemes will take people without having a medical.

With a simple whole life policy in which you carry on paying the monthly premiums until you die, whereupon a fixed sum is paid out, you may end up paying in much more than the final payout. If you discover you have paid over the limit, as it were, it is very unlikely that you will be able to terminate the scheme in a way that gets much of your money back.

An alternative to taking out an insurance policy specifically to cover funeral costs would be to include provision in your main life cover. If you already have life insurance, you could increase the cover as necessary.

To ensure the money is accessible when it will be needed (ie to pay for the funeral and not tied up in your estate) you should arrange for the policy to be written 'in trust' to a family member, or to your funeral guardian, who will be arranging the funeral. That person will then be able to gain access to the money without having to wait for probate to be settled.

Savings Accounts

You could put the money for your funeral into a high-interest savings account. But funeral costs seem likely to keep increasing at a higher rate than the interest you would be able to earn. You would have to top up the fund from time to time to make sure there was enough in it to meet the costs.

So that your funeral guardian, or whoever takes responsibility, can draw from the fund when it is needed, you should set the account up in joint names with that person. Producing the death certificate can then access the money.

Prepaid Funeral Plans

Costs Rising Faster Than Inflation

With a prepaid plan you make your choices, pay your money and commit the basic essentials of arranging your funeral into the charge of a funeral director, to be delivered at some future date unknown. You buy at today's prices something that will be costing more when it is delivered. The idea is that the funeral

GOLDEN CHARTER
FUNERAL PLANS

INVESTOR IN PEOPLE

SAIF

The only plan recommended by the National Society of Allied & Independent Funeral Directors

THE *CARING* APPROACH TO A *SENSITIVE* SUBJECT

THERE COMES A TIME in life when it's natural to consider your own funeral...and to think about loved ones and what you'd like to leave them. Not the burden of funeral costs, obviously. Or the ordeal of deciding on the arrangements.

Golden Charter gives you peace of mind in knowing everything is taken care of. The plan you select can be personalised in any way you wish. You may choose the funeral director.

And once you've paid, by single payment or flexible instalments, you are guaranteed that your family or estate will never be asked for a penny more for the arrangements selected.

Furthermore your thoughtfulness will live on forever.

A tree will be planted on your behalf by the Woodland Trust.

Golden Charter is a British company at the heart of Britain's largest funeral planning network. A legally separate trust fund makes sure your money is secure.

For our free brochure, which includes prices, send the coupon today. If you'd like a friendly chat, with no pressure to buy a plan, call us free - on

0800 833 800

Rest assured, no one will visit your home unless you want them to.

Please send me your Golden Charter brochure with prices.

NO STAMP
REQUIRED
To: FREEPOST
Golden Charter

Mr/Mrs/Ms	Initial:	Surname:
Address:		
Postcode:	Tel no:	

DTGF0799

MEMBER OF THE FUNERAL PLANNING COUNCIL

director invests your money where it will earn enough interest to pay for the expected increases in costs caused by inflation and other factors.

Funeral prices have gone up by almost 75 per cent in the past 10 years; well in excess of inflation. A large part of the costs are outside the funeral director's domain and described as disbursements. These are the fees for burial, cremation, ministers, doctors and other expenses.

The prices for graves and grave digging are increasing generally as cemetery managers seek to adjust fees to cover costs of maintenance and this is particularly so in urban districts where cemeteries are filling up. Cremation fees are increasing to cover the costs of meeting environmental pollution control measures. Ministers' and doctors' fees are also rising faster than inflation.

Exclusions

To overcome the highly probable problem of disbursements rising faster than the interest earned, many prepaid plans do not include disbursements; others peg their obligation to an inflation-only increase in the cost of disbursements. If they rise more than that, which seems likely, the difference will have to be made up by your relatives at the time of the funeral.

Most prepaid plans cover the cost of essential products and services but omit incidentals, which will have to be paid for from additional funds at the time of the funeral. Likely to be excluded from the plan are flowers, invitations, press announcements, printing the order of service, hire of hall, following car(s), use of chapel of rest, reception and church costs such as heating, hymn sheets, organist, verger, choir and bell-ringing.

Value for money

The funeral director's own operating costs and overheads could also rise faster than the interest earned on your invested prepayment. This could mean profits being reduced or even a loss made in meeting the obligations to deliver the quality of funeral you paid for several years ago. There would be pressure to cut back on the value of the goods and services actually delivered. Would your relatives notice if a 'wood effect' coffin were substituted for the more expensive 'solid wood' coffin that you paid for? Or if there were two rather than four bearers?

It is recommended that funeral directors place prepaid funeral money in a trust fund and, in fact, many of the plans are provided and managed by companies set up especially to do this. They collect and invest the money in a separate fund and release payment to the funeral director only when the service is delivered.

This can result in a three-cornered contract between the plan provider/fund-holder (who may also market and sell the prepaid plan), the funeral director (who is to provide the service) and you the paying customer (who will be dead when the time comes for the service to be delivered).

If, for example, interest earned has not kept pace with rising costs, the funeral director may decide that it is not financially viable to provide the service for the price offered by the fund-holder. The contract is between you and the service provider, the funeral director, who now refuses to carry out the contract on the grounds that he or she would lose money at the price offered.

Perhaps the contract would be between you and the plan provider, who may be expected to hunt around for a different funeral director who is prepared to deliver your funeral for the price on offer. But there could be no funeral director acceptable to your relatives or, indeed, willing to take the contract.

The contract was with you and cannot be enforced by you, or anyone acting for you, because you are dead. You can't take legal action to get your money back, nor can your relatives – except possibly by the executor after probate, when it is too late.

Generally, prepaid plan operators are prepared to make a refund if the service is not delivered. This may be, for example, because a family has moved away or those arranging the funeral were not aware that a plan was in place or ownership of the funeral director's has changed. But the refund is unlikely to be for more than the amount paid into the scheme. It would almost certainly not cover the full price of the funeral and, furthermore, an administration charge of about £70 would be most likely deducted from any refund. The same applies if you simply change your mind and withdraw from the plan.

Insurance-linked Plans

There are insurance schemes under which you pay a regular premium for life cover that is paid direct to a plan provider at the time of your death. The plan provider in turn nominates a funeral director's to carry out the service and pays that company direct. The size of your premiums depends on the type of funeral you select.

These schemes only pay out fully in the first few years in the case of accidental death. You may pay more in premiums than the value of the chosen funeral if you live longer than 10 years or so.

The Plan Providers

Some funeral directors operate their own schemes, others customize a plan run by a large operator by putting their name on it. However, the majority of plans are provided by specialist companies that sell direct to the public as well as through funeral directors participating in their schemes.

Three main providers dominate the market and together they are responsible for more than 80 per cent of all prepaid funerals. They are the Co-ops, Golden Charter and Service Corporation International (SCI).

Four plans are linked solely or jointly with SCI. Two owned and sold by SCI are Chosen Heritage and Dignity Personal Funeral Plan. SCI also owns 75 per cent of Advance Planning, which provides the Age Concern scheme, and is joined with Sun Life in an insurance-linked plan. The plans differ in detail and compete in the market. SCI have more than 600 funeral homes, 21 crematoria and 4 cemeteries.

The Co-ops sell funeral bonds as an integrated part of their funeral business, that is, without involvement of a third party plan provider. The Co-op Funeral Care Plan is an insurance scheme underwritten by Cornhill Direct and jointly marketed with the Co-op Funeral Service. The policy covers funeral costs after one year and is available to people between 60 and 80 years of age. The Co-op has about 900 funeral homes and 2 crematoria.

Golden Charter provides its plan to independent funeral directors and has links with the Society of Allied Independent

Funeral Directors (SAIF). The company claims to have more than 2,000 funeral homes within its network.

If you decide on a prepaid funeral plan, your choice of funeral director is going to be restricted to one of those participating in the particular plan you have bought into. This is an important point, especially if you are buying one of the plans sold by way of direct mail, telephone selling or national advertising. You will be allocated a funeral director nominated by the plan provider. The funeral director may be some distance from your home and you won't have had the opportunity to visit and assess the facilities personally.

Some providers intimate that you will be able to choose your own funeral director to deliver the service; but this will be subject to the funeral director agreeing to the plan provider's terms and conditions and meeting its operating criteria.

Where crematoria and cemeteries are owned by the same firm as the funeral director there is a likely implication that you will be expected to use its crematoria or cemetery, which may not be the most convenient.

Benefits of Prepaid Funeral Plans

There are clear benefits in prepaid plans: for funeral directors in that they secure future business and for the plan providers in that they profit from investing the funds. For your part:

▌ You will save your relatives some of the hassle and some of the cost of arranging your funeral – but they may prefer to make their own arrangements for you.

▌ You should be protected from inflationary price increases – but you will lose interest on your savings.

▌ You can shop around and compare prices in advance – but most prepayment schemes are arranged as packages with two or three price tiers offering not a lot of choice.

▌ Paying in advance would reduce your capital, which may be significant if you were seeking entitlement to social security benefits.

▌ If you are worried about settling your affairs then arranging your funeral and paying for it in advance can bring peace of mind on that score.

Costs

The costs of prepaid schemes are pretty much in line with those of at-need funerals. There is an increase if you elect to pay by instalments, though some don't charge extra if you complete payments within a year.

Funeral packages range from about £1,000–£2,000. You can customize a plan with some schemes by adding extras and some, such as the National Association of Funeral Directors' (NAFD) Perfect Assurance Plan, allow you to entirely tailor-make the plan with any participating funeral director. With a bespoke plan you can pay any amount up to several thousands of pounds.

Choices in a Prepaid Plan

Typically, a prepaid plan will offer three packages. Here is an example:

1. The lowest-cost basic funeral, which will have a euphemistic name like 'bronze'. This provides for: collection of the body from the place of death to the funeral director's, within a radius of 100 miles; advice on documentation; laying out and preparation of the body; supply of a basic coffin; a hearse to a local crematorium or cemetery; support and administration staff; no following car.

2. The normal mid-price service, called 'silver'. This will be as above but could also supply a better-quality veneered coffin, a limousine for mourners, the use of the chapel of rest or other extra services.

3. A superior option offered at the highest price and called 'gold'. This will be like the silver plan but could also include embalming, supply of a solid-timber coffin, two following

limousines, transport to church/place for service and then to local crematorium or cemetery plus other services.

Government Plans to Regulate

The Office of Fair Trading has conducted three investigations into the funeral trade in the last 10 years and, most recently, one specifically looking at the prepaid business. This resulted in the publication in January 1999 of a consultation document from HM Treasury exploring avenues for regulation of the prepaid funeral industry.

About 40–50,000 plans are sold each year and there are about 250,000 plans in place. They each cost, on average, £1,200. Payment is made either as a lump sum or by instalments over a period of up to 10 years. The people who buy them are typically about 70 years old and of modest means. The purchase is a significant outlay for them to make.

There are no regulations about how your money is invested or protected. You may see the payment as a long-term investment but you are not in fact making an investment. You are paying in advance for services to be delivered in the future. If you stop the plan for any reason you will get back only the amount paid, less an administration fee. Any interest earned by your money stays with the plan provider or trustee. MPs are campaigning for the payments to be held in a trust and treated as savings, thus giving some investment return to the purchaser.

Of greater concern is the risk that your money may not be available when the time comes to pay for the funeral because of such reasons as fraud, bad investments or the company going bust. The better companies keep the money in a trust independent of their control and with actuaries supervising to ensure there will be funds to cover the liabilities. But there have been instances of fraud, with prepayments being stolen, and there are some plans where the payments are simply kept in a client account at a bank.

Two self-regulatory organizations have been set up by the trade itself: the Funeral Planning Council (FPC) and the National Association for Prepaid Funeral Plans (NAPFP). Each has a code of practice for its members and stipulates how your money should be held and invested. Most of the larger plan-provider companies are members of one or the other but membership is not compulsory and some providers have not joined.

The Treasury is proposing that all plans should be regulated by the Financial Services Authority.

The Essentials of Planning Finance for a Funeral

1. Make special arrangements for money to be available to pay for your funeral at the time it is needed (ie before probate) and not out of your estate.

2. If you want to save or invest to pay for your funeral then there are various ways to do this. The heavily marketed prepayment funeral plans are not the only choice available.

3. The government is planning to regulate prepaid funeral plans.

18 Coping with Bereavement

Support or Professional Counselling

Funeral directors, once known as undertakers, are assuming a new sobriquet as bereavement counsellors. Of 22 prepaid plans featured in a *Which?* survey, all but one was shown to have 'confidential advice on social and personal matters available for relatives'. The three Age Concern plans included provision of 24-hour bereavement support.

In the litigious United States I was told that funeral directors do not get involved in any sort of counselling. Clients requiring help or advice outside the bounds of arranging the funeral are referred to professional counsellors who, presumably, are fully insured in case they get anything wrong.

Bereavement can inflict serious illness on surviving relatives and friends, which may need professional treatment. In severe cases, suicides have been attributed to unresolved grief.

But such instances are thankfully extremely rare. Most people manage to cope with bereavement largely on their own. Neighbours and friends are generally not very good at responding to another person's grief. They don't know what to say, tend to avoid you, cross over the road or start talking about deaths they have known when you want to talk about the one you have just experienced. The church is not there for many people.

Anything from tea and sympathy to advice about filling in benefit claim forms may be expected from UK funeral directors. They are increasingly recognizing the demand and appreciating the public relations value in providing such a service.

Grieving Process Mapped Out

Professional and academic research into the grieving process is comparatively recent and opinions change as the information resource builds up. It has been generally accepted that there are various 'stages of grief' that most people experience.

At first there is disbelief, then a suspension of reality, a numbness that can enable you to concentrate on the urgent practicalities of what has to be done. But coming to terms with the reality is important. Viewing the body and taking part in the ritual of the funeral can help bring about the confirmation and realization of what has happened and start the adjustment to a new way of life.

The next stage is one of feeling loss and longing for the person who has died. Other common feelings are anger that it should have happened to you, anger against other people for letting it happen, guilt about unfinished business and guilt about feeling relief.

Between four and six weeks after the death, periods of depression can set in, with bouts of sudden grief as memories are sparked off by events. Daydreaming, going over your times together in your mind's eye, is an essential part of adjusting. Gradually, the pain of grief will fade and you can start planning for the future, though the sense of loss will never disappear.

This sort of 'map of grieving' forms the basis for many training courses in bereavement counselling and will no doubt help funeral directors understand the behaviour of their clients.

Private and Individual Grief

But grieving is very much an individual thing and not the same for everyone. If you don't have these feelings, or don't seem to be passing through the stages of the map of grieving, don't think you have to worry about it.

Studies of widows and widowers have found that a great many are not greatly distressed by the bereavement and that severe depression need not necessarily follow a loss. Not being too upset can be quite normal and possibly a sign of spirituality or resilience. Worry about repressed feelings can also be needless as studies have shown that people who let their feelings out had more negative emotions 14 months after the death than those who had bottled them up.

It is not abnormal for grief to be continuing as an intrusion to daily living two or three years after the death, but the pain will be receding. You will be gradually passing through phases of what the experts call 'mourning detachment'.

Memorialization as Therapy

Cemeteries and gardens of remembrance can be seen as places created especially to help people through the stages of adjustment. Dr Frances Clegg is a clinical psychologist who made a special study of memorials and cemeteries. She believes they are there largely for psychological and therapeutic reasons.

If it weren't for a human need for commemoration after death, separate places of burial would cease to exist. We would only need to put bodies or remains into pits, sprinkle on some appropriate chemical, restore the ground and put it to some useful purpose; build a multi-storey car park or shopping mall on the site. This suggestion is quite offensive to many people and perhaps reflects a deep human need for special places for the deceased; places where they can be remembered with reverence. It is the needs of bereaved people that have resulted in the creation of cemeteries and gardens of remembrance as institutions.

The purchase of a memorial can be an extremely therapeutic activity for bereaved people. Furthermore, it seems that the more effort that is put into choosing and designing a memorial, in making it have some unique relevance to the deceased, the greater will be the therapeutic value.

Spending on a funeral or memorial is sometimes thought to be a way of making amends for something left undone, forgotten or neglected in a relationship with the deceased. Memorialization is probably therapeutic even when the bereaved person doesn't feel particularly guilty or neglectful. And it seems that a memorial is particularly helpful when it is sited near to where the body or cremated remains have been placed. Not only are the remains cherished by the act of burial, but the memorial stone itself can also be cherished; and for many people this last act of caring for the deceased is extremely important.

The period of attachment to a grave and frequency of visits varies according to many factors. Practical things come to bear such as how near the grave is to the grieving person's home, how easy it is to travel to the site, the cost of travel, the time available and so on. These may override an individual's particular wishes and desires. Generally, however, a predictable pattern of relationship with graves emerges.

In the first few days after the funeral, visits may be frequent, even daily, then they gradually tail-off to monthly and then to special occasions such as the anniversary of the death, a birthday, Mothers' Day, Fathers' Day, Easter and Christmas. On Mothering Sunday and Easter weekends the modern sections of cemeteries and crematoria are normally carpeted in cut flower tributes. Some establishments make special arrangements to collect and display the masses of blooms in set pieces, laying out heart- or cross-shapes on the lawns.

After two or three years, grave visits become less frequent, perhaps only once a year. After 10–15 years, visits are a rare occurrence and graves begin to assume an appearance of neglect. This can be interpreted as a good result from a psychological point of view. No longer needing to visit the grave, the bereaved person can be assumed to have adjusted to the change in life, to have completed mourning detachment. It has also been observed that after 10–15 years, a widow or widower who had been tending the grave is likely to have become too infirm to continue or may have also died.

Some people interrelate quite actively with a memorial and gravesite. They will talk alone at the graveside, sometimes aloud, clean and polish the headstone and create a grave garden. Such a relationship may help in coming to terms with grief and perhaps obviate any need for other forms of therapy.

Bereavement Support Groups

Unresolved grief can lead to a pathological condition requiring professional counselling. Few people suffer to such an extent but many are grateful for bereavement support and hundreds of groups have been set up with local branches throughout the country.

Some groups are especially for those who have been bereaved in particularly distressing circumstances. The Stillbirth and Neonatal Death Society (SANDS), for parents of babies who are stillborn or of newborn babies who have died, says, 'When a parent dies you mourn your past; when a baby dies you mourn your future'. SANDS has many befriending groups that have created memorial sites at cemeteries, crematoria and hospitals.

There is a group for parents bereaved by cot death. Parents of older children who have died may find support with Compassionate Friends. Widows and widowers can turn to CRUSE.

The National Association of Bereavement Services, 20 Norton Folgate, London E1 6DB (tel: 020 7247 1080) maintains a database of bereavement help organizations nationwide and can put you in contact with the most appropriate group and the branch nearest to your home.

YOU CAN HELP

Meet Elisa. She had tubes and electrodes permanently bolted into her head. For each test she was starved for 24 hours. Then for up to four hours at a time she was restrained - her headpiece bolted to the side of her cage - while she performed certain tasks. And yet many scientists themselves criticise the relevance of work on monkey brains to humans.

Elisa's species is described as having a 'generally docile and friendly nature' - one of the reasons why she was chosen. She is just one of millions of animals that suffer and die in UK laboratories every year.

The National Anti-Vivisection Society (NAVS) is the leading organisation of its kind. We work tirelessly to expose the cruelty and futility of animal experiments, to end animal experiments.

We organise public and schools educational programmes; we conduct undercover investigations of laboratories; and produce detailed scientific reports to MPs and the media.

Your bequest will help us to help laboratory animals.

For a free guide to making a will, please
call the NAVS on 0208-846 9777.
National Anti-Vivisection Society,
261 Goldhawk Road, London W12 9PE.

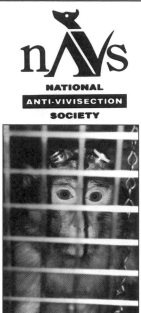

NATIONAL
ANTI-VIVISECTION
SOCIETY

HELP TO END THEIR SUFFERING

At eighteen months old Trudy became the most famous chimp in the country, this year. Her trainer was convicted of beating her, not once or twice but on three separate occasions. Thanks to the Animal Defenders, who filmed the beatings, Trudy is now saved.

The Animal Defenders undertook an exhaustive undercover investigation into the daily life for circus animals.

ANIMAL DEFENDERS

Our findings are devastating: physical and verbal abuse - animals hit with sticks, whips, broomhandles, anything that might come to hand; severe deprivation and confinement - lions and tigers in small cages for up to 80% of their day while elephants spent up to 96% of their time in chains.

With the best will in the world, circuses cannot meet the needs of their animals.

Existing legislation fails circus animals. We are campaigning to end all animal circuses and to bring performing animal training centres (winter quarters), like Trudy's previous home, under the Zoo Licensing Act 1981. We must protect the Trudys of the future.

And we need your help.

Your bequest will help us to help circus animals.

For a free guide to making a Will, please
call the Animal Defenders on 0208-846 9777.
Animal Defenders, 261 Goldhawk Road, London W12 9PE.

Animal Defenders - The Campaign to End Animal Circuses

The Animal Defenders was originally founded in 1990 as the youth wing of the National Anti-Vivisection Society. Having gone from strength to strength, it is now a welfare and conservation group in its own right.

With its key focus currently on the use of animals in circuses, the Animal Defenders is campaigning to end all animal circuses and to bring performing animal training centres (circus winter quarters) under the Zoo Licensing Act 1981.

The group are responsible for the successful convictions of top circus trainer Mary Chipperfield, her husband Roger Cawley and their employee Michael Stephen Gills, who were caught on film beating animals in their care.

The convictions arose from an 18-month undercover investigation into animal circuses. Over 7,000 hours of observation and 800 hours of video footage of 13 UK circuses, including three winter quarters, revealed that daily life for circus animals is one of environmental deprivation, stress, physical and verbal abuse.

Circus animals spend almost their entire time on the road, moving from one makeshift encampment to another. They can spend unbearably long hours shut in transporters - this is the same for any species: lions, tigers, elephants, even horses. For example, one pony spent nearly 26 hours in its transporter, despite its journey taking just five hours.

Our campaign is supported by over 200 MPs and a host of celebrities including Sir Elton John, Sir John Gielgud, Phil Collins, Jenny Seagrove and Twiggy.

Our work also extends beyond the UK:

The Animal Defenders undertakes international rescues. In 1996, we were called to Mozambique where a group of circus animals, including lions, tigers, horses, dogs and a python, had been left to starve. Having arranged homes for all the animals we later discovered that at least one of the lions had been identified as being from an extinct subspecies, the Barbary. We are now working on a long-term project to eventually reintroduce the Barbary lions into the protected wild. It is unthinkable that such a rare animal may have just starved to death, abandoned by its circus owner.

In 1998, we relocated two more rescued Barbary lions from Italy to the breeding project in South Africa. We also worked with a South African animal welfare group, the NSPCA, to help their campaign to prevent 30 wild-caught baby elephants from being sent to circuses and zoos across the world.

The vital work of the Animal Defenders relies solely on donations and legacies from our supporters and cannot hope to continue without it. The Animal Defenders is a non-profitmaking organisation.

Please contact the Animal Defenders to
find out more about our work and how you
can help us. Call us today on 0208-846 9777,
fax 0208-846 9712 or write to us at
261 Goldhawk Road, London W12 9PE.

Pets

Few Pets Have a Decent Funeral

Half the households in the country own a pet and for 10 million of them it's a dog or a cat. Rabbits, birds, guinea pigs and hamsters each account for around 1.5 million pets and there are 30 million pet fish! This is not counting exotics like alligators, snakes and stick insects.

When a companion pet dies, the bereavement experienced is often as acute as when a family member dies. Indeed, for many people the pet is a member of the family. Shoebox funerals in the garden are a part of growing up for many children. For adults as much as for children, the loss of a companion pet can be traumatic. There are books, videos and helpline counselling for bereaved pet owners – and there are pet crematoria and cemeteries.

But not many pets end up with a 'decent' funeral. There are an estimated 1.5 million deaths a year among the pet dog and cat population. It is probable that these bodies are disposed of as follows: 300,000 are buried in garden graves at home, 1,000 are buried in pet cemeteries, 100,000 are individually cremated and the remainder are disposed of as waste.

When you take your pet to the vet for the last time, for the unavoidable euthanasia, you have the choice of leaving the animal with the vet or undertaking for yourself the task of disposal. Given a small pet and a large garden, this is not too difficult. But for the millions in flats or those with tiny gardens or no skills with a spade, the easy option is for a parting at the veterinary clinic.

If you think your animal companion deserves more than a routine incineration and disposal by the vet, why not consider burying it in a pet cemetery.

Pet Cemeteries and Crematoria

Pet cemeteries are not new. One of the most famous is the Victorian site in London's Hyde Park, long since full and closed for further burials. It was reserved exclusively for dogs and most of them with upper-class owners. But pet cemeteries are not numerous and those that exist manage very few burials and commemorations of either animals or their cremated remains.

The Association of Private Pet Cemeteries and Crematoria (APPCC) reckon an average of about 25 interments take place in a year in each cemetery, a figure that has changed little in the past 20 years.

Pet crematoria are a fairly recent development with about 40 covering the whole of the UK. Most have burial grounds and memorial gardens and their operators are anxious to distance themselves from the bulk incineration and landfill activities of the animal disposal industry.

There are no middle-people in the pet bereavement service. No funeral directors to take over arrangements for dead companion animals. The pet crematoria staff undertake to lay out, wash, groom and encoffin the pet in readiness for the funeral. Owners are welcome to attend a funeral service, to say their farewells and, if they wish, to see the coffin into the cremator or lowered into the grave.

Members of the APPCC make a point of offering a dignified personal service for companion animals and of treating them in a dignified and caring manner at all times. Most will provide a choice of two types of cremation.

All will offer individual cremation in which the pets are cremated alone in an enclosed chamber. All ash is carefully collected before the next cremation commences. Clients are guaranteed that the ashes they receive, or that are placed into a memorial garden, will be all and only those of their pet.

With communal cremation, two or more pets are cremated together with no separation of ashes. The ashes are buried or scattered in licensed locations, these areas being either memorial gardens or natural areas. Often, owners opt for this service for animals that lived as part of a pack, on the basis that they were always with other pets.

All APPCC members with cemeteries carry out burials in identifiable plots and clients have visiting rights to the graves.

Burials Together

Often people want to be buried with their pets or have their pets buried with them. Many family mausolea are believed to contain pets. A mausoleum in Edinburgh's Eastern Cemetery houses the remains of a magician performer and the dog that was part of his stage act. An annex to this cemetery still functions as a pet cemetery with a collection of fascinating memorials.

The family pet dog Lucy, killed in the murder of mother and daughter Lin and Megan Russell in 1996, is buried with them in a Welsh churchyard.

A few years ago, the Rossendale Pet Crematorium and Cemetery in Lancashire obtained permission from the council to allow owners to be buried with their pets. Ashes have often been sprinkled on pet graves, and at least one inhumation has taken place there.

However, the majority of cemeteries and churchyards will not admit animal burials – and many will not even allow them in walking. It is, in fact, against the law to bury animals in a people cemetery and, in theory, it could lead to the cemetery being classified as a waste site.

The Costs

The fees for pet burial range from about £180–£350, depending on the size of the pet and type of coffin. Individual cremation prices range from about £60–£120, again depending on size of animal and type of coffin.

You should also expect to pay a maintenance fee, which may be in the form of an up-front lump sum or a renewable amount for a yearly or longer term. If you don't keep up payments then the pet grave may be repossessed and reused.

There will also be the cost of a memorial, which will depend on the type and size. You are unlikely to be charged a fee for the right to erect a memorial on the grave. You would normally be expected to buy your memorial and coffin from the operator of the pet cemetery/crematorium.

For information about pet cemeteries and crematoria contact The Association of Private Pet Cemeteries and Crematoria, Chestnut Lodge, Furnace Wood, East Grinstead, West Sussex RH19 2PU (helpline: 01252 844478).

Home Burials

Hundreds of thousands of dogs and cats are buried in family gardens, not to mention hamsters, guinea pigs, rats, budgerigars and sundry other pet creatures and stray animals. Officialdom seems to express little interest in this activity although it would be prudent to comply with the Environment Agency's recommendation that graves should be more than 250 metres from any well or borehole, 10 metres from ponds or streams and 1.5 metres from underground pipes and cables. Animal carcasses buried in a field normally have to be 250 metres from any human-consumption water supply, 30 metres from any other spring and 10 metres from any field drain.

With regard to human graves in a private garden, it is generally considered that more than three would constitute a change of use of the property. It seems your local Environment Agency may use its discretion to decide when a garden becomes a pet cemetery.

Clinical Waste Sites

Pet cemeteries are classified as landfill sites under the Environmental Protection Act and are licensed as such. Dead pets, unlike dead people, are classified as controlled waste and there is some argument that they may fall into the category of clinical waste. Such a ruling would make it virtually impossible for you to hold a dignified and sympathetic funeral for your pet.

It has been accepted that only if a pet died under treatment from a vet, or was put down after suffering from a highly contagious disease such as rabies or anthrax, would it be classified as clinical waste.

However, the Environment Agency is seeking to classify pet cemeteries as clinical waste landfill sites. This would suggest that a dead pet could be clinical waste and should therefore be disposed of by incineration or under strictly controlled conditions. Therefore, logically, burial of pets in gardens would be illegal, but an exception is made for pets buried in the garden of the place where they had their home.

The Cost of Controls

Because the pet cemetery is a landfill site, the operator pays approximately £100 a year for a waste management licence and has to lodge a bond for about £500 with the Environment Agency to provide for returning the land to normal condition on closure of the site. If deceased pets were reclassified as clinical waste then the site would require the installation of gas monitoring equipment, at a cost of £2,000, as well as yearly calibration.

Pet cemetery operators usually carry out collection of the deceased pets and, unlike funeral directors transporting human bodies, they must have a licence to do this.

Most cemeteries and churchyards will not allow pets to be buried in their grounds. If you really wanted to have a companion pet buried with you, it has been suggested that a burial in your own garden or private land would be the solution.

Or you could consider a green burial in a nature or woodland cemetery where the management may be more accommodating to the idea (see Chapter 15). However, if the Environment Agency insists on classifying pets as clinical waste, such alternatives may no longer be an option. Even with pets as controlled waste, helpful green cemeteries could be reclassified as landfill sites.

Scampy was left tied to a fence overnight

"FRIENDS OF THE ANIMALS"

**408 Bearwood Road
Bearwood, Warley
West Midlands
B66 4EX**

**Telephone
0121 420 4201
Reg. Charity No.
1000249**

Will YOU please give a helping hand to some of the thousands of sick, injured and neglected animals that 'Friends of the Animals' save EVERY year. The Charity operates a policy of non-destruction, and our four branches - in the Midlands and South - help: dogs, cats, horses, donkeys, badgers, hedgehogs, other wildlife and all birds.

We are especially strong on education and 'preventative' work; and to this end, have had more than 7,000 animals spayed/neutered. Thousands more have been wormed and inoculated - many for the first time in their lives! Veterinary treatment (currently £381,000-00) is our biggest outgoing.

All too often we are literally, the animals' VERY last chance of life.

Branches in: Birmingham, Portsmouth, Ringwood and the Isle of Wight. Please make a donation to help us continue this work and to expand and open other branches. *Newsletter sent with pleasure.*

20 *How to Complain*

Complaints About Funerals

No Licensing or Regulation

The first place to go with any problem or complaint about your funeral is to the funeral directors that provided the service. They have a business and a reputation to protect and are mostly anxious to see problems resolved quickly and satisfactorily.

There is no national licensing scheme or regulating organization to control funeral directors. There are self-regulatory codes of practice and your funeral directors may be members of one of several trade associations that operate such a code. This will be shown by a symbol printed on the letterhead or a sticker on the door or window. If you are not satisfied by the response you receive to your complaint, you can take the matter up with the appropriate trade association. However, this is a matter of members criticizing their own colleagues and customers have not always felt they were getting a fair deal.

The Funeral Ombudsman Scheme (FOS) was started in April 1994 in the wake of criticism from the Office of Fair Trading and the Consumers Association of the way the self-regulatory schemes and codes of conduct were being operated. It was established by the Funeral Standards Council (FSC), a group formed in June 1993 by a number of Co-op funeral businesses and Golden Charter, a provider of prepaid funeral plans to independent funeral directors.

The Co-op had previously been a major supporter of the National Association of Funeral Directors (NAFD). This is an historic trade association evolved from the British Institute of Undertakers, which existed from 1898 to 1905 when it changed its name to the British Undertakers' Association and changed again in 1935 to the NAFD when undertakers professed to be funeral directors.

The NAFD have their own, long-established procedure for dealing with complaints about their members and eschew involvement with the independent ombudsman. After examination by a professional standards board, complainants to the NAFD may be referred to the Chartered Institute of Arbitrators (CIA).

The FSC claimed the initiative to improve on the NAFD code of practice and the way it was being enforced. They also joined with another newly established organization, the Funeral Planning Council (FPC), in developing a code of practice for prepaid funeral plans with access to the FOS for plan holders.

The rival group of funeral directors formed the National Association of Prepaid Funeral Plans (NAPFP), which has its own code of practice and gives people purchasing plans from NAPFP access to the CIA services.

Yet another group of funeral directors claiming to represent independent family-owned businesses set up another trade association, the Society of Allied Independent Funeral Directors (SAIF). Since 1998, all SAIF funeral directors are regulated by the FOS code of practice. Prepaid plans from Golden Charter, a member of the FPC, already came under the ombudsman's remit.

The Funeral Ombudsman Scheme

By the end of 1998, the proportion of funerals covered by the FOS had risen to around 70 per cent. During 1998, numbers of crematoria, around 30, came under the scheme through associate membership of the FSC.

In 1998, the funeral ombudsman received 144 formal complaints against funeral directors. The vast majority of cases were resolved by conciliation, a settlement negotiated between the client and the company. In cases where the ombudsman had to reach a formal adjudication, the average compensation to complainants was about £700.

The ombudsman can only deal with a complaint if the firm is a member of the FSC, SAIF or the FPC. You must first refer your complaint to the funeral directors or prepaid funeral plan provider concerned. The matter has to be raised with the ombudsman within six months of your receiving the final offer from the company concerned. You cannot use the ombudsman if you have already gone to law over the matter but if you do not agree with the ombudsman's decision you can then take legal proceedings.

There is no charge to you for use of the ombudsman scheme. If you refer your complaint to the FOS, evidence from both you and the company will be considered and an attempt made to reach a settlement by common agreement. If that is not possible the ombudsman will make a decision that is binding on the company. Compensation of up to £50,000 can be awarded.

The FSC commissioned Barbara Saunders, chairman of the Council of the Insurance Ombudsman Bureau, to advise on the structure of the ombudsman scheme. The Council of the Funeral Ombudsman was formed with membership of independent consumer representatives, who form a majority, together with representatives from the FSC and FPC. Chairman of the Council is Jill Moore OBE, a former member of the National Consumer Council.

The Council of the Funeral Ombudsman appointed Professor Geoffrey Woodroffe to the post of Ombudsman. He is Director of the Centre for Consumer and Commercial Law Research at Brunel University. Professor Woodroffe is a qualified solicitor and has extensive experience as consumer consultant to a variety of organizations including the European Commission, the Office of Fair Trading, the Consumers' Association and the National Consumer Council. He is also the author of several books on consumer law.

The contact address is: The Funeral Ombudsman, 31 Southampton Row, Holborn, London WC1B 5HJ (tel: 020 7430 1112).

Complaints About Crematoria

Nearly all crematoria in the UK are members of the Federation of

British Cremation Authorities (FBCA) and most managers and operatives are members of the Institute of Burial and Cremation Administration (IBCA). They operate according to a strict code of conduct and you should be able to get a copy of this from your crematorium.

Most crematoria, nearly 200, are owned by local authorities. Take your complaint first of all to the manager at the crematorium. It is at this point that the huge majority of problems can be resolved. Managers administer the service according to regulations and bylaws drawn up by government officers and laid down by the council. If you are not satisfied by the response of the crematorium manager you can go to the director of the department in the town hall that controls crematorium and cemetery services. This department has different titles ranging from parks and leisure to environment and waste control.

Behind them is the bureaucracy of local government and, ultimately, your vote for an elected member of the council. You can take your complaint to your elected council representative or to the chairman of the cemeteries and crematoria committee of the local council.

About 30 of the 43 crematoria in private ownership are associate members of the FSC and so offer you recourse to the Funeral Ombudsman Scheme. Concerning complaints with those not in the FSC, if you don't get a satisfactory response from the manager, you should go to the managing director or chairman of the proprietary company.

Complaints About Cemeteries

Local authorities operate the majority of cemeteries and the complaints procedure will be the same as for municipal crematoria. The same companies that own private crematoria also own most of the private cemeteries so, if they are members of the FSC, you should be able to have access to the funeral ombudsman.

The operation and administration procedures for crematoria and cemeteries have generally been drafted more for the convenience of the management and operatives than for the needs of the bereaved. This was highlighted in a report by the Audit

Commission in 1989. Adverse criticism continued and in 1996 the IBCA published its Charter for the Bereaved in a move to improve the situation.

Crematoria and cemeteries are being encouraged to adopt the charter, so becoming 'Charter Members' and adhering to certain standards of service to the bereaved. The charter identifies 33 'rights', which you can expect to be delivered by your crematorium or cemetery, and another 33 items that may become rights after consultation and discussion.

The charter is a 72-page document that sets out in some detail the service that IBCA believes cemeteries and crematoria should provide, useful addresses and information about the IBCA and laws and regulations involved with bereavement. You can obtain a copy for £25 from The Charter Organizer, Bereavement Services, Cemetery Office, Richardson Street, Carlisle CA2 6AL (tel: 01228 25033; fax: 01228 595165).

Complaints About Churchyards

The minister incumbent at the church is the person directly responsible for the churchyard and any complaints should be addressed there in the first instance. Overall control is with the bishop but legal affairs, such as granting a faculty for a right of burial or erection of a monument, are looked after by the chancellor of the diocese. Some aspects of churchyard management come under the ambit of the parochial church council (PCC).

Complaints About Parish Burial Grounds

Many rural burial grounds, and churchyards that have been closed to further interments, are the responsibility of parish councils. They rarely have a manager and administrative matters are looked after by the clerk to the council. Complaints should be addressed to the clerk, and if not dealt with satisfactorily, to the chairperson of the parish council.

Advice can be obtained from The Association of Burial

Authorities at 155 Upper Street, Islington, London N1 1RA (tel: 020 7288 2522).

Complaints About Memorials

Restrictive regulations are a common cause of complaint in respect of memorials and these should be addressed to the landowners, the church or local authority. Monumental masons have no control of these regulations. However, if your complaint concerns workmanship then you should go first of all to the mason who supplied and installed the memorial. Members of the National Association of Memorial Masons (NAMM) subscribe to a code of practice and standards of quality and if your mason is a member but does not satisfactorily respond to your complaint, you can bring this to the attention of this trade association.

Even if your mason is not a member of NAMM and you are in dispute about workmanship or value for money, NAMM is prepared to send an expert to examine the problem and give an opinion. This may be enough to enable you to reach a settlement or, at least, it will provide useful information should you have to go to court.

This arrangement is not entirely satisfactory as another member of the trade makes the assessment and you may not think this sufficiently independent. Complaints could be better addressed if monumental masons joined the FSC and so gave you access to the Funeral Ombudsman Scheme. This would, of course, be open to you if you bought your memorial from a funeral director that is a member of the FSC.

Contact NAMM at 27a Albert Street, Rugby, Warwickshire CV21 2SG (tel: 01788 542264).

HELP TO END THEIR SUFFERING

At eighteen months old Trudy became the most famous chimp in the country, this year. Her trainer was convicted of beating her, not once or twice but on three separate occasions. Thanks to the Animal Defenders, who filmed the beatings, Trudy is now saved.

The Animal Defenders undertook an exhaustive undercover investigation into the daily life for circus animals.

ANIMAL DEFENDERS

Our findings are devastating: physical and verbal abuse - animals hit with sticks, whips, broomhandles, anything that might come to hand; severe deprivation and confinement - lions and tigers in small cages for up to 80% of their day while elephants spent up to 96% of their time in chains.

With the best will in the world, circuses cannot meet the needs of their animals.

Existing legislation fails circus animals. We are campaigning to end all animal circuses and to bring performing animal training centres (winter quarters), like Trudy's previous home, under the Zoo Licensing Act 1981. We must protect the Trudys of the future.

And we need your help.

Your bequest will help us to help circus animals.

For a free guide to making a Will, please call the Animal Defenders on 0208-846 9777. Animal Defenders, 261 Goldhawk Road, London W12 9PE.

Animal Defenders - The Campaign to End Animal Circuses

The Animal Defenders was originally founded in 1990 as the youth wing of the National Anti-Vivisection Society. Having gone from strength to strength, it is now a welfare and conservation group in its own right.

With its key focus currently on the use of animals in circuses, the Animal Defenders is campaigning to end all animal circuses and to bring performing animal training centres (circus winter quarters) under the Zoo Licensing Act 1981.

The group are responsible for the successful convictions of top circus trainer Mary Chipperfield, her husband Roger Cawley and their employee Michael Stephen Gills, who were caught on film beating animals in their care.

The convictions arose from an 18-month undercover investigation into animal circuses. Over 7,000 hours of observation and 800 hours of video footage of 13 UK circuses, including three winter quarters, revealed that daily life for circus animals is one of environmental deprivation, stress, physical and verbal abuse.

Circus animals spend almost their entire time on the road, moving from one makeshift encampment to another. They can spend unbearably long hours shut in transporters - this is the same for any species: lions, tigers, elephants, even horses. For example, one pony spent nearly 26 hours in its transporter, despite its journey taking just five hours.

Our campaign is supported by over 200 MPs and a host of celebrities including Sir Elton John, Sir John Gielgud, Phil Collins, Jenny Seagrove and Twiggy.

Our work also extends beyond the UK:

The Animal Defenders undertakes international rescues. In 1996, we were called to Mozambique where a group of circus animals, including lions, tigers, horses, dogs and a python, had been left to starve. Having arranged homes for all the animals we later discovered that at least one of the lions had been identified as being from an extinct subspecies, the Barbary. We are now working on a long-term project to eventually reintroduce the Barbary lions into the protected wild. It is unthinkable that such a rare animal may have just starved to death, abandoned by its circus owner.

In 1998, we relocated two more rescued Barbary lions from Italy to the breeding project in South Africa. We also worked with a South African animal welfare group, the NSPCA, to help their campaign to prevent 30 wild-caught baby elephants from being sent to circuses and zoos across the world.

The vital work of the Animal Defenders relies solely on donations and legacies from our supporters and cannot hope to continue without it. The Animal Defenders is a non-profitmaking organisation.

Please contact the Animal Defenders to find out more about our work and how you can help us. Call us today on 0208-846 9777, fax 0208-846 9712 or write to us at 261 Goldhawk Road, London W12 9PE.

YOU CAN HELP

Meet Elisa. She had tubes and electrodes permanently bolted into her head. For each test she was starved for 24 hours. Then for up to four hours at a time she was restrained - her headpiece bolted to the side of her cage - while she performed certain tasks. And yet many scientists themselves criticise the relevance of work on monkey brains to humans.

Elisa's species is described as having a 'generally docile and friendly nature' - one of the reasons why she was chosen. She is just one of millions of animals that suffer and die in UK laboratories every year.

The National Anti-Vivisection Society (NAVS) is the leading organisation of its kind. We work tirelessly to expose the cruelty and futility of animal experiments, to end animal experiments.

We organise public and schools educational programmes; we conduct undercover investigations of laboratories; and produce detailed scientific reports to MPs and the media.

Your bequest will help us to help laboratory animals.

For a free guide to making a will, please call the NAVS on 0208-846 9777. National Anti-Vivisection Society, 261 Goldhawk Road, London W12 9PE.

nAVS

NATIONAL ANTI-VIVISECTION SOCIETY

Useful Addresses

AB Wildlife Trust Fund (advice on green burials), 7 Knox Road, Harrogate, North Yorkshire HG1 3EF (tel: 01423 530900)

Age Concern England, Astral House, 1268 London Road, Norbury, London SW16 4ER (tel: 020 8679 8000; fax: 020 8679 6069; e-mail: age@ace.org.uk; Web site: www.ace.org.uk)

Age Concern Northern Ireland, 3 Lower Crescent, Belfast BT7 1NR (tel: 028 9024 5729; fax: 028 9023 5497)

Age Concern Scotland, 113 Rose Street, Edinburgh EH2 3DT (tel: 0131 220 3345; fax: 0131 220 2779)

Age Concern Wales, 4th Floor, Cathedral Road, Cardiff CF1 9SD (tel: 029 2037 1156; fax: 029 2039 9562; e-mail: accymru@ace.org.uk)

Alzheimer's Disease Society, Gordon House, 10 Greencoat Place, London SW1P 1PH (tel: 020 7306 0606; fax: 020 7306 0808)

Asian Family Counselling Service, 76 Church Road, Hanwell, Middlesex W7 1LB (tel: 020 8567 5616)

Association of Burial Authorities, 155 Upper Street, Islington, London N1 1RA (tel: 020 7288 2522)

Association of Private Pet Cemeteries and Crematoria (APPCC), Chestnut Lodge, Furnace Wood, East Grinstead, West Sussex RH19 2PU (tel/fax: 01342 712976; helpline: 01252 844478)

Britannia Shipping Company (sea burials), Britannia House, Newton Poppleford, Nr Sidmouth, Devon EX10 0EF (tel: 01395 568652; fax: 01395 567511)

British Humanist Association, 47 Theobalds Road, London WC1X 8SP (tel: 020 7430 0908; fax: 020 7430 1271; e-mail: robert@humanism.org.uk)

British Organ Donors Society (BODY), Balsham, Cambridge CB1 6DL (tel/fax: 01223 893636; e-mail: body@argonect.co.uk; Web site: http://www.argonet.co.uk)

CancerLink, 11–21 Northdown Street, London N1 9BN (tel: 020 7833 2818; helpline: 0800 132905)

CancerLink (Scotland), 9 Castle Terrace, Edinburgh EH1 2DP (tel: 0131 228 5567; fax: 0131 228 8956; e-mail: <cancerlink@cislink. demon.co.uk>)

Cemetery Friends, National Federation of, 47 Chestnut Grove, South Croydon CR2 7LH (tel: 020 8651 5090)

Charter for the Bereaved, Charter Organizer, Bereavement Services, Cemetery Office, Richardson Street, Carlisle CA2 6AL (tel: 01228 25033; fax: 01228 595165)

Charter, The Dead Citizens', National Funerals College, University of Bristol, 3 Priory Road, Bristol BS8 1TX (tel: 0117 928 9024; fax: 0117 974 1960; e-mail: Malcolm.Johnson@bristol.ac.uk)

Church's Group on Funeral Services at Cemeteries and Crematoria, Church House, Great Smith Street, London SW1P 3NZ (tel: 020 7898 1000)

Commonwealth War Graves Commission, 2 Marlow Road, Maidenhead, Berkshire SL6 7DX (tel: 01628 634221; fax: 01628 771208)

Compassionate Friends, 53 North Street, Bristol BS3 1EN (tel/fax: 0117 966 5202; helpline: 0117 953 9639)

Council for the Care of Churches, Fielden House, Little College Street, London SW1P 3SH (tel: 020 7898 1866)

Cremation Society, 2nd Floor, Brecon House, 16–16a Albion Place, Maidstone ME14 5DZ (tel: 01622 688292/3; fax: 01622 686698)

CRUSE Bereavement Care, Cruse House, 126 Sheen Road, Richmond TW9 1UR (tel: 020 8940 4818; fax: 020 8940 7638; helpline Mon to Fri 9.30 am–5 pm: 020 8332 7227)

Death, Dying and Grief Resources (Web site: http://www.cyberspace.com/~webster/death.html)

FACTS Health Centre (for advice and support following death after AIDS), 23–25 Crouch End, London N8 9SY (tel: 020 8348 9195)

Federation of British Cremation Authorities (FBCA), 41 Salisbury Road, Carshalton, Surrey SM5 3HA (tel: 020 8669 4521)

Foundation for Study of Infant Death (FSID), 14 Halkin Street, London SW1X 7DP (tel: 020 7235 0965; fax: 020 7823 1986; e-mail: fsid@dial.pipex.com; Web site: http://www.vois.org.uk/fsid; 24-hour helpline: 020 7235 1721)

Funeral Ombudsman Scheme, 26–28 Bedford Row, London WC1R 4HE (tel: 020 7430 1112; fax: 020 7430 1012)

Funeral Planning Council (FPC), Melville House, 70 Drymen Road, Bearsden, Glasgow G61 2RP (tel: 0141 942 5885; fax: 0141 942 2323)

Funeral Standards Council (FSC), 30 North Road, Cardiff CF1 3DY (tel: 029 2038 2046)

Garden of Remembrance on the Internet, The World Wide Cemetery, PO Box 723, Station F. Toronto, Canada N4Y 1T0 (Web site: <http://www.cemetery.org/>)

General Register Office, Overseas Registration Section, Smedley Hydro, Trafalgar Road, Birkdale, Southport PR8 2HH (tel: 01704 569824)

General Register Office, PO Box 2, Southport, Merseyside PR8 2JD (tel: 0151 471 4200; fax: 0151 471 4523; Certificates: 01704 550013)

General Register Office (Scotland), New Register House, Edinburgh EH1 3YT (tel: 0131 334 0380; fax: 0131 314 4400; Web site: http://www.open.go.uk/gros/gros home.htm)

Help the Aged, St James's Walk, Clerkenwell Green, London EC1R 0BE (tel: 020 7253 0253; fax: 020 7250 4474; SeniorLine weekdays 9 am–4 pm: 020 8800 6565)

Home Office, Constitutional Policy Directorate, Room 972, 50 Queen Anne's Gate, London SW1H 9AT (tel: 020 7273 2888/3574; fax: 020 7273 4231)

INQUEST, Ground Floor, Alexandra National House, 330 Seven Sisters Road, London N4 2PJ (tel: 020 8802 7430; fax: 020 8802 7450; e-mail: INQUEST@compuserve.com)

Institute of Burial and Cremation Administration (IBCA), Kelham Hall, Kelham, Nr Newark, Notts NG23 5QX (tel/fax: 01636 708 311)

Jewish Bereavement Counselling Service, PO Box 6748, London N3 3BX (tel/fax: 020 8349 0839)

Lesbian and Gay Bereavement Project, Vaughan Williams Centre, Colindale Hospital, London NW9 5HG (tel: 020 8200 0511; helpline Mon to Thurs 1.30–5.00 pm: 020 8455 8894)

London Lighthouse, 111–117 Lancaster Road, London W11 1QT (tel: 020 7792 1200)

Macmillan Cancer Relief Fund, 15–19 Britten Street, London SW3 3TZ (tel: 020 7351 7811; fax: 020 7376 8090)

Useful Addresses

Marine Environmental Protection, Ministry of Agriculture, Fisheries and Food (MAFF), Nobel House, 17 Smith Square, London SW1P 3JR (tel: 020 7238 5869; fax: 020 7238 5724)

Memorials by Artists, Snape Priory, Saxmundham, Suffolk IP17 1SA (tel: 01728 689073)

Memorials Insurance, Stone Guard, Bridge Insurance Brokers (Manchester) Ltd, Indemnity House, Chatham Street, Manchester M1 3AY (tel: 0161 236 3141)

Miscarriage Association, c/o Clayton Hospital, Northgate, Wakefield, West Yorkshire WF1 3JS (tel: 01924 200799; fax: 01924 298834; e-mail: susan.ellis@btinternet.com; Web site: http://www.btinternet.com/~miscarriageassociation/ma/default.htm)

National Association of Bereavement Services (NABS), 20 Norton Folgate, London E1 6DB (tel: 020 7247 0617; helpline: 020 7247 1080)

National Association of Funeral Directors (NAFD), 618 Warwick Road, Solihull, West Midlands B91 1AA (tel: 0121 711 1343; fax: 0121 711 1351)

National Association of Memorial Masons (NAMM), 27a Albert Street, Rugby, Warwickshire CV21 2SG (tel: 01788 542264; fax: 01788 542276)

National Association of Prepaid Funeral Plans (NAPFP), 618 Warwick Road, Solihull, West Midlands B91 1AA (tel: 0121 711 1343; fax: 0121 711 1351)

National Association of Widows, 54–57 Allison Street, Digbeth, Birmingham B5 5TH (tel: 0121 643 8348; e-mail: wat@dial.pipex.com)

National Secular Society, 47 Theobalds Road, London WC1X 8SP (tel: 020 7404 3126; fax: 020 7430 1271; e-mail: kpw@secularism.org.uk; Web site: http://www.secularism.org.uk)

Natural Death Centre, 20 Heber Road, London NW2 6AA (tel: 020 8208 2853; fax: 020 8452 6434; e-mail: rhino@dial. pipex.com; Web site: http://www.newciv.org/GIB/natdeath/ ndhbook.html)

NHS Organ Donor Register, UK Transplant Support Service Authority, Foxden Road, Stoke Gifford, Bristol BS34 8RR (tel: 0117 975 7575; fax: 0117 975 7523/7537)

Office of Fair Trading, Field House, 15–25 Breams Buildings, London EC4A 1PR (tel: 020 7242 2858; fax: 020 7269 8543)

Parkinson's Disease Society of the UK, 215 Vauxhall Bridge Road, London SW1V 1EG (tel: 020 7931 8080; fax: 020 7233 9908; helpline Mon to Fri 10 am–4 pm: 020 7233 5373)

Pensions Scheme Registry, PO Box 1NN, Newcastle upon Tyne NE99 1NN (tel: 0191 225 6394)

Pet Bereavement Support Service (helpline 8.30 am–5.00 pm: 0800 096 6606)

Probate Registry, Personal Applications Dept, 2nd Floor, Principal Registry, Family Division, Somerset House, Strand, London WC2R 1LP (tel: 020 7936 6983 or 020 7936 6939)

Public Search Room, Family Records Centre, 1 Myddleton Street, London EC1R 1UW (tel: 020 8392 5300; fax: 020 8392 5307; certificate enquiries: 020 7233 9233; Web site: http://www. open.gov.uk/pro/prohome.htm)

Regale Memorials and Urns, 155 Upper Street, Islington, London N1 1RA (tel: 020 7288 2522)

Registrar General (Northern Ireland), GRO Oxford House, 49–55 Chichester Street, Belfast BT1 4HH (tel: 028 9025 2000; fax: 028 9035 2044)

Registry of Shipping and Seamen, PO Box 165, Cardiff CF4 5FU (tel: 02920 747333; fax: 02920 747877; e-mail: marine. information.centre.msa.sp@gtnet.gov.uk)

Royal National Institute for the Blind (RNIB), 224 Great Portland Street, London W1N 6AA (tel: 020 7388 1266; fax: 020 7388 2034; e-mail: rnib@rnib.org.uk; Web site: http://www.rnib.org.uk)

Samaritans, 10 The Grove, Slough, Berkshire SL1 1QP (tel: 01753 532713; fax: 01753 819004; e-mail: joe@samaritans.org; Web site: http://www.samaritans.org.uk; helpline: 0345 909090)

The Scottish Office, Home Department, V1 Spur, Saughton House, Broomhouse Drive, Edinburgh EH11 3XD (tel: 0131 244 3581; Web site: http://www.scotland.gov.uk)

Shadow of Suicide (SOS), 53 North Street, Bristol BS3 1EN (tel: 0117 953 9639)

Society of Allied and Independent Funeral Directors (SAIF), Crowndale House, 1 Ferdinand Place, London NW1 8EE (tel: 020 7267 6777; fax: 020 7267 1147; e-mail: info@saif.org.uk; Web site: http://www.saif.org.uk)

Stillbirth and Neonatal Death Society (SANDS), 28 Portland Place, London W1N 4DE (tel: 020 7436 7940; fax: 020 7436 3715; helpline: 020 7436 5881; Web site: http://members.aol.com/babyloss/sands.htm)

Terrence Higgins Trust, 52–54 Grays Inn Road, London WC1X 8JU (tel: 020 7831 0330; helpline 12 noon–10 pm: 020 7242 1010)

War Pensions Agency, Norcross, Blackpool FY5 3WP (tel: 01253 858858; fax: 01253 330561)

The Woodland Trust, Ref 1744 Freepost, Grantham, Lincs NG31 6BR (tel: 01476 581111; fax: 01476 590808)

Glossary of UK Funerary and Cemetery Terminology

altar tomb See *chest tomb*.

ashuary (new) Place or chamber for the common burial or deposit of cremated remains after a period of deposit in a columbarium or vault. See *ossuary*.

bier Platform or stand on which a corpse or a coffin rests before a burial.

body slab See *ledger*.

body stone A stone covering the length of a grave, shaped narrower at the foot, gabled like a roof or rounded.

box tomb See *chest tomb*.

burial See *deposition*.

burial ground Generic name for an extramural place of burial.

casket (a) Container for a corpse which is rectangular rather than tapered, usually made of wood in UK. See *coffin*. (b) A box-like container for cremated remains.

catacomb Building or structure above or below ground comprising niches arranged in rows on several storeys into which encoffined corpses and urns of ashes are deposited and usually walled up.

catafalque Raised platform on which a body lies in state before and/or during a funeral service.

cemetery A place, other than a churchyard, for disposal of the dead and their memorialization.

cemetery section Division of a cemetery comprising a group of graves and memorials.

cenotaph A sepulchral monument without remains.

chapel of rest Where a body is kept prior to a funeral, perhaps for viewing; euphemism for a mortuary.

chappelle A roofed building located above a vault, used for ceremonies of remembrance and committal and as a memorial.

charnel house See *ossuary*.

chest tomb Stone or brick box set above a grave or vault. Also box tomb.

churchyard See *graveyard*. Usually Church of England.

coffin A container for a corpse, usually made of wood and tapered from the shoulders towards the feet and towards the head.

columbarium Building having a room or rooms with shelves or niches to take urns with ashes either on display or sealed with a plaque. Also a structure above ground comprising niches arranged in rows and on several storeys into which urns are deposited and usually sealed with a plaque.

columbarium wall Not a columbarium with niches but a wall upon which memorial plaques can be fixed. Often near a scattering lawn.

cremated remains The calcified remains of a cremated body, usually pulverized or broken.

cremation section Division of a cemetery comprising a group of graves and memorials dedicated to after-cremation commemoration. See *cemetery section*.

crematory Room in a crematorium where the cremators are located.

cremulator Machine that reduces to a powder the calcified bones remaining after a cremation.

deposition (a) of a body Burial in a grave or placement in a vault or walled grave or in a mausoleum or catacomb; (b) of cremated remains (ashes) by *scattering* Distribution on the surface of the ground; by *strewing* Distribution beneath a layer of turf or directly on to the soil underground; by *burial* Placing in a container in a hole in the ground (a grave) or a vault or walled grave below ground; by *placement* Placing in a container in a columbarium niche or mausoleum or catacomb above ground.

exhumation (a) of a corpse Disinterment or removal after deposition; (b) of cremated remains Digging up after burial.

faculty A permit issued by the Church of England to allow the introduction of memorials and other developments in a church and churchyard.

footstone Like a headstone and associated with it, but smaller and set at the foot of a grave, usually with a limited inscription.

grave Excavation to receive a corpse or corpses for inhumation, place of inhumation and mound over it.

grave numbering   A system of allocating and recording grave locations.

gravestone   Generic name for a memorial at the place of burial.

graveyard   Area belonging to and often adjacent to or embracing a church or chapel used for disposal of the dead and cremated remains and their memorialization.

headboard   A wooden board with carved and/or painted inscription and often ornamentation set at the head of a grave in place of a headstone.

headstone   An upright slab carrying an inscription, and often ornamentation, set at the head of a grave.

inhumation   Burial of a corpse, usually encoffined, by covering with earth in a grave.

interment   Burial in the ground. See also *inhumation*.

kerbs or kerbset   Strips of stone set to surround a grave and containing a grave garden, chippings, paving or body slab.

landing stone   A single piece of stone or concrete placed flat over a grave as a foundation upon which a monument is constructed.

lawn cemetery   A cemetery comprising rows of headstones with mown grass in between, intended to simplify ground maintenance. Opportunities for memorial objects are strictly limited.

lawn memorial   A headstone of strictly regulated dimensions such as installed in a lawn cemetery; usually of the plinth-and-plate design.

leaping board   A memorial in the form of a wooden plank raised on two posts and running the length of a grave. Inscription may be painted and/or carved.

ledger A stone normally covering the length and width of an earth or walled grave. May be flat, tapered (sloping) or with oval or peon top. Also body slab.

lich gate or lych gate Roofed gate to a churchyard, formerly used as a temporary shelter for the bier during a funeral.

loculus Shelved recess in catacomb for encoffined body.

mausoleum Roofed building with shelves or niches (loculi) to take encoffined corpses, usually reserved for a family or group in UK.

memorial Generic term for a monument to a dead person or persons.

memorial garden (for cremated remains) Lawn or garden where ashes are deposited by scattering, interment or strewing, often with associated memorials.

monument Generic name for any form of sepulchral commemoration.

mortuary chapel Building in cemetery for temporary safe-keeping of a corpse.

niche A recess intended to accommodate a cremation urn, usually sealed with an inscribed tablet. It may contain one or several urns.

officiant Person other than a member of the clergy who performs a funeral service.

ogee The shape of a curve on the top of a headstone having a cross section in the form of a flattened letter 's'.

ossuary A place or chamber for the common burial or deposit of the bones of the dead. An urn for bones. Also *charnel house*.

pedestal tomb Like a chest tomb but taller, smaller in girth and can be square, three-cornered, oval or round.

peon Inverted 'v' shape on top of a memorial like the gable of a house.

plaque Engraved small stone tablet or metal or plastic plate set into walls or flat on the ground in grass or gravel. Often used where cremated remains are interred.

recordia panel A stone tablet upon which the names of a number of people are recorded for memorialization; usually their cremated remains are deposited nearby.

riven Natural rough finish to a stone achieved by splitting it along the grain.

sarcophagus Stone coffin, especially one with carvings.

scattering lawn Grassed area where cremated remains are scattered.

strewing The placing of cremated remains beneath the turf. See _deposition_.

table tomb Raised ledger supported at each corner by small columns standing on a landing stone.

tablet As plaque but larger.

tomb Excavated chamber for deposit of a corpse.

tombstone Memorial stone over a tomb.

urn Container for cremated remains or a decorative feature on a monument.

vault An underground chamber for the deposit of corpses or cremated remains.

walled grave A grave which is lined with brick, stone, concrete or similar material.

Reference

Litten, Julian (1991) *The English Way of Death*, Robert Hale, London

Index

Index of Advertisers

269

The Lifeplanner Series

The Lifeplanner series addresses personal finance and consumer issues in a jargon-free, readable way, taking the fear out of planning your life. So whether you are thinking about buying a house, having a baby, getting married or planning your retirement the Lifeplanner series will help you do so wisely.

Titles available are:

Balancing Your Career, Family and Life
Getting Married
Landing Your First Job
Making the Most of Being a Student
Making the Most of Retirement
The Young Professional's Guide to Personal Finance
Your Child's Education
Your First Home: A Practical Guide to Buying and Renting
Your First Investment Portfolio

Available from all good booksellers. For further information on the series, please contact:

Kogan Page
120 Pentonville Road
London
N1 9JN
Tel: 0171 278 0433
Fax: 0171 837 6348
e-mail: kpinfo@kogan-page.co.uk
or visit our website: www.kogan-page.co.uk